Caroline Lee Hentz

Love after Marriage

And Other Stories of the Heart

Caroline Lee Hentz

Love after Marriage
And Other Stories of the Heart

ISBN/EAN: 9783744673815

Printed in Europe, USA, Canada, Australia, Japan

Cover: Foto ©Thomas Meinert / pixelio.de

More available books at **www.hansebooks.com**

LOVE AFTER MARRIAGE;

AND

OTHER STORIES OF THE HEART.

BY

MRS. CAROLINE LEE HENTZ.

AUTHOR OF "LINDA; OR, THE YOUNG PILOT OF THE BELLE CREOLE," "THE BANISHED SON,"
"COURTSHIP AND MARRIAGE; OR, THE JOYS AND SORROWS OF AMERICAN LIFE,"
"THE PLANTER'S NORTHERN BRIDE; OR, SCENES IN MRS. HENTZ'S CHILDHOOD,"
"EOLINE; OR, MAGNOLIA VALE; OR, THE HEIRESS OF GLENMORE,"
"ERNEST LINWOOD; OR, THE INNER LIFE OF THE AUTHOR,"
"HELEN AND ARTHUR; OR, MISS THUSA'S SPINNING-WHEEL,"
"RENA; OR, THE SNOW BIRD," "THE LOST DAUGHTER,"
"MARCUS WARLAND; OR, THE LONG MOSS SPRING,"
"ROBERT GRAHAM;" A SEQUEL TO "LINDA," ETC.

THIS volume contains some of the most charming stories ever written by Mrs.
Caroline Lee Hentz, among which will be found: "Love After Marriage." "The
Victim of Excitement." "The Blind Girl's Story." "The Parlour Serpent."
"The Shaker Girl." "A Rainy Evening." "Three Scenes in the Life of a Belle."
"The Fatal Cosmetic." "The Abyssinian Neophyte." "The Village Anthem."
"The Brown Serpent." "My Grandmother's Bracelet," and "The Mysterious
Reticule."

PHILADELPHIA:

T. B. PETERSON & BROTHERS;

306 CHESTNUT STREET.

MRS. CAROLINE LEE HENTZ'S WORKS.

Each Work is complete in one large duodecimo volume.

LINDA; OR, THE YOUNG PILOT OF THE BELLE CREOLE.

ROBERT GRAHAM. A SEQUEL TO "LINDA."

RENA; OR, THE SNOW BIRD. A TALE OF REAL LIFE.

EOLINE; OR, MAGNOLIA VALE; OR, THE HEIRESS OF GLENMORE.

MARCUS WARLAND; OR, THE LONG MOSS SPRING.

ERNEST LINWOOD; OR, THE INNER LIFE OF THE AUTHOR.

THE PLANTER'S NORTHERN BRIDE; OR, SCENES IN MRS. HENTZ'S CHILDHOOD.

HELEN AND ARTHUR; OR, MISS THUSA'S SPIN- NING-WHEEL.

COURTSHIP AND MARRIAGE; OR, THE JOYS AND SORROWS OF AMERICAN LIFE.

LOVE AFTER MARRIAGE.

THE LOST DAUGHTER.

THE BANISHED SON.

Price $1.75 each in Morocco Cloth; or $1.50 in Paper Cover.

Above books are for sale by all Booksellers. Copies of any or all of the above books will be sent to any one, to any place, post-age pre-paid, on receipt of their price by the Publishers,

T. B. PETERSON & BROTHERS,

306 CHESTNUT STREET, PHILADELPHIA, PA.

CONTENTS.

LOVE AFTER MARRIAGE.

A STRANGER was ushered into the parlour, where two young ladies were seated, one bonneted and shawled, evidently a morning visiter, the other in a fashionable undress, as evidently a daughter or inmate of the mansion. The latter rose with a slight inclination of the head, and requested the gentleman to take a chair. "Was Mr. Temple at home?" "No! but he was expected in directly." The young ladies exchanged mirthful glances, as the stranger drew nearer, and certainly his extraordinary figure might justify a passing sensation of mirth, if politeness and good feeling had restrained its expression. His extreme spareness and the livid hue of his complexion indicated recent illness, and as he was apparently young, the almost total baldness of his head was probably owing to the same cause. His lofty forehead was above the green shade that covered his eyes in unshadowed majesty, unrelieved by a single lock of hair, and the lower part of his face assumed a still more cadaverous hue, from the reflection of the green colour above. There was something inexpressibly forlorn and piteous in his whole appearance, notwithstanding an air of gentlemanly dignity pervaded his melancholy person. He drew forth his pocket-book, and taking out a folded paper, was about to present it to Miss Temple, who, drawing back with a suppressed laugh, said—"A petition, sir, I suppose?" —then added in a low whisper to her companion—"the poor fellow is perhaps getting up a subscription for a wig." The whisper was very low, but the stranger's shaded though penetrating eyes were fixed upon her face, and the motion of her lips assisted him in a knowledge of their sound; he replaced

(17)

the paper in his pocket-book—"I am no petitioner for your bounty, madam," said he, in a voice, whose sweetness fell like a reproach on her ear, "nor have I any claims on your compassion, save being a stranger and an invalid. I am the bearer of a letter to your father, from a friend of his youth, who, even on his death-bed, remembered him with gratitude and affection; will you have the goodness to present to him my name and direction?"

Then laying his card upon the table, he made a low bow and retreated, before Miss Temple had time to apologize, if indeed any apology could be offered for her levity and rudeness. She approached the table and took up the card— "Gracious Heavens!" she exclaimed—"it cannot be possible?—Sydney Allison—that bald, yellow, horrid-loooking creature—Sydney Allison! they described him as the perfection of manly beauty—I never will believe it—he is an impostor—the wretch!"

The young lady who was with her, beheld with astonishment, the passion that lighted up Miss Temple's face, and her looks besought an explanation. "Have you not heard," said Miss Temple, "since you came to this city, that I was betrothed; that I had been so from a child, to a young gentleman residing in Cuba, whose uncle was the bosom friend of my father? You must have heard it, for my father has always taken pains to circulate the report, so that no one might presume upon my favour. And this is the delectable bridegroom! the one who has been represented as clothed in every grace calculated to fascinate a female heart—and I, fool that I was, I believed it, and looked forward with rapture to the hour of our first meeting." Here she paused, and throwing herself back in her chair, burst into a passion of tears.

Mary Manning, her more rational companion, endeavoured to soothe the excited feelings of her friend, and suggested to her, that whatever disappointment she might feel with regard to his personal appearance, his character might be such as to awaken a very ardent attachment. "Indeed," added Mary, "I thought there was something quite interesting in his address, and his voice was remarkably persuasive in its tones. He has evidently been very ill, and his bad looks are owing to this circumstance. He will become handsomer by and by. Besides, my dear Augusta, what is mere beauty in a man? It is the prerogative of a woman, and you are so highly gifted

in that respect yourself, you should be willing that your husband should excel in those qualities which men generally arro-
gate to themselves."

"Husband!" repeated Augusta; "I would as soon take a
death's-head for my husband. I care nothing about mere
beauty, provided there is intelligence and spirit. But with
such a bald, livid-looking wretch at my side, such a living
memento of mortality, I should sink into my grave in a fort-
night. I never will marry him, unless I am dragged to the
altar." Here Mr Temple entered the room, and interrupted
her rash speech. Miss Manning too retired, feeling that her
presence might be an intrusion. He looked astonished at
the agitation of his daughter, who handed him the card, and
turning away leaned against the mantel-piece, the image of
woe.

"Sydney Allison arrived!" exclaimed Mr. Temple; "where
is he? when was he here? and why is he gone?—why—what
is the matter with you, Augusta? The first wish of my heart
seems accomplished, and I find you weeping. Tell me the
meaning of all this?"

"Oh! father," sobbed Augusta, covering her face with her
handkerchief, "he is *so* ugly, and you told me he was so *very*
handsome."

Mr. Temple could not forbear laughing at the piteous tone
in which Augusta uttered this melancholy truth, though he
immediately resumed, in an accent of displeasure, "I am
ashamed of your folly—I have always given you credit for
being a girl of sense, but you talk like a little fool;—ugly!
if a man is not ugly enough to frighten his horse, he is handsome enough. Besides, it is nothing but a whim; I saw him
when a child, and he was an uncommonly beautiful boy. I
hope you did not behave in this manner before him—why did
you suffer him to go away?"

"Why, I did not know him," said Augusta, in considerable
trepidation, for she feared her father's anger; "and he looked
so thin and woe-begone, I thought he was some foreigner asking charity, and when he took out a paper I thought it a petition, and said something about one—so he was angry, I believe,
and went away, saying he had letters for you, from a friend.
who was dead."

"And is he dead!—the good old man!—the best, the
earliest friend I ever had in the world—dead and gone!"
Mr. Temple leaned his face over on his hands, and sat in

silence several moments, as if struggling with powerful emotions After a while, Mr. Temple lifted his hands, and fixed his darkened eyes upon his daughter. He took her hand with affection and solemnity. "Augusta, you are the child of affluence as well as of indulgence; you are my only child, and all the wealth, which now surrounds you with luxury, will be at your disposal after my death."

" Oh ! father, do not speak of such a thing."

" Do not interrupt me.   Mr. Allison, the uncle of this young man, was my benefactor and friend, when all the world looked dark upon me. He extricated me from difficulties which it is unnecessary to explain—gave me the means of making an ample fortune, and asked no recompense, but a knowledge of my success. It was through his influence I was united to your now angel mother—yes! I owe everything to him—wealth, reputation, and a brief, but rare portion of domestic bliss. This dear, benevolent, romantic old man, had one nephew, the orphan child of his adoption, whom he most tenderly loved. When commercial affairs carried me to Cuba, about ten years ago, Sydney was a charming boy,"—here Augusta groaned—"a charming boy; and when I spoke with a father's pride of my own little girl whom I had left behind, my friend gladdened at the thought, that the union which had bound our hearts together would be perpetuated in our children; we pledged our solemn promise to each other, that this union should take place at a fitting age; you have long been aware of this betrothal, and I have seen with great pleasure, that you seemed to enter into my views, and to look forward with hope and animation to the fulfilment of this contract. The engagement is now doubly binding, since death has set his awful seal upon it. It must be fulfilled. Do not, by your unprecedented folly, make me unhappy at a moment like this."

" Forgive me, my dear father, but indeed when you see him, you will not wonder at the shock I have received. After all you had said of him, after reading his uncle's letters so full of glowing descriptions, after dwelling so long on the graceful image my fancy drew, to find such a dreadful contrast."

" Dreadful contrast! why surely he cannot be transformed into such a monster."

" You have not seen him yet," said she mournfully.

" No! you remind me of my negligence. After the strange

reception you have given him, it is doubly urgent that I should hasten to him. Have a care, Augusta, you have always found me a very indulgent father, but in this instance I shall enforce implicit obedience. I have only one fear, that you have already so disgusted him with your levity, that he may refuse, *himself*, the honour of the alliance."

" *He* refuse *me !*" murmured Augusta, in a low voice, as she glanced at herself in a mirror that shone above the mantelpiece. As the nature of her reflections may be well imagined, it may be interesting to follow the young man, whose figure had made so unfortunate an impression on his intended bride, and learn something of the feelings that are passing through his mind.

Sydney Allison returned to his lonely apartment at the hotel with a chilled and aching heart. The bright day-dream, whose beauty had cheered and gilded him, even while mourning over the death-bed of his uncle, while languishing himself on the bed of sickness, and while, a sea-sick mariner, he was tossed upon the boisterous waves—this dream was fled. She, who had always risen upon his imagination as the morning star of his destiny—this being he had met, after years of romantic anticipation—what a meeting! He was well aware of the sad ravages one of the violent fevers of a tropical clime had made upon his beauty, but, never attaching much value to his own personal attractions, he could not believe that the marks of a divine visitation would expose him to ridicule, or unkindness; of an extremely sensitive disposition, he was peculiarly alive to the stings of satire, and the sarcastic whisper of Miss Temple wounded him to the quick.

"What!" said he, to himself, as he folded his arms in melancholy abstraction, in the solitude of his chamber, "what, if the dark luxuriance of waving hair which once shadowed my temples, is now gone, is not thought and intelligence still lingering on my brow? Are there no warm and animated veins of feeling in my heart, because the tide of health no longer colours my wan and faded cheek? These enfeebled eyes, which I must now shelter from the too dazzling light, can they not still emit the rays of tenderness, and the beams of soul? This proud beauty! May she live to know what a heart she has wounded!"

He rose and walked slowly across the floor, pausing before a large looking-glass, which fully reflected his person. He could not forbear a smile, in the midst of his melancholy, at the ludicrous contrast to his former self, and acknowledge it was preposterous to expect to charm at first sight, under the present disastrous eclipse. He almost excused the covert ridicule of which he had been the object, and began to pity the beautiful Augusta for the disappointment she must have endured. It was under the influence of these feelings Mr. Temple found him.

"My dear fellow," said the latter, warmly grasping his hand, and gazing earnestly at him—"My poor boy! how ill you must have been!—your uncle, too"—the warm-hearted man was incapable of uttering another syllable, not more moved at that moment, by the recollection of his friend, than affected by the transformation of the blooming boy, whose waving locks were once so singularly beautiful.

His sympathy was so unaffected, his welcome so warm, and his affection expressed in so heartfelt a manner, that Sydney, who had just been arming himself with proud philosophy against the indifference and neglect of the world, melted into woman's softness. He had been so long among strangers, and those of rougher natures—had experienced so cold a disappointment in his warmest hopes—he had felt so blighted, so alone—the reaction was too powerful, it unmanned him. Mr. Temple was a remarkable instance of a man who retained a youthful enthusiasm and frankness of character, after a long and prosperous intercourse with the world of business. The rapid accumulation of wealth, instead of narrowing, as it too often does, enlarged his benevolent heart. When, in a long and confidential conversation with Sydney, he learned that Mr. Allison had left but a small fortune for his support, instead of the immense one he had been led to expect, he was more than ever anxious to promote his union with his daughter. However mysterious it seemed that Mr. Allison's property should be so diminished, or have been so much overrated, he rather rejoiced at the circumstance, as it gave him an opportunity of showing his gratitude and disinterestedness. But Sydney was proud. He felt the circumstance of his altered fortunes, and, though not a poor man, was no longer the heir of that wealth which was his in reversion when Mr. Temple had plighted his daughter to him. In his short interview with her he had gained such an insight into her character, that he recoiled from the idea of appearing before her as her betrothed lover.

"Receive me as a friend," said he to Mr. Temple; "let

your daughter learn to look upon me as such, and I ask no more; unless I could win her *affections*, nothing would induce me to accept of her hand—under existing circumstances, I believe that impossible. Much as I feel your kindness, and sacred as I hold the wishes of the dead, I hold your daughter's happiness paramount to every other consideration. This must not be sacrificed for me. Promise me, sir, that it shall not. I should be more wretched than words can express, if I thought the slightest force were imposed upon her sentiments."

"Be satisfied on that score; say nothing about it; only let her get fully acquainted with you, and there will be no occasion to employ *force*. You must forget the mistake of the morning. This yellow fever makes sad work of a man when it gets hold of him, but you will soon revive from its effects."

* * * * * * * * * *

Sydney Allison became a daily visiter at Mr. Temple's Had he assumed the privileges of a lover, Augusta would have probably manifested, in a wounding manner, the aversion she felt for him in that character; but it was impossible to treat with disdain one who never presumed to offer any attentions beyond the civilities of friendship. Though rendered vain from adulation, and selfish from indulgence, and though her thoughtless vivacity often made her forgetful of the feelings of others, Augusta Temple was not destitute of redeeming virtues. Nature had gifted her with very ardent affections, and opened but few channels in which those affections could flow. She had the great misfortune to be the only child of a rich, widowed, and doting parent, and from infancy had been accustomed to see every one around her subservient to her will. She had reached the age of womanhood without knowing one real sorrow, or meeting with a being who had excited in any degree the affections of her heart. Her warm and undisciplined imagination had dwelt for years on one image. She had clothed it in the most splendid hues that fancy ever spread upon her palette; and had poor Sydney appeared before her in his original brightness, the reality would probably have been dim, to the visions of ideal beauty by which she had been so long haunted. In the greatness of her disappointment, she became unjust and unreasonable, violent in her prejudices, and extravagant in the manifestations of them. But after the first ebullition of her grief, she grew more guarded, from the dread of her father's anger; and as Sydney continued the same reserved and dignified deportment, she began to think her father's prediction was fulfilled, and that their aversion was mutual. She did not derive as much comfort from this supposition as might be anticipated. She had dreaded his importunity, but she could not endure his indifference. It was in vain Mr. Temple urged his young friend to a different course of conduct; he always answered, " Let her cease to dread m as a lover, then she may learn to prize me as a friend."

One evening, there was a concert at Mr. Temple's. Sydney, who was passionately fond of music, forgot every cause of inquietude, while abandoned to its heavenly influence. He stood near the fair songstress of the hour, keeping time to the harmony, while in a pier-glass opposite, he had a full view of the groups behind. Augusta was a little in the rear, leaning on the arm of Miss Manning. He could gaze on her image thus reflected, without her being conscious of the act, and he sighed as he paid involuntary homage to her brilliant beauty. Her figure was of superb proportions, her features formed on the model of oriental symmetry, while her eyes glittered through their dark sweeping lashes, like sunbeams through the forest foliage. She stood with her head a little averted, and her profile presented the softened outline of the lineaments ascribed to the beautiful daughters of Judah. He forgot himself entirely, in the contemplation of her loveliness, when he saw her turn, with an arch smile, and hold up her hands in a whimsical attitude in the direction of his head, as if in the act of warming them; for the full blaze of the chandeliers seemed concentrated in that point, and all eyes, lured by Augusta's gesture, were turned upon his illuminated skull. For one moment Sydney lost his self-possession, and the angry spot was seen distinctly burning on his sallow cheek. The next, he smiled superior to such weakness, and retreating a few steps, bowed for her to pass forward. She had relied on the shade that covered his eyes, for security from detection, unconscious of the piercing glances that were darting beneath. Her conscience now upbraided her for her folly, and she felt with bitterness how low she must be in the opinion of the man whose admiration she secretly coveted, notwithstanding the ridicule she dared to throw upon his person. After the company dispersed, she remained alone in the drawing-room, dissatisfied with herself and sickening at the pleasure that surrounded her. The door softly opened. It was Sydney, who had returned for his gloves, which he had left on the mantel-piece. It was the first time she had found herself alone with him, and she felt excessively embarrassed. In that tone, which even *she* acknowledged to be irresistibly sweet, he apologized for his intrusion, and taking his gloves, was retiring, when she, ever impulsive, arrested his motions.

"Stay one moment, Mr. Allison—you have great reason to despise me—I have treated you with unpardonable levity and rudeness. Though I can hardly hope your forgiveness, I cannot withhold this acknowledgment of my errors; your calm forbearance has done more for my reformation, than a thousand reproofs."

Surprised and softened by this unexpected avowal from the cold sarcastic Augusta, whose fluctuating complexion and agitated voice bore witness to her sincerity, Allison was at first incapable of replying.

"Your present candour," at length he said, "would indemnify me for much greater suffering than you have ever inflicted on me. Allow me, Miss Temple, to take advantage of this first moment of confidence, to disarm you of all fear on my account. The relative situation in which we have been placed by others, has given us both much embarrassment; but be assured my only wish is to be looked upon as your friend. Consider yourself as entirely unshackled. In brighter hours I might have aspired to the distinction our parents designed for me; but, worn down by sickness, the shadow of my former self, I feel but too sensibly, that the only sentiment I can now inspire in the female heart, is that of compassion."

Augusta was so much impressed by his delicacy and generosity, she began to hate herself for not having more justly appreciated his worth. She raised her eyes to his face and sighed—"Ah!" said she to herself, "I must respect and esteem, but I can never love him." Mr. Temple, who had been absent the whole evening, returned at this moment, and his countenance expressed his pleasure in finding them thus alone, in apparently confidential conversation with each other.

"Do not go, Allison," said he; "I have been oppressed with business to-night, and I want a little social enjoymen before I sleep. Besides, I do not feel quite well."

They now observed that he looked unusually pale, and pressed his hand upon his head, as if in pain.

"Father," said Augusta, "you do indeed look ill; you have fatigued yourself too much. A glass of wine will revive you."

She brought him the glass, but just as he took it from her hand with a smile, a sudden spasm came over him, and he fell back in his chair, speechless and convulsed. Augusta's piercing shriek alarmed the servants, who, rushing in, beheld their master supported in the arms of Allison, gasping for breath, while Augusta was trying to loosen his cravat with hands nerveless from terror. A physician was directly summoned, who bled him profusely, and after a few hours consciousness was restored. He was removed to his chamber, and Allison remained with him during the remainder of the night. Augusta sat by her father's bedside holding his hand, almost stunned by the suddenness of the calamity. Never, since her recollection, had her father known an hour's sickness; and now to be prostrated at once, in the midst of florid health, it was awful. She dared not ask the physician if there was danger, lest he should confirm her worst fears. She looked at Allison, and, in his pale and anxious countenance, she saw a reflection of her own anxiety and sorrow. Towards morning Mr. Temple opened his eyes, and looked earnestly round him.

"My children," said he, "come near me—both—both."

"Father," cried Augusta, "we *are* near thee—oh! my father, say that you are better—only say that you will *live*."

As she uttered the last word she bowed her head upon the bed cover, and sobbed as if her heart were breaking.

"My child," said Mr. Temple, faintly, "you must call upon God to sustain you, for there is need. I feel that the hand of death is on me. Sudden and awful is the summons—but it must be obeyed. Doctor, I would see my minister. Not to give peace to my parting soul—for all is peace *here*," said he, laying his hand feebly on his heart, "peace with God and man—but there is one thing I would witness before I die."

Sydney, who stood at the bed's head, trembled at the import of these words; Augusta in her agony comprehended them not.

"Sydney, my son, give me your hand; Augusta, is this your hand I hold? My children, if you would bless my last hour, you must let my dying eyes behold your union. It will gladden my friend, when I meet him in another world, to tell him his last wishes are consummated. Do you consent, my children?"

He looked up to Sydney, with that earnest expression which is never seen except in the eye of the dying, and pressed their hands together in his, already cold and dewy with the damps of death. Sydney sunk upon his knees, unutterably affected. All the happiness of his future life was at stake, but it seemed as nothing at that moment.

"Your daughter, sir?" was all he could utter.

"Augusta," repeated Mr. Temple, in a voice fearfully hollow, "will you not speak?"

"Oh! my father," she murmured, "do with me as you will, only take me with you."

The reverend figure of the minister was now added to the group that surrounded that bed of death. Strange and awful was the bridal ceremony, performed at such a moment, and attended by such solemnities. Sydney felt that he was mysteriously and irresistibly impelled on to the fulfilment of his destiny, without any volition of his own; and he supported, with a firm arm, the sinking form of her he was now to call his own. It was with bloodless lips and deadened perceptions Augusta repeated her vows; but low as they were, they fell like music on the ear that was so shortly to close to all earthly sound.

"There is a blessing above, mingling with mine," faintly articulated the dying man. "I bless you, my dear children, and ye will be blessed."

These were the last words he ever uttered. Augusta fell almost lifeless on her father's bosom, but what was a moment before the temple of an immortal spirit, was now but dust and ashes. At the same moment an orphan and a bride, she was incapable of comprehending the startling realities of her situation. The images that flitted through her mind, were like the phantasmagoria of a dream—a vague impression of something awful and indescribable having occurred, a wild fear of something more awful still impending, filled her imagination and paralyzed her frame. But Allison had a full and aching sense of the responsibilities so unexpectedly imposed upon him. He mourned for the venerated and generous friend so suddenly snatched away; but he grieved most of all, that his last act had placed in his keeping that to which he felt he had no legitimate right. No selfish repinings filled his heart—but to find himself *married*, joined irrevocably to a woman who had given him so many proofs of personal aversion; who never, till that evening, had evinced towards him the slightest sensibility—a woman whom he did not love, and whose superior fortune burdened him with a painful sense of obligation—

there was something inexpressibly galling and humbling in
these circumstances, to the sensitive and high-minded Allison.
Tenderness, however, mingled with the bitterness of his reflections; and even then, he could have taken her to his heart,
and wept over her tears of sympathy and sorrow, had he not
dreaded that she would recoil from his embraces.   He did not
intrude on the sacredness of her grief, and for days she buried
herself in the solitude of her chamber.   She admitted no one
but her chosen friend, Miss Manning, who represented her as
inconsolable, either sunk in a torpor, from which nothing could
arouse her, or in a state of nervous excitement still more dis-
tressing.   He waited, hoping that time would restore her to
comparative composure, and that she would be willing to receive from him the consolations of friendship.   Finding, at
length, that she persevered in her system of solitary grief,
and that time, while it must, according to its immutable laws,
soften her anguish for her father's death, probably increased
her dread of the shackles that bound her, his resolution was
taken.   In a short time everything was arranged for his departure to a foreign land.   The ship, in which he was bound
a passenger, was ready to sail, when he requested a parting
interview with Augusta.   A parting interview!—Augusta was
roused at that sound, from the selfishness of her grief.   He
was going into banishment, and she was the cause.   For the
first time since the bridal ceremony, the thought forced itself
into her mind, that *he* too might have cause for sorrow, and
that *his* happiness might be sacrificed as well as her own.
Allison was greatly shocked, to see the change wrought in her
radiant face.   He was so much agitated, he forgot everything
he purposed to say, and remembered only the strangeness of
their situation.   He endeavoured to repress his own emotion,
that he might not increase hers; while she, unused to self-control, abandoned herself to a passion of tears.   He approached
her with tenderness and solemnity, and entreated her to listen
to him, as a *friend*, as one willing to promote her happiness
by any sacrifice she might require.   " I go," said he, " Augusta, to another clime, whose genial influence may restore
me again some portion of my former vigour.   I go, too, in the
hope, that in my absence you will learn submission to a destiny
which my presence renders insupportable.   If you knew the
anguish that fills my heart, when I think of myself as the
involuntary cause of your wretchedness, you would pity me,
even as much as you abhor.   Hear me, Augusta, while I re-

peat with all the solemnity of the vows that bound us to each other, that I will never claim the name of husband, till your own free affections hallow the sacred title. In the mean time I leave you with one who will be to you as a loving sister, in whose father you will find a faithful and affectionate guardian —will you not part from me, at least in kindness?"

Augusta sat, with her arms thrown around Miss Manning, weeping, yet subdued. All the best impulses of her nature were wakened and active. She would have given worlds to say something expressive of her remorse and regret for her selfishness and waywardness. Clasping her hands together she exclaimed, "Oh! forgive me, Sydney, that I cannot love you;" then, conscious that she was only wounding more deeply when she wished to heal, she only uttered, "what an unfortunate wretch I am!"

' We are both unfortunate," said he, moved beyond his power of control—"but we may not be always miserable. Something whispers me, that we shall meet again with chastened feelings, capable of appreciating all that is excellent in each other, and both earnest in the endeavour to merit the blessing that hallowed our nuptial tie. I leave you that you may be restored to tranquillity—I may never return—I pray to God, that he may find me a grave in that ocean to whose bosom I am about to commit myself, if I am only to live for the misery of others."

"No, no," cried Augusta, "this must not be, you must not become an exile for me."

"Listen to her," said Miss Manning, earnestly, her whole soul wrought up into the most painful excitement, at the sight of their mutual distress—"indeed, sir, you are doing what is rash and uncalled for—oh! why, with so much to bind you together, with qualities capable of inspiring the strongest attachment in each other, will ye close up your hearts in this manner, and resolve to be miserable?"

"I cannot now remain if I would, as I have taken steps which cannot well be recalled—your father, Miss Manning, knows and approves my intention. He is the delegated guardian and protector of Augusta. I will not, I cannot prolong the pain of these moments. Farewell, Augusta! think of me, if possible, with kindness—should I live to return, I will be to you friend, brother, or husband, as your own heart shall dictate."

He pressed her cold and passive hand in his—turned, and
103

was gone. Augusta would have spoken, but she seemed as
if under the influence of a nightmare. Her faculties were
spell-bound; she would have returned the parting pressure of
his hand, but her fingers seemed icicles. She shuddered with
superstitious dread. Her father's upbraiding spirit appeared
to her imagination, armed with the terrors of the grave, and
threatening her with the retribution of heaven. Poor Augusta! her mind required the stern, but salutary discipline of
adversity, and that discipline was preparing. How she pro-
fited by the teachings of this monitress, whose lessons, however
hard, have such high and celestial bearings, the events of after
years may show.

     *   *   *   *   *   *   *   *   *   *

Augusta and her friend are once more presented to the
view of the reader, but the destiny of the former is changed.
They are seated in a parlour side by side, but it is not the
same, rich in all the adornments of wealth and fashion, that
Augusta once occupied. It is in a neat rural cottage, in the
very heart of the country, embosomed in trees and flowers.
A few words will explain the past. Mr. Temple's open,
generous, uncalculating disposition had exposed him to the
designs of the mercenary and treacherous. He never could
refuse to endorse a note for a friend, or to loan money when
it was asked with a look of distress. He believed his resources
as exhaustless as his benevolence; but by the failure of several
houses with which he was largely connected, his estate was
involved in ruin, and his daughter left destitute of fortune.
Mr. Manning suffered so much himself in the general loss, he
was obliged to sell all that he still possessed in the city and
retire into the country, with limited means of subsistence.
But, though limited, he had sufficient for all the comforts of
life, and what he deemed its luxuries—books, music, the
socialities of friendship, and the exercise of the kindly chari-
ties. A cherished member of this charming family, Augusta
no longer the spoiled child of fortune, but the chastened dis
ciple of sorrow, learned to estimate the true purposes of her
being, and to mourn over her former perversity. With such
ennobled views of life and its enjoyments, she began to think
she might be happy with a husband, with such irreproachable
worth and exalted attributes as Sydney Allison, even though
he had the misfortune to be bald and sallow. But him she
had banished, and when would he return? He had written

to her once or twice, in the most affectionate manner, as a
brother would write; he had spoken of amended health and
reviving spirits, but he spoke of his return as of something
indefinite and even remote. She too had written, and her
letters were transcripts of the progressive elevation of her
character, and expressed with candour and warmth the just
appreciation she now had of his own. She was uncertain
whether they had ever reached him. It was long since she
had received any tidings, and she felt at times that sickness
of the heart, which suspense unfed by hope creates.

"I bring you a messenger, who I trust is the bearer of glad
tidings," said Mr. Manning, entering, with a benevolent smile,
and ushering in a young gentleman, whom he introduced by
the name of Clarence. "Augusta, you will greet him with
joy, for he comes with letters from Mr. Allison, your husband."

Augusta sprang forward, scarcely waiting to go through the
customary form of introduction, and took the letter with a
trembling hand. "Tell me, sir, do you know him, and is he
well?" The stranger bent his dark and lustrous eyes upon
her face, with a look of undisguised admiration.

"I know him intimately, madam; when I last saw him,
he was in perfect health, and animated by the prospect of a
speedy return."

Augusta waited to hear no more, but retired to her own
chamber, to peruse the epistle she had so anxiously anticipated. It was in answer to her last, and breathed the language of hope and confidence. There was a warmth, a fervour
of sentiment, far different from his former cold, but kind com-
munications. He rejoiced in the knowledge of her altered
fortune, for he could prove his disinterestedness, and show
her that he loved her for herself alone, by returning and devoting himself to the task of winning her affections. "Say
not, my Augusta," said he in conclusion, "that I cannot win
the prize. All the energies of my heart and soul are enliste
for the contest. I could look on your beauty, all dazzling a
it is, without much emotion; but the humility, the trust, th
gentleness and feeling expressed in your letter has melted me
into tenderness. Dare I indulge in the blissful dream, that
even now gilds this page with the hues of heaven? Augusta,
the sad, reluctant bride, transformed into the fond and faithful wife, cherished in my yearning bosom, and diffusing there
the life, the warmth, the fragrance of love!"

Augusta's tears rained over the paper. "Oh! Allison,' she cried, "the task shall not be in vain; I *will* love thee for thy virtues, and the blessing my dying father called down, may yet rest upon us." She was about to fold the letter, when a postscript on the envelope met her eye. "Receive Clarence," it said, "as my friend—he knows all my history, and the peculiarity of our situation—he is interested in you, for my sake—as a stranger and my especial friend, may I ask for him the hospitable attentions of Mr. Manning's family?"

When she descended into the room, where Clarence was seated, she could not repress a painful blush, from the consciousness that he was familiar with her singular history. "He must despise me," thought she; but the deference, and respect of his manner forbade such an impression. Gradually recovering from her embarrassment, and finding him directing his conversation principally to Mr. Manning, she had leisure to observe one who possessed strong interest in her eyes, as the friend of Allison. And seldom does the eye of woman rest upon a more graceful or interesting figure, or a more expressive and glowing countenance. There was a lambent brightness in his eyes, a mantling bloom upon his cheek, that indicated indwelling light and conscious youth. His hair clustered in soft waves round his temples, relieving by its darkness the unsunned whiteness of his forehead. Yet the prevailing charm was manner, that indescribable charm, that, like sunshine in the summer landscape, gilded and vivified the whole. The acquisition of such a guest gave life and animation to the domestic circle. Mr. Manning was a man of varied information, and the society of this accomplished traveller recalled the classic enthusiasm of his earlier days. Mary, though usually reserved to strangers, seemed fascinated into a forgetfulness of herself, and found herself a partaker of a conversation to which at first she was only a timid listener. Augusta, while she acknowledged the stranger's uncommon power to please, was preoccupied by the contents of her husband's letter, and longed to be alone with Mary, whose sympathy was always as spontaneous as it was sincere. She was not disappointed in the readiness of Mary's sympathy; but after having listened again and again, and expressed her hope and joy that all would yet be for the happiest and the best, she returned to the subject next in interest, the bearer of this precious document. "Ah! my dear Augusta," said she, "if Allison's noble spirit had been enshrined in such a temple, you had not been parted now." Augusta felt the comparison *odious*. It brought before her the person of Allison in too melancholy a contrast with the engaging stranger. "I thought it was Mary Manning," answered she in a grave tone, "who once reproved me for attaching too much importance to manly beauty—I never thought you foolish or unkind till this moment."

"Forgive me," cried Mary, with irresistible frankness; "foolish I may be, indeed I know I am; but intentionally unkind to you—never—never." It did not require the recollection of all Mary's tried friendship and sincerity, for Augusta to accord her forgiveness. Mary was more guarded afterwards in the expression of her admiration, but Augusta, in her imagination, had drawn the horoscope of Mary's destiny, and Clarence shone there, as the star that was to give it radiance. A constant guest of her father's, she thought it impossible for him to witness Mary's mild, yet energetic virtues, without feeling their influence. She was interesting without being beautiful, and Clarence evidently delighted in her conversation. To her, he was always more reserved, yet there was a deference, an interest, a constant reference to her wishes and opinions, that was as delicate as it was flattering. He was the companion of their walks, and nature, never more lovely than in this delightful season, acquired new charms from the enthusiasm with which he sought out and expatiated on its beauties. Mr. Manning was passionately fond of music, and every evening· Mary and Augusta were called upon for his favourite songs. Now the music was finer than ever, for Clarence accompanied them with his flute, and sometimes with his voice, which was uncommonly sweet and melodious. One evening Augusta was seated at the piano; she was not an excelling performer, but she played with taste and feeling, and she had endeavoured to cultivate her talent, for she remembered that Allison was a lover of music. She had played all Mr. Manning's songs, and turned over the leaves, without thinking of any particular tune, when Clarence arrested her at one, which he said was Allison's favourite air. "Let us play and sing that," said he, repeating the words, "your husband loves it, we were together when he first heard it; it was sung by an Italian songstress, whom you have often struck me as resembling. The manner in which your hair is now parted in front, with those falling curls behind, increases the resemblance; it is very striking at this moment."

Augusta felt a strange pang penetrate her heart, when he asked her for her husband's favourite. There was something, too, in his allusion to her personal appearance that embarrassed her. He had paid her no compliment, yet she blushed as if guilty of receiving one. "I cannot play it," answered she, looking up, "but I will try to learn it for his sake." She could not prevent her voice from faltering; there was an expression in his eyes, when they met hers, that bowed them down, in shame and apprehension. It was so intense and thrilling—she had never met such a glance before, and she feared to interpret it.

"Shall I sing it for you?" asked he; and leaning over the instrument, he sang in a low, mellow voice, one of those impassioned strains, which the fervid genius of Italy alone can produce. The words were eloquent of love and passion, and Augusta, charmed, melted by their influence, could not divest herself of a feeling of guilt as she listened. A new and powerful light was breaking upon her; truth held up its blazing torch, flashing its rays into the darkest corners of her heart; and conscience, discovering passions, of whose very existence she had been previously unconscious. She saw revealed in prophetic vision, the misery of her future existence, the misery she was entailing on herself, on others, and a cold shudder ran through her frame. Mary, alarmed at her excessive paleness, brought her a glass of water, and asked her if she were ill. Grateful for an excuse to retire, she rose and took Mary's arm to leave the room; but as she passed through the door, which Clarence opened and held, she could not avoid encountering again a glance so tender and impassioned, she could not veil to herself the language it conveyed. Augusta had thought herself miserable before, but never had she shed such bitter tears as bathed her pillow that night. Just as she had schooled herself to submission; just as she was cherishing the most tender and grateful feelings towards her husband, resolving to make her future life one long task of expiation, a being crossed her path, who realized all her early visions of romance, and who gently and insidiously had entwined himself into the very chords of her existence; and now, when she felt the fold, and struggled to free herself from the enthralment, she found herself bound as with fetters of iron and clasps of steel. That Clarence loved her, she could not doubt. Enlightened as to the state of her own heart, she now recollected a thousand covert marks of tenderness and regard. He had been admitted to the most unreserved intercourse with her, as the friend of her husband. Like herself, he had been cherishing sentiments of whose strength he was unaware, and which, when revealed in their full force, would make him tremble. She now constantly avoided his society. Her manners were cold and constrained, and her conscious eyes sought the ground. But Clarence, though he saw the change, and could not be ignorant of the cause, was not rebuked or chilled by her coldness. He seemed to call forth, with more animation, the rich resources of his mind, his enthusiasm was more glowing, his voice had more music, and his smile more brightness. It was evident she alone was unhappy; whatever were his feelings, they inspired no remorse. She began to believe her own vanity had misled her, and that he only looked upon her as the wife of his friend. She had mistaken the luminousness of his eyes for the fire of passion. Her credulity abased her in her own estimation.

One afternoon Clarence found her alone. She had declined accompanying Mary and her father in a walk, because she thought Clarence was to be with them. "I did not expect to find you alone," said he, taking a seat by her side— "but since I have gained such a privilege, may I ask, without increasing your displeasure, in what I have offended? You shun my society—your averted looks, your altered mien" —he paused, for her embarrassment was contagious, and the sentence remained unfinished. The appeal was a bold one, but as a *friend* he had a right to make it.

"You have not offended me," at length she answered, "but you know the peculiar circumstances of my life, and cannot wonder if my spirits sometimes droop, when reflecting on the misery of the past, and the uncertainty of the future."

"If," said he, "the uncertainty of the future makes you unhappy as it regards yourself, you may perhaps have cause of uneasiness, but as it respects Allison, as far as I know his sentiments, he has the fullest confidence, and the brightest hopes of felicity. I once looked upon him as the most unfortunate, but I now view him as the most blessed of men. When he told me the circumstances of his exile, how lone and hopeless seemed his lot! Now, when I see all that wooes him to return, angels might covet his destiny."

"You forget yourself," cried Augusta, not daring to take in the full meaning of his words—"it is not the office of a

friend to flatter—Allison never flattered—I always revered
him for his truth."

" Yes !" exclaimed Clarence, " he has truth and integrity.
They call him upright, and honourable, and just; but is he
not cold and senseless to remain in banishment so long,
leaving his beautiful wife in widowhood and sorrow ! and was
•he not worse than mad to send me here the herald of himself,
o expose me to the influence of your loveliness, knowing that
to see you, to be near you, must be to love, nay, even to worship."

" You have driven me from you for ever !" cried Augusta,
rising in indignant astonishment, at the audacity of this
avowal.   " Allison shall learn in what a friend he has confided."

" I am prepared for your anger," continued he, with increasing impetuosity, " but I brave it ; your husband will
soon return, and I shall leave you.   Tell him of all my boldness, and all my sincerity ; tell him too all the emotions that
are struggling in your heart for me, for oh ! you cannot deny
it, there is a voice pleading for my pardon, in your bosom
now, and telling you, that, if it is a crime to love, that one
crime is mutual."

" Then I am indeed a wretch !" exclaimed Augusta, sinking
down into a chair, and clasping her hands despairingly over
her face ; " but I deserve this humiliation."   Clarence drew
nearer to her—she hesitated—he trembled.   The triumphant
fire that revelled in his eyes was quenched ; compassion, tenderness, and self-reproach softened their beams.   He was in
the very act of kneeling before her, to deprecate her forgiveness, when the door softly opened, and Mary Manning entered.
Her step was always gentle, and she had approached unheard.
She looked at them first with a smile, but Augusta's countenance was not one that could reflect a smile ; and on Mary's
face, at that moment, it appeared to her as a smile of derision.
Clarence lingered a moment, as if unwilling to depart, yet uncertain whether to remain or go—then asking Mary for her
father, he hastily retired, leaving Augusta in a state of such
agitation, that Mary, seriously alarmed, entreated her to explain the cause of her distress.

" Explain !" cried Augusta.   " You have witnessed my
humiliation, and yet ask me the cause.   I do not claim your
sympathy, the grief I now feel admits of none ; I was born
to be unhappy, and whichever way I turn, I am wretched."

"Only tell me one thing, dear Augusta, is all your grief owing to the discovery of your love for Clarence, and to the sentiments with which you have inspired him? There is no humiliation in loving Clarence—for who could know him and not love him?"

Augusta looked in Mary's face, assured that she was utter-'ng the language of mockery. Mary, the pure moralist, the mild, but uncompromising advocate for duty and virtue, thus to palliate the indulgence of a forbidden passion! It could only be in derision; yet her eye was so serene, and her smile so kind, it was impossible to believe that contempt was lurking beneath. "Then you *do* love him, Mary, and I am doubly treacherous!"

Mary blushed—"with the affection of a sister, the tender-ness of a friend, do I regard him; I admire his talents, I venerate his virtues."

"Virtues! oh! Mary, he is a traitor to his friend; what reliance is there on those virtues, which, having no root in the heart, are swept away by the first storm of passion?"

"Passion may enter the purest heart," answered Mary; "guilt consists in yielding to its influence. I would pledge my life that Clarence would never give himself up to the in-fluence of a guilty passion."

"Talk not of him, let me forget his existence, if I can; I think of one, who will return from his long exile, only to find his hopes deceived, his confidence betrayed, his heart broken."

Here Augusta wept in such anguish, that Mary, finding it in vain to console her, threw her arms around her, and wept in sympathy; yet still she smiled through her tears, and again and again repeated to her, that heaven had long years of hap-piness yet in store.

Augusta, in the solitude of her own chamber, recovered an appearance of outward composure, but there was a deadly sickness in her soul, that seemed to her like a foretaste of mortality. The slightest sound made her tremble, and when Mary returned to her, softly, but hurriedly, and told her he father wished to see her, she went to him, with a blanched cheek and trembling step, like a criminal who is about to hear her sentence of doom.

"I have something to communicate to you," said he, kindly taking her hand, and leading her to a seat. "But I fear you will be too much agitated."

"Is he come?" cried she, grasping his arm with sudden energy; "only tell me, is he come?"

"Your husband *is* arrived; I have just received tidings that he is in the city, and will shortly be here."

Augusta gasped for breath, she pressed her hands on her bosom, there was such a cold, intolerable weight there; she felt the letter of her husband, which she had constantly worn s a talisman against the evil she most dreaded. That tender, confiding letter, which, when she had first received it, she had hailed as the precursor of the purest felicity.

"It is all over now," sighed she, unconscious of the presence of Mr. Manning. "Poor unhappy Allison, I will tell him all, and then I will lie down and die."

"I hear a carriage approaching," said Mr. Manning; "the gate opens—support yourself, my dear child, and give him the welcome he merits." Augusta could not move, her limbs were powerless, but perception and sensibility remained; she saw Mr. Manning leave the room, heard steps and voices in the passage, and then the door reopen. The shades of twilight were beginning to fall, and a mist was over her eyes, but she distinctly recognised the figure that entered—what was her astonishment, to behold, instead of the lank form, bald brows, and green shade, marked in such indelible characters on her memory—the graceful lineaments, clustering looks, and lustrous eyes of Clarence? She looked beyond in wild alarm for her husband. "Leave me," she exclaimed, "leave me, or you drive me to desperation!"

But Clarence eagerly approached her, as if defying all consequences, and reckless of her resentment. He clasped her in his arms, he pressed her to his heart, and imprinted on her brow, cheek, and lips, unnumbered kisses. "My bride, my wife, my own beloved Augusta, do you not know me? and can you forgive me for this trial of your love? I did not mean to cause you so much suffering, but I could not resist the temptation of proving whether your love was mine, through duty or inclination. I have been the rival of myself, and I have exulted in finding, that love in all its strength has still been mastered by duty. Augusta, I glory in my wife."

Augusta looked up, in bewildered rapture, hardly knowing in what world she existed. She had never dreamed of such a transformation. Even now it seemed incredible—it could not be true—her present felicity was too great to be real—"Can Allison and Clarence be one?"

"Yes, my Augusta, these arms have a right to enfold thee, or they would not clasp you thus. No miracle has been wrought, but the skeleton is reclothed with flesh, the locks of youth have been renewed, the tide of health has flowed back again into the wasted veins, lending a glow to the wan cheek, and a brightness to the dim eye; and more than all, the worn .nd feeble spirit, always sympathizing with its frail companion, as replumed its drooping wings, and been soaring in regions .f hope, and joy, and love."

Without speaking metaphorically, Augusta's heart actually ached with its excess of happiness.

"I have not room here," she cried, "for such fulness of joy," again laying her hand where that precious letter was deposited, but with such different emotions. "My friends must participate in my happiness, it is selfish to withhold it from them so long."

"They know it already," said Allison, smiling; "they have known my secret from the first, and assisted me in concealing my identity."

Augusta now understood Mary's apparent inconsistency, and vindicated her from all unkindness and wilful palliation of guilt. "I am not quite an impostor," continued her husband, "for my name is Sydney Clarence Allison—and let me still wear the appellation you have learned to love. It was my uncle's, and he left a condition in his will that I should assume it as my own. I find myself, too, the heir of sufficient wealth to be almost a burden; for my uncle, romantic to the last, only caused the report of the failure of his wealth, that I might prove the sincerity of your father's friendship. My wife, my own Augusta, is not his blessing resting on us now?"

Mr. Manning and his daughter sympathized largely in the happiness of their friends. Their only sorrow was the approaching separation. Mary, whose disposition was naturally serious, was exalted on this occasion to an unwonted vein of humour. When she saw Augusta's eyes turning with fond admiration towards her husband, she whispered in her ear— "Is it possible, that bald, yellow, horrid-looking creature is your husband? I would not marry him, unless I were dragged to the altar."

And Allison, passing his hand over his luxuriant hair, reminded her, with a smile, of the *subscription* and the *wig*.

THE

VICTIM OF EXCITEMENT.

INTEMPERANCE is a vice which is generally considered of
the masculine sex. In the pictured scenes of the ravages it
has wrought woman is seldom introduced but as the patient
victim of brutality, or as the admonishing angel of transgress-
ing man. There are instances on record, however, of a sad
reverse. Not alone in the lower classes of life, amid the
dregs of society, but in higher walks, where intelligence, wit,
beauty, and wealth, virgin worth, wedded love, and Christian
grace, are all cast as unvalued offerings at the beastly shrine
of intemperance. One of these fatal examples (of which, to
the honour of our sex be it said, there are so few) once came
under the observation of the writer. Her character and history
form the subject of the following sketch.

Mr. Manly first met Anne Weston in a ball-room. It was on
the evening of the Fourth of July, and the fairest ladies of the
country were assembled to celebrate the national jubilee. He
was a lawyer, and had been the orator of the day; an eloquent
one, and therefore entitled to distinguished attention. He came
from an adjoining town, of which he had recently become an
inhabitant, and now found himself in a scene which scarcely
presented one familiar countenance. He was a very proud
man, and had the air of one who felt himself too superior to
the multitude to mingle in the general amusement. He stood
with folded arms, as remote as possible from the dancers
despising those who were engaged in that exercise on such a
sultry night. In vain the obsequious master of ceremonies
begged to introduce him to this and that fair lady. He de-

40

clined the honour with a cold bow, declaring his utter disinclination to dancing. He was told that his disinclination
would cease as soon as Miss Weston arrived. She was the
belle of the place, the daughter of the richest gentleman in
town—had received the most finished education, and refused
the most splendid offers. In short, she was irresistible, and
it was predicted that he would find her so. It cannot be
denied, that the fame of this all-conquering lady had pre-
viouly reached his ears, but unfortunately he had a detesta-
tion of belles, and predetermined to close his eyes, and shut
his ears, and steel his heart against her vaunted attractions.
He had never yet sacrificed his independence to woman. He
had placed his standard of female excellence very high. He
had seen no one that reached its altitude. "No," said he to
himself, "let me live on in singleness of heart and loneliness
of purpose, all the days of my life, rather than unite myself
with one of those vain, flimsy, garrulous, and superficial beings
who win the smiles, and fix the attention of the many. I
despise a weak woman, I hate a masculine one, and a pedantic
one I abhor. I turn with fear from the glittering belle, whose
home is the crowded hall, whose incense the homage of fools,
whose altar the shrine of fashion. Can *she* sit down contented
in the privacy of domestic love who has lived on the adulation
of the world, or be satisfied with the affection of one true heart,
who has claimed as her due, the vows of all? No, better the
fool, the pedant, than the belle. Who can find that woman,
whose price is above rubies? Ah! 'tis certain I never shall
marry." He was aroused from these reflections, by a movement in the hall, and he felt a conviction that the vaunted lady
was arrived. In spite of his boasted indifference, he could
not repress a slight sensation of curiosity to see one who was
represented as so transcendent. But he moved not, he did
not even turn his eyes towards the spot where so many were
clustering. "The late hour of her arrival," said he, "shows
equal vanity and affectation. She evidently wishes to be conspicuous—studies everything for effect." The lady moved
towards that part of the hall where he was stationed. She
held the arm of one gentleman, and was followed by some
half-dozen others. He was compelled to gaze upon her, for
they passed so near, the folds of her white muslin dress
fluttered against him. He was pleased to see that she was
much less beautiful than he had expected. He scarcely thought
her handsome Her complexion was pale, even sallow, and

her face wanted that soft, flowing outline, which is necessary
to the perfection of beauty. He could not but acknowledge,
however, that her figure was very fine, her motions graceful,
and her air spirited and intellectual. "I am glad she is not
beautiful," said he, "for I might have been tempted to have
admired her, against my sober judgment. Oppressed by the
heat of the apartment, he left the hall and sauntered for a
ong time in the piazza, till a certain feeling of curiosity, to
now whether a lady whose bearing expressed so much pride
of soul, could be foolish enough to dance, led him to return.
The first object he beheld, was the figure of Miss Weston,
moving in most harmonious time, to an exhilarating air, her
countenance lighted up with an animation, a fire, that had as
magical an effect upon her features, as the morning sunbeams
on the face of nature. The deepest colour was glowing on her
cheek,—her very soul was shining forth from her darkening
eyes. She danced with infinite spirit, but equal grace. He
had never witnessed anything to compare with it, not even on
the stage. "She dances entirely too well," thought he; "she
cannot have much intellect, yet she carries on a constant conversation with her partner through all the mazes of the dance.
It must be admirable nonsense, from the broad smiles it elicits.
I am half resolved to be introduced and invite her to dance—
from mere *curiosity*, and to prove the correctness of my
opinion." He sought the introduction, became her partner
in the dance, and certainly forgot, while he listened to her
" admirable nonsense," that she was that object of his detesta-
tion—a *belle*. Her conversation was sprightly, unstudied, and
original. She seemed more eager to listen than to talk, more
willing to admire than to be admired. She did not tell him
that she admired his oration, but she spoke warmly on the
subject of eloquence, and quoted in the happiest manner, a
passage of his own speech, *one* which he himself judged
superb. It proved her to have listened with deep attention.
He had never received so delicate or gratifying a compliment.
His vanity was touched, and his pride slumbered. He called
forth those powers of pleasing, with which he was eminently
endowed, and he began to feel a dawning ambition to make
the conquest of a heart which so many had found indomitable.
He admired the simplicity of her dress, its fitness and elegance.
A lady's dress is always indicative of her character. Then
her voice was singularly persuasive in its tones, it breathed
of feminine gentleness and sensibility, with just enough spirit

and independence for a woman. Mr. Manly came to these wise conclusions before the end of the first dance—at the termination of the second, he admired the *depth*, as well as the brilliancy of her mind, and when he bade her adieu for the night, he was equally convinced of the purity of her feelings and the goodness of her heart. Such is the strength of man's wisdom, the stability of his opinions, the steadiness of his purpose, when placed in competition with the fascinations of a woman who has made the determination to please. In after years Mr. Manly told a friend of a dream which that night haunted his pillow. He was not superstitious, or disposed to attach the slighest importance to dreams. But this was a vivid picture, and succeeding events caused him to recall it, as one having the power of prophecy. He lived over again the events of the evening. The winning accents of Miss Weston mingled in his ear with the gay notes of the violin. Still, ever and anon, discordant sounds marred the sweet harmony. The malicious whisper, the stifled, deriding laugh, and the open scoff came from every corner. Sometimes he saw, through the crowd, the slow finger of scorn pointing at him. As he turned, with a fierce glance of defiance, Miss Weston seemed to meet him still, holding a goblet in her hand, which she pressed him to drain. Her cheeks and lips burned with a scarlet radiance, and her eyes sparkled with unnatural brightness. "Taste it not," whispered a soft voice in his ear, "it is poison." "It is the cup of immortality," exclaimed the syren, and she drained the goblet to its last drop. In a few moments her countenance changed—her face became bloated, her features disfigured, and her eyes heavy and sunken. He turned with disgust from the former enchantress, but she pursued him, she wound her arms around him. In the vain struggle of liberating himself from her embrace, he awoke. It was long before he could overcome the sensation of loathing and horror excited by the unhallowed vision, and even when, overcome by heaviness and exhaustion, he again slept, the same bloated phantom presented her intoxicating draught. The morning found him feverish and unrefreshed. He could not shake off the impression of his dream, and the image of Miss Weston seemed deprived of the witchery that had enthralled his imagination the preceding evening. He was beginning to despise himself, for having yielded up so soon his prejudices and pride, when an invitation to dine at Mr. Weston's, interrupted the severe tenor of his thoughts. Polite ness obliged him to accept, and in the society of Miss Weston, graceful, animated, and intellectual, presiding with unaffected dignity and ease at her father's board, he forgot the hideous metamorphose of his dream.

From that day his fate was sealed. It was the first time his heart had ever been seriously interested, and he loved with all the strength and ardour of his proud and ardent character. The triumph, too, of winning one whom so many had sought in vain, threw a kind of glory over his conquest, and exalted his estimation of his own attributes. The wedding-day was appointed. The evening previous to his nuptials, Anne Weston sat in her own chamber, with one of the chosen friends of her girlhood, Emily Spencer. Anne had no sisters, and from childhood, Emily had stood to her almost in that dear relation. She was to accompany her to her new home, for Anne refused to be separated from her, and had playfully told Mr. Manly, "that if he married *her*, he must take Emily too, for she could not and would not be parted from her."

The thought of the future occupied the minds of the two friends. Anne sat in silence. The lamp that partially illumined the apartment, gave additional paleness to her pale and spiritual countenance. Her thoughts appeared to have rolled within herself, and, from the gloom of her eye, did not appear to be such as usually rest in the bosom of one about to be wedded to the object of her affection and her trust.

"I fear," said she at length, as if forgetting the presence of her friend, "that I have been too hasty. The very qualities that won my admiration, and determined me to fix his regard, now cause me to tremble. I have been too much accustomed to self-indulgence, to bear restraint, and should it ever be imposed by a master's hand, my rebellious spirit would break the bonds of duty, and assert its independence. I fear I am not..formed to be a happy wife, or to *constitute* the happiness of a husband. I live too much upon excitement, and when the deep monotony of domestic life steals on, what will become of me?"

"How can there be monotony," answered Emily, warmly, "with such a companion as Manly? Oh, trust him, Anne, love him as he merits to be loved, as you yourself are loved, and your lot may be envied among women."

"He has awakened all the capabilities my heart has of loving," cried Anne, "but I wish I could shake off this dull weight from my spirits." She rose as she spoke, approached a side table, and, turning out a glass of rich cordial, drank it, as if conscious, from experience, of its renovating influence Emily's anxious gaze followed her movements. A deep sigh escaped her lips. When her friend resumed her seat, she drew nearer to her, she took her hand in hers, and, while her colour heightened, and her breath shortened, she said—

"Anne Weston, I should not deserve the name of friend, if in this hour, the last, perhaps, of unrestrained confidence between us, I did not dare—"

"Dare what?" interrupted Anne, shame and resentment kindling in her eye.

"To tell you, that the habit you indulge in, of resorting to artificial means to exhilarate your spirits, though now attended with no obvious danger, may exercise most fatal influence on your future peace. I have long struggled for resolution to utter this startling truth, and I gather boldness as I speak. By all our friendship and sincerity, by the past splendour of your reputation, by the bright hopes of the future, by the trusting vows of a lover, and the gray hairs of a father, I pray you to relinquish a habit, whose growing strength is now only known to me." Emily paused, strong emotions impeded her utterance. "What is it you fear?" asked Anne, in a low, stern voice; "speak, for you see that I am calm."
"You know what I dread," continued Emily. "I see a speck on the bright character of my friend. It may spread and dim all its lustre. We all know the fearful strength of habit, we cannot shake off the serpent when once its coils are around us. Oh, Anne, gifted by nature with such brilliancy of intellect and gayety of heart, why have you ever had recourse to the exciting draught, as if art could exalt the original buoyancy of your spirits, or care had laid his blighting hand upon you?"

"Forbear," cried Anne, impetuously, "and hear me, before you blast me with your contempt. It was not till bitter disappointment pressed, crushed me, that I knew art could renovate the languor of nature. Yes, I, the courted and admired of all, was doomed to love one whose affections I could not win. You knew him well, but you never knew how my ineffectual efforts to attach him maddened my pride, or how the triumph of my beautiful rival goaded my feelings. The world guessed not my secret, for still I laughed and glittered with mocking splendour, but with such a cold void within! I could not bear it. My unnatural spirits failed me. I *must*

still shine on, or the secret of my humiliation be discovered.
I began in despair, but I have accomplished my purpose. And
now," added she, "I have done. The necessity of shining
and deceiving is over. I thank you for the warmth of friendship that suggested your admonition. But, indeed, Emily,
your apprehensions are exaggerated. I have a restraining
power within me that must always save me from degradation.
Habit, alone, makes slaves of the weak; it becomes the slave
of the strong in mind. I know what's due to Manly. He
never shall blush for his choice in a wife."

She began with vehemence and ended with deliberation.
There was something in the cold composure of her manner
that forbid a renewal of the subject. Emily felt that she had
fulfilled her duty as a friend, and delicacy commanded her to
forbear a renewal of her admonitions. Force of feeling had
betrayed her into a warmth of expression she now regretted.
She loved Anne, but she looked with many misgivings to being
the sharer of her wedded home. She had deeply studied the
character of Manly, and trembled to think of the reaction that
might one day take place in his mind, should he ever discover
the dark spot on the disk of his sun—of his destiny. Though
she had told Anne that the secret of her growing love for the
exciting draught was *known* only to herself, it was whispered
among the servants, suspected by a few discreet individuals,
and had been several times hinted in a private circle of
friends. It had never yet reached the ears of Manly, for
there was something in his demeanour that repelled the most
distant approach to familiarity. He married with the most
romantic and enthusiastic ideas of domestic felicity. Were
those bright visions of bliss realized? Time, the great dis-
enchanter, alone could answer.

*   *   *   *   *   *   *   *   *

It was about five years after the scenes we have recorded,
that Mr. and Mrs. Manly took up their residence in the town
of G———. Usually, when strangers are about to become
inhabitants of a new place, there is some annunciation of their
arrival; but they came, without any previous intimation being
given for the speculation of the curious, or bringing any
letters of introduction for the satisfaction of the proud. They
hired an elegant house, furnished it rich and fashionably, and
evidently prepared for the socialities of life, as enjoyed in the
highest circles. The appearance of wealth always commands

the respect of the many, and this respect was heightened by
their personal claims to admiration. Five years, however,
had wrought a change in both, not from the fading touch of
time, for they were not of an age when the green leaf begins
to grow sere, but other causes were operating with a power
as silent and unpausing. The fine, intelligent face of Mrs.
Manly had lost much of its delicacy of outline, and her cheek,
that formerly was pale or roseate as sensibility or enthusiasm
ruled the hour, now wore a stationary glow, deeper than the
blush of feminine modesty, less bright than the carnation of
health. The unrivalled beauty of her figure had given place
to grosser lineaments, over which, however, grace and dignity
still lingered, as if unwilling to leave a shrine so worshipped.
Mr. Manly's majestic person was invested with an air of deeper
haughtiness, and his dark brow was contracted into an expression of prevailing gloom and austerity. Two lovely children,
one almost an infant, who were carried abroad every fair day
by their nurse, shared the attention their parents excited; and
many appealed to *her* for information respecting the strangers.
She was unable to satisfy their curiosity, as she had been a
member of their household but a short time, her services
having been hired while journeying to the place. The other
servants were hired after their arrival. Thus, one of the most
fruitful sources from which the inquisitive derive their aliment,
was denied to the inhabitants of G———. It was not long
before the house of Mr. and Mrs. Manly was frequented by
those whose society she most wished to cultivate. The suavity
of her manners, the vivacity of her conversation, her politeness and disinterestedness, captivated the hearts of all. Mr.
Manly too received his guests with a cordiality that surprised,
while it gratified. Awed by the external dignity of his deportment, they expected to be repulsed, rather than welcomed,
but it was universally acknowledged, that no man could be
more delightful than Mr. Manly, when he chose to unbend.
As a lawyer, his fame soon rose. His integrity and eloquenc
became the theme of every tongue. Amidst all the admiration
they excited, there were some dark surmises. The malicious,
the censorious, the evil-disposed are found in every circle, and
in every land. It was noticed that Mr. Manly watched his
wife with painful scrutiny, that she seemed uneasy whenever
his glance met hers, that her manner was at times hurried and
disturbed, as if some secret cause of sorrow preyed upon her
mind. It was *settled* in the opinion of many, that Mr. Manly

was a domestic tyrant, and that his wife was the meek victim of this despotism. Some suggested that he had been convicted of crime, and had fled from the pursuit of justice, while his devoted wife refused to separate her destiny from his. They gave a large and elegant party. The entertainment was superior to anything witnessed before in the precincts of G———. The graceful hostess, dressed in unwonted splendour, moved through her drawing-rooms, with the step of one accustomed to the homage of crowds, yet her smiles sought out the most undistinguished of her guests, and the most diffident gathered confidence from her condescending regards. Still the eye of Mr. Manly followed her with that anxious, mysterious glance, and her hurried movements often betrayed inexplicable perturbation. In the course of the evening, a gentleman refused wine, on the plea of belonging to the Temperance Society. Many voices were lifted in condemnation against him, for excluding one of the gladdeners of existence, what, the Scriptures themselves recommended, and the Saviour of men had consecrated by a miracle. The subject grew interesting, the circle narrowed round the advocate of Temperance, and many were pressing eagerly forward to listen to the debate. The opinion of Mrs. Manly was demanded. She drew back at first, as if unwilling to take the lead of her guests. At length she seemed warmed by the subject, and painted the evils of intemperance in the strongest and most appalling colours. She painted woman as its victim, till every heart recoiled at the image she drew. So forcible was her language, so impressive her gestures, so unaffected her emotions, every eye was riveted, and every ear bent on the eloquent mourner of her sex's degradation. She paused, oppressed by the notice she attracted, and moved from the circle, that widened for her as she passed, and gazed after her, with as much respect as if she were an Empress. During this spontaneous burst of oratory, Mr. Manly remained aloof, but those who had marked him in their minds as the harsh domestic tyrant, were now confirmed in their belief. Instead of admiring the wonderful talents of his wife, or sympathizing in the applause she excited, a gloom thick as night lowered upon his brow, his face actually grew of a livid paleness, till at last, as if unable to control his temper, he left the drawing-room.

"Poor Mrs. Manly," said one, "how much is her destiny to be lamented! To be united to a man who is incapable of

appreciating her genius, and even seems guilty of the meanness of annoying her."

Thus the world judges; and had the tortured heart of
Manly known the sentence that was passing upon him, he
would have rejoiced that thé shaft was directed to *his* bosom,
rather than *hers*, which he would fain shield from the proud
man's contumely, though it might never more be the resting-
lace of love and confidence. Is it necessary to go back and
elate the history of those years which had elapsed since Anne
Weston was presented to the reader as a triumphant belle, and
plighted bride! Is it not already seen that the dark speck
had enlarged, throwing into gradual, but deepening shade, the
soul's original brightness, obscuring the sunshine of domestic
joy, converting the home of love into a prison-house of
shame, and blighting, chilling, palsying the loftiest energies
and noblest purposes? The warning accents of Emily Spencer
were breathed in vain. That fatal habit had already become
a passion—a passion which, like the rising tide, grows deeper
and higher, rolling onward and onward, till the landmarks of
reason, and honour, and principle, are swept over by its waves
—a tide that ebbs not but with ebbing life. She had looked
"upon the wine when it was red, when it gave its colour to
the cup," till she found, by fatal experience, that it biteth like
a serpent, and stingeth like an adder. It were vain to attempt
à description of the feelings of Manly when he first discovered
the idol of his imagination under an influence that, in his
opinion, brutalized a man. But a woman!—and that woman
—his wife! In the agony, the madness of the moment, he
could have lifted the hand of suicide, but Emily Spencer
hovered near and held him back from the brink to which he
was rushing. She pleaded the cause of her unhappy friend,
she prayed him not to cast her off. She dwelt on the bright
and sparkling mind, the warm, impulsive heart that might yet
be saved from utter degradation by his exerted influence. She
pledged herself to labour for him, and with him, and faithfully
did she redeem her pledge. After the first terrible shock,
Manly's passionate emotion settled down into a misanthropic
gloom. Sometimes when he witnessed the remorse which
followed such self-abandonment, the grace and beauty with
which she would emerge from the disfiguring cloud, and the
strong efforts she would make to reinstate herself in his estimation, a ray of brightness would shine in on his mind, and
he would try to think of the past as a frightful dream. Then

his prophetic dream would return to him, and he shuddered at its confirmation—once it seemed as if the demon had withdrawn its unhallowed presence, unable to exist in the holy atmosphere that surrounds a mother's bosom.

For a long time the burning essence was not permitted to mingle with the fountain of maternal tenderness. Even Manly's blasted spirit revived, and Emily hoped all, and believed all. But Anne had once passed the Rubicon, and though she often paused and looked back with yearnings that could not be uttered, upon the fair bounds she had left, the very poignancy of her shame goaded her on, though every step she took, evidenced the shame that was separating her from the affections of a husband whom she loved and respected, and who had once idolized her. It has been said that when woman once becomes a transgressor, her rapid progress in sin mocks the speed of man. As the glacier, that has long shone in dazzling purity, when loosened from its mountain stay, rushes down with a velocity accelerated by its impenetrability and coldness, when any shameful passion has melted the virgin snow of a woman's character, a moral avalanche ensues, destroying " whatsoever is venerable and lovely, and of good report."

Manly occasionally sought to conceal from the world the fatal propensities of his wife. She had occupied too conspicuous a station in society—she had been too highly exalted —to humble herself with impunity. Her father, whose lavish indulgence probably paved the way to her ruin, was unable to bear himself up under the weight of mortification and grief thus unexpectedly brought upon him. His constitution had long been feeble; and now the *bowl was, indeed, broken at the fountain.* The filial hand which he once hoped would have scattered roses on his dying pillow, struck the death-blow. Physicians talked of a chronic disease; of the gradual decay of nature; but Anne's conscience told her she had winged the dart. The agony of her remorse seemed a foretaste of the quenchless fire, and the undying worm. She made the most solemn promises of reformation—vowed never again to taste the poisonous liquor. She threw herself on the forgiveness of her husband, and prayed him to remove her where her name was never breathed; that she might begin life anew, and establish for their children an unblemished reputation. On the faith of these ardent resolutions, Manly broke his connexion with every former friend—sold all his possessions, and sought a new home, in a place far removed from the scene of their present unhappiness. Circumstances in her own family prevented Emily Spencer from accompanying them, but she was to follow them the earliest opportunity, hoping miracles from the change. •

Mrs Manly, from the death of her father, came into the possession of a large and independent fortune. She was not sordid enough to deem money an equivalent for a wounded reputation; but it was soothing to her pride, to be able to fill her husband's coffers so richly, and to fit up their new establishment in a style so magnificent. Manly allowed her to exercise her own taste in everything. He knew the effect of external pomp, and thought it was well to dazzle the judgment of the world. He was determined to seek society; to open every source of gratification and rational excitement to his wife, to save her from monotony and solitude. His whole aim seemed to be, "that she might not be led into temptation." If with all these cares for her safety, he could have blended the tenderness that once softened his proud manners, could he have banished from his once beaming eye the look of vigilance and distrust; could she have felt herself once more enthroned in his heart, gratitude might, perhaps, have completed the regeneration begun by remorse. But Anne felt that she was an object of constant suspicion and fear; she felt that he had not faith in her good resolutions. She was no longer the sharer of his counsels—the inspirer of his hopes— or the companion in whom his soul delighted. His ruling passion supported him in society; but in those hours when they were necessarily thrown upon each other's resources, he was accustomed to sit in gloomy abstraction, brooding over his own melancholy thoughts. Anne was only too conscious of the subject of these reveries, and it kept alive a painful sense of her humiliation. She had, hitherto, kept her promise sacred, through struggles known only to herself, and she began to feel impatient and indignant that the reward for which she looked was still withheld. Had she been more deeply skilled in the mysteries of the human heart, she might have addressed the Genius of the household shrine, in the language of the avenging Moor, who first apostrophizes the torch that flares on his deed of darkness:

" If I quench thee, thou flaming minister,
I can again thy former light restore,

Should I repent me—but once put out thine,
I know not where is the Promethean heat
That can thy light relume."

Mr. Manly was called away by professional business, which would probably detain him many weeks from home. He regretted this necessity; particularly before the arrival of Emily, whose coming was daily expected. He urged his wife to invite some friends to remain as her guests during his absence, to enliven her solitude. His request, so earnestly repeated, might have been gratifying to her feelings, if she had not known the distrust of her faith and strength of resolution it implied. The last words he said to her, at parting, were, "Remember, Anne, everything depends on yourself." She experienced a sensation of unspeakable relief in his absence. The eagle glance was withdrawn from her soul, and it expanded and exulted in its newly acquired freedom. She had a constant succession of visiters, who, remarking the elasticity of her spirits, failed not to cast additional obloquy on Mr. Manly, for the tyranny he evidently exercised over his wife. Emily did not arrive, and Mrs. Manly could not regret the delay. Her presence reminded her of all she wished to forget; for her days of triumph were returned, and the desire of shining rekindled from the ashes of scorn, that had for a while smothered the flame.

It wanted about a week of Mr. Manly's return. She felt a strong inclination to renew the splendours of her party. She had received so many compliments on the subject:—"Mrs. Manly's delightful party!" "Her conversational powers!" "Such a literary banquet!" &c. Invitations were given and accepted. The morning of the day, which was somewhat warm and oppressive, she was summoned by the kitchen council, where the business of preparation was going on. Suddenly, however, they came to a stand. There was no brandy to give flavour to the cake; and the cook declared it was impossible to make it without, or to use anything as a substitute.

Mrs. Manly's cheeks flushed high with shame. Her husband had retained the key of the closet that contained the forbidden article. He was afraid to trust it in her keeping. The mildest cordials were alone left at her disposal, for the entertainment of her guests. What would her husband think if she purchased, in his absence, what he had himself secreted from her? What would the servants believe if she refused to pro-

vide them with what was deemed indispensable? The fear of
her secret being detected, combined with resentment at her
husband's unyielding distrust, decided her conduct. She
bought—she *tasted*. The cook asserted there was something
peculiar in its flavour, and asked her to judge for herself.
Would it not excite suspicion, if she refused? She broke her
solemn vow—she *tasted*—and was *undone*. The burning
thirst once kindled, in those who have been victims to this
fatal passion, it rages with the strength of madness. In the
secrecy of the closet where she hid the poison, she yielded to
the tempter, who whispered, that, as she had been *compelled*
to taste, her promise had been innocently broken: there could
be no harm in a *little more*—the last that should ever pass
her lips. In the delirium of the moment, she yielded, till, incapable of self-control, she continued the inebriating draught.
Judgment—reason—at length, perception, vanished. The
approach of evening found her still prostrate on her bed, a
melancholy instance of the futility of the best human resolutions, unsupported by the divine principle of religion. The
servants were at first struck with consternation. They thought
some sudden disease had overtaken her. But the marks of
intemperance, that, like the brand on the brow of Cain, single
out its votaries from the rest of mankind, those revolting traces,
were but too visible. They knew not what to do. Uncertain
what guests were invited, they could not send apologies, nor
ask them to defer their visit. The shades of evening were
beginning to fall; the children were crying, deprived of the
usual cares of their nurse; and in the general bustle, clung
to their mother, whose ear was deaf to the appeal of nature.
The little one, weary of shedding so many unavailing tears, at
last crawled up on the bed, and fell asleep by her side, though
there was scarcely room for her to stretch her little limbs,
where she had found the means of climbing. As her slumbers
deepened, her limbs relaxed from the rigid posture they had
assumed: her arms dropped unconsciously over the bed, and
she fell. In her fall she was thrown against one of the posts,
and a sharp corner cutting her head, inflicted a deep wound.
The screams of the little sufferer roused the household, and
pierced even the leaden slumbers of intemperance. It was
long, however, before Mrs. Manly came to a clear perception
of what was passing around her. The sight of the streaming
blood, however, acted like a shock of electricity. She sprang
up, and endeavoured to stanch the bleeding wound. The effu-

sion was soon stopped; the child sunk into a peaceful sleep, and the alarm subsided.

Children are liable to so many falls, and bruises, and wounds, it is not strange that Mrs. Manly, in the confused state of her mind, should soon forget the accident, and try to prepare herself for the reception of her guests, who were already assembling in the drawing-room. Every time the bell rung, she started, with a thrill of horror, conscious how unfit she was to sustain the enviable reputation she had acquired. Her head ached almost to bursting, her hands trembled, and a deadly sickness oppressed her. The visions of an upbraiding husband, a scoffing world, rose before her—and dim, but awful, in the dark perspective, she seemed to behold the shadow of a sin-avenging Deity. Another ring—the guests were thronging. Unhappy woman! What was to be done? She would have pleaded sudden indisposition—the accident of her child—but the fear that the servants would reveal the truth—the hope of being able to rally her spirits—determined her to descend into the drawing-room. As she cast a last hurried glance into the mirror, and saw the wild, haggard countenance it reflected, she recoiled at her own image. The jewels with which she had profusely adorned herself, served but to mock the ravages the destroying scourge had made upon her beauty. No cosmetic art could restore the purity of her complexion; nor the costliest perfumes conceal the odour of the fiery liquor. She called for a glass of cordial— kindled up a smile of welcome, and descended to perform the honours of her household. She made a thousand apologies for her delay; related, in glowing colours, the accident that happened to her child, and flew from one subject to another, as if she feared to trust herself with a pause. There was something so unnatural in her countenance, so overstrained in her manner, and so extravagant in her conversation, it was impossible for the company not to be aware of her situation. Silent glances were exchanged, low whispers passed round; but they had no inclination to lose the entertainment they anticipated. They remembered the luxuries of her table, and hoped, at least, if not a "feast of reason," a feast of the good things of earth.

It was at this crisis Emily Spencer arrived. Her travelling dress, and the fatigue of a journey, were sufficient excuses for her declining to appear in the drawing-room; but the moment she saw Mrs. Manly, her eye, too well experienced, perceived the backsliding of Anne, and hope died within her bosom. Sick at heart, wounded, and indignant, she sat down in the chamber where the children slept—those innocent beings, doomed to an orphanage more sad than death even makes. Anne's conscious spirit quailed before the deep reproach of Emily's silent glances. She stammered out an explanation of the bloody bandage that was bound around the infant's head, assured her there was no cause of alarm, and hurried down to the *friends* who had passed the period of her absence in covert sarcasm, and open animadversion on her conduct.

Emily sat down on the side of the bed, and leaned over the sleeping infant. Though Mrs. Manly had assured her there was no cause of alarm, she felt there was no reliance on her judgment; and the excessive paleness and languor of its countenance, excited an anxiety its peaceful slumbers could not entirely relieve. "It is all over," thought she, "a relapse in sin is always a thousand times more dangerous than the first yielding. She is at this moment blazoning her disgrace, and there will be no restraining influence left. Oh! unfortunate Manly! was it for this you sacrificed home, friends, and splendid prospects, and came a stranger to a strange land!" Absorbed in the contemplation of Manly's unhappy destiny, she remained till the company dispersed, and Mrs. Manly dragged her weary footsteps to her chamber. Completely exhausted by her efforts to command her bewildered faculties, she threw herself on the bed, and sunk into a lethargy; the natural consequence of inebriation. The infant, disturbed by the sudden motion, awakened, with a languid cry, expressive of feebleness and pain. Emily raised it in her arms, endeavoured to soothe its complaining; but it continued restless and wailing, till the blood gushed afresh through the bandage. Greatly alarmed, she shook Mrs. Manly's arm, and called upon her to awake. It was in vain; she could not rouse her from her torpor. Instantly ringing the bell, she summoned the nurse, who was revelling, with the other servants, over the relics of the feast, and told her to send immediately for a physician. Fortunately there was one in the neighbourhood, and he came speedily. He shook his head mournfully when he examined the condition of the child, and pronounced its case beyond the reach of human skill. The injury produced by the fall had reached the brain. The very depth of its slumbers was but a fatal symptom of approaching dissolution. The tears of Emily fell

fast and thick on the pallid face of the innocent victim. She
looked upon its mother—thought upon its father, and pressed
the child in agony to her bosom. The kind physician was
summoned to another chamber of sickness. He had done all
he could to mitigate, where he could not heal. Emily felt
that this dispensation was sent in mercy. She could not pray
for the child's life, but she prayed that it might die in the
arms of its father; and it seemed that her prayer was heard.
It was a singular providence that brought him that very night
—a week sooner than he anticipated—urged on by a restless
presentiment of evil; a dread that all was not well. Imagination, however, had not pictured the scene that awaited him.
His wife, clothed in her richest raiments, and glittering with
jewels, lying in the deep torpor of inebriation. Emily, seated
by the side of the bed, bathed in tears, holding in her lap the
dying infant, her dress stained with the blood with which the
fair locks of the child were matted. What a spectacle! He
stood for a moment on the threshold of the apartment, as if a
bolt had transfixed him. Emily was not roused from her
grief by the sound of his footsteps, but she saw the shadow
that darkened the wall, and at once recognised his lineaments.
The startling cry she uttered brought him to her side, where,
kneeling down over his expiring infant, he gazed on its
altering features and quivering frame with a countenance so
pale and stern, Emily's blood ran cold. Silently and fixedly
he knelt, while the deepening shades of dissolution gathered
over the beautiful waxen features and the dark film grew over
the eyes, so lately bright with that heavenly blue, which is
alone seen in the eyes of infancy. He inhaled its last, cold,
struggling breath; saw it stretched in the awful immobility
of death; then slowly rising, he turned towards the gaudy
figure that lay as if in mockery of the desolation it had
created. Then Manly's imprisoned spirit burst its bonds.
He grasped his wife's arm, with a strength that might have
been felt, even were her limbs of steel, and calling forth her
name in a voice deep and thrilling as the trumpet's blast, he
commanded her to rise. With a faint foretaste of the feeling
with which the guilty soul shall meet the awakening summons
of the archangel, the wretched woman raised herself on her
elbow, and gazed around her with a wild and glassy stare.
" Woman," cried he, still retaining his desperate grasp, and
pointing to the dead child, extended on the lap of the weeping
Emily, ' woman! is this your work? Is this the welcome

you have prepared for my return? Oh! most perjured wife and most abandoned mother! You have filled, to overflowing, the vials of indignation; on your own head shall they be poured, blasting and destroying. You have broken the last tie that bound me—it withers like flax in the flame. Was it not enough to bring down the gray hairs of your father to the grave? to steep your own soul in perjury and shame, but that fair innocent must be a sacrifice to your drunken revels? One other victim remains. Your husband—who lives to curse the hour he ever yielded to a syren, who lured him to the brink of hell!"

He paused suddenly—relaxed his iron hold, and fell back perfectly insensible. It is an awful thing to see man fall down in his strength, struck, too, by the lightning of passion. Anne sprang upon her feet. The benumbing spell was broken. His last words had reached her naked soul. She believed him dead, and that he had indeed died *her* victim. Every other thought and feeling was swallowed up in this belief; she threw herself by his side, uttering the most piercing shrieks, and rending her sable tresses, in the impotence of despair. Poor Emily! it was for her a night of horror; but her fortitude and presence of mind seemed to increase with the strength of the occasion. She turned her cares from the dead to the living. She bathed with restorative waters the pale brow of Manly; she chafed his cold hands, till their icy chill began to melt in the warmth of returning animation. All the while his wretched wife continued her useless and appalling ravings.

The morning dawned upon a scene of desolation. In one darkened room lay the snowy corpse, dressed in the white garments of the grave; in another, the almost unconscious Manly, in the first stages of a burning fever; Anne, crouched in a dark corner, her face buried in her hands; and Emily, pale and wan, but energetic and untiring, still the ministering and healing spirit of this house of grief. Yes! darkness and mourning was in that house; but the visitation of God had not come upon it: Pestilence had not walked in the darkness, nor Destruction, at the noon-day hour. Had Anne resisted the voice of the tempter, her child might have still smiled in his cherub beauty; her husband might have still presided at his board, and she, herself, at his side; if not in the sunshine of love, in the light of increasing confidence. Her frame was worn by the long, silent struggles of contending passions, hopes, and fears. This last blow prostrated her in

the dust. Had *Anne resisted the voice of the tempter*, all
might yet have been well; but having once again steeped her
lips in the pollution, the very consciousness of her degradation
plunged her deeper in sin. She fled from the writhing of
remorse to the oblivious draught. She gave herself up, body
and soul, irredeemably. She was hurrying on, with fearful
strides, to that brink from which so many immortal beings
have plunged into the fathomless gulf of perdition.

Manly rose from the couch of sickness an altered man : his
proud spirit was humbled—chastened—purified. Brought to
the confines of the unseen world, he was made to feel the
vanity—the nothingness of this—and while his soul seemed
floating on the shoreless ocean of eternity, the billows of
human passion sunk before the immensity, the awfulness of
the scene. The holy resolutions, formed on what he believed
his death-bed, did not vanish with returning health. He saw
the bitter cup prepared for him to drain, and though he prayed
that it might be permitted to pass from him, he could say, in
the resignation of his heart, "Not my will, oh, Father! but
thine be done." He looked upon his degraded wife rather
with pity, than indignation. He no longer reproached her,
or used the language of denunciation. But sometimes, in her
lucid intervals, when she witnessed the subdued expression of
his once haughty countenance—his deep paleness—the mildness of his deportment to all around him ; the watchful guard
he held over his own spirit; and all this accompanied by an
energy in action—a devotedness in duty—such as she had
never seen before—Anne trembled, and felt that he had been
near unto his Maker, while she was holding closer and closer
companionship with the powers of darkness. The wall of
separation she had been building up between them, was it
to become high as the heavens—deep as the regions of irremediable woe ?

Emily was no longer their guest. While Manly lingered
between life and death, she watched over him with all a sister's
tenderness. Insensible to fatigue—forgetful of sleep—and
regardless of food, she was sustained by the intensity of her
anxiety; but as soon as his renovated glance could answer her
attentions with speechless gratitude, and he became conscious
of the cares that had done more than the physician's skill in
bringing him back to life, she gradually yielded to others the
place she had occupied as nurse—that place, which she who
should have claimed it as her right, was incapacitated to fill.

When Manly was restored to health, Emily felt that she could no longer remain. There was no more fellowship with Anne; and the sympathy that bound her to her husband she could not, with propriety, indulge. Manly, himself, did not oppose her departure; he felt it was best she should go. She took with her the little Anne, with the grateful consent of her father. The opposition of the mother was not allowed to triumph over what Manly knew was for the blessing of his child. "Let her go," said he, mildly, but determinately; "she will not feel the want of a mother's care."

* * * * * * * * * *

It was a dark and tempestuous night. The winds of autumn swept against the windows, with the mournful rustle of the withered leaves, fluttering in the blast: the sky was moonless and starless. Everything abroad presented an aspect of gloom and desolation. Even those who were gathered in the halls of pleasure, felt saddened by the melancholy sighing of the gust; and a cold, whispered mortality breathed into the hearts of the thoughtless and gay. It was on this night that Manly sat by the dying couch of Anne. Every one is familiar with the rapid progress of disease, when it attacks the votary of intemperance. The burning blood soon withers up the veins; the fountain, itself, becomes dry. Fearfully rapid, in this instance, had been the steps of the destroyer. Here she lay, her frame tortured with the agonies of approaching dissolution, and her spirit strong and clear from the mists that had so long and so fatally obscured it. She saw herself in that mirror which the hand of truth holds up to the eye of the dying. Memory, which acquires, at that awful moment, such supernatural power, brought before her all the past—the *wasted past*—the *irretrievable past.* Her innocent childhood—her bright and glowing youth; her blasted womanhood, seemed embodied to her eyes. Her father rose from his grave, and standing by her bedside, waving his mournful locks, warned her of her broken oath. Her little infant, with his fair hair dabbled with blood, came gliding in·its shroud, and accused her of being its murderer. Her husband! As her frenzied spirit called up this last image, she turned her dim eye to him, who was hanging over her couch with a countenance of such grief and compassion, the dry agony of her despair softened into a gush of remorseful tenderness:· "Oh! no—no!" cried she, in difficult accents, "you do not curse me; you live to pardon the wretch who has undone herself and you. Oh! could I live over the past; could I carry back to our bridal the experience of this awful hour, what long years of happiness might be ours!"

The recollection of what she had been—of what she *might have been*—contrasted with what she then was, and with what she still *might be*, was too terrible. Her agonies became wordless. Manly knelt by her side : he sought to soothe her departing spirit by assurances of his own pardon ; and to lead her, by penitence and prayer, to the feet of Him, "in whose sight the heavens are not clean." He poured into her soul the experience of his, when he had travelled to the boundaries of the dark valley : his despair—his penitence, and his hopes. He spoke of the mercy that is boundless—the grace that is infinite—till the phantoms, accusing conscience called up, seemed to change their maledictions into prayers for her behalf. Her ravings gradually died away, and she sunk into a troubled sleep.

As Manly gazed upon her features, on which death was already fixing its dim, mysterious impress,—those features whose original beauty was so fearfully marred by the ravages of intemperance,—the waters of time rolled back, and revealed that green, enchanted spot in life's waste, where he was first gilded by her presence. Was that the form whose graceful movements then fascinated his senses ; or those the eyes, whose kindling glances had flashed like a glory over his soul? The love, then so idolatrous and impassioned—so long crushed and buried—rose up from the ruins to hallow the vigils of that solemn night.

The morning dawned, but the slumbers of Anne were never to be broken, till the resurrection morn. In the bloom of life —the midst of affluence—with talents created to exalt society, and graces to adorn it; a heart full of warm and generous impulses ; a husband as much the object of her pride as of her affections ; children, lovely in their innocence, she fell a sacrifice to one brutalizing passion. Seldom, indeed, is it that woman, in the higher walks of life, presents such a melancholy example ; but were there but *one*, and that one Anne Weston, let her name be revealed, as a beacon, whose warning light should be seen by the daughters of the land.

*   *   *   *   *   *   *   *   *   *

Another year glided by. The approach of another autumn,

found Manly girded for enterprise. He had marked out a new path, and was about to become a dweller of a young and powerful city, born on one of the mighty rivers of the West. His child could there grow up, unwithered by the associations of her mother's disgrace. Amidst the hopes and anticipations gathering around a new home, in a new land, his own spirit might shake off the memories that oppressed its energies. He was still young. The future might offer something of brightness, to indemnify for the darkness of the past.

He once more sought the native place of his unhappy wife; for his child was there, under the cherishing care of Emily Spencer. He passed that ball-room, in whose illuminated walls his destiny was sealed. The chamber selected for the traveller's resting-place was the one where the prophetic dream had haunted his pillow. His brow was saddened by the gloom of remembrance, when he entered the dwelling-place of his child; but when he saw the bright, beautiful little creature, who sprang into his arms, with spontaneous rapture, and witnessed the emotion that Emily strove vainly to conquer, he felt he was not alone in the world : and the future triumphed over the past. He unfolded all his views, and described the new scenes in which he was soon to become an actor, with reviving eloquence.

" Are you going to carry me there too, father ?" said the little girl, whose earnest blue eyes were riveted on his face.

" Are you not willing to go with me, my child? or must I leave you behind ?"

" I should like to go, if you will take Emily, but I cannot leave her behind," cried the affectionate child, clinging to that beloved friend, who had devoted herself to her with all a mother's tenderness.

" We will not leave her," exclaimed Manly, a warm glow spreading over his melancholy features, " if she will go with us, and bless our western home."

Emily turned pale, but she did not speak—she could not, if her existence had depended upon it. She was no sickly sentimentalist, but she had ardent affections, though always under the government of upright principles. Her mind was well balanced, and though passion might enter, it was never suffered to gain the ascendancy. From her earliest acquaintance with Manly, she had admired his talents, and respected his character; but the idea of *loving* the husband of her friend, never entered her pure imagination. It was not till she saw

105

him borne down by domestic sorrow, on the bed of sickness, thrown by the neglect of his wife on her tenderness and care, that she felt the danger and depth of her sympathy. The moment she became aware of her involuntary departure from integrity of feeling she fled, and in the tranquillity of her own home, devoted to his child the love she shuddered to think began to flow in an illegitimate channel. That Manly ever cherished any sentiments towards her, warmer than those of esteem and gratitude, she did not believe, but now he came before her, freed by heaven from the shackles that bound him, and duty no longer opposed its barrier to her affections, her heart told her she could follow him to the ends of the earth, and deem its coldest, darkest region, a Paradise, if warmed and illumed by his love ! The simplicity of child-hood had unveiled the hearts of each to the other. It was not with the romance of his earlier passion that Manly now wooed Emily Spencer to be his wife. It was love, approved by reason, and sanctified by religion. It was the Christian, seeking a fellow labourer in the work of duty; the father, yearning for a mother to watch over an orphan child—the man awakened to the loftiest, holiest purposes of his being.

In a beautiful mansion, looking down on one of the most magnificent landscapes unfolded in the rich valley of the West, Manly and Emily now reside. All the happiness capable of being enjoyed around the household shrine is theirs—and the only shade that ever dims their brows, is caused by the re-membrance of the highly gifted—but ill-fated Anne.

\

THE BLIND GIRL'S STORY.

ALL is still and solitary—the lamp burns on the table, with wasting splendour. The writing-desk is open before me, with the last letter unfolded—the letter I have cherished so fondly, though every word seems an arrow to my conscience. I cannot solace myself by the act, yet I must give utterance to the feelings with which my heart is bursting. On these unwritten sheets I will breathe my soul—I will trace its early history, and, perchance, *his* eye may see them when mine are veiled in a darkness deeper than that which once sealed them. Yet what shall I write? How shall I commence? What great events rise up in the records of memory, over which imagination may throw its rich empurpling dyes? Alas! mine is but a record of the heart—but of a *blind* girl's heart—and that Being who bound my eyes with a fillet of darkness, till the hand of science lifted the thick film, and flooded them with the glories of creation, alone knows the mysteries of the spirit he has made. *His* eye is upon me at this moment, and as this awful conviction comes over me, a kind of deathlike calmness settles on the restless sea of passion. Oh! when I was blind, what was my conception of the All-seeing eye! It seemed to me as if it filled the world with its effulgence. I felt as if I, in my blindness, were placed in the hollow of that rock where Moses hid, when the glory of the Lord passed by Would that no daring hand had drawn me from that protect ing shade! The beams that enlighten me have withered u the fountains of joy, and though surrounded by light, as with a garment, my soul is wrapped in the gloom of midnight. I was a blind child—blind from my birth—with one brother, older than myself, and a widowed father—for we were mo-therless—motherless, sisterless—yet blind. What a world of dependence is expressed in these few words! But, though

(63)

thus helpless and dependent, I was scarcely conscious of my peculiar claim to sympathy and care.

My father was wealthy, and my childhood was crowned with every indulgence that wealth could purchase, or parental tenderness devise. My brother was devotedly attached to me, giving up all his leisure to my amusement—for I was looked upon as hallowed by the misfortune which excluded me from communion with the visible world—and my wishes became laws, and my happiness the paramount object of the household. Heaven, perhaps, as a kind of indemnification for depriving me of one of the wonted blessings of life, moulded me in a form which pleased the fond eyes of my relatives, and, as it was my father's pride to array me in the most graceful and becoming attire, my sightless eyes being constantly covered by a silken screen, I was a happy child. If it had not been for the epithet, *poor*, so often attached to my name, I should never have dreamed that mine was a forlorn destiny. " My *poor* little blind girl," my father would exclaim, as he took me in his lap, after his return from his business abroad— " My *poor* little sister," was the constant appellation given me by my affectionate brother, yet I was happy. When he led me in the garden, through the odorous flowers, I felt a kind of aching rapture at the sweetness they exhaled—their soft, velvet texture, was ecstasy to the touch, and the wind-harps that played amid the branches of the trees were like the lyres of angels to my ears. Then the songs of birds, with what thrilling sensations would I listen to these harmonists of nature, these winged minstrels of God's own choir, as they lifted their strains of living harmony in the dim corridors of the woods ! They painted to me the beauty of the world, and I believed them—but I could conceive of nothing so beautiful as sound. I associated the idea of everything that was lovely with music. It was my passion, and also my peculiar talent. Every facility which art has furnished to supply the deficiencies of nature was given me, and my progress was considered astonishing by those who are not aware of the power and acuteness of touch bestowed upon the sightless. I love to linger on the days of my childhood, when sunshine flowed in upon my heart in one unclouded stream. The serpent slumbered in the bottom of the fountain—had no one gone down into its depths, its venom might have slumbered yet.

My first cause of sorrow was parting with my brother— " my guide, my companion, my familiar friend." He was sent to a distant college, and I felt for a while as if I were alone in the world, for my father was in public life, and it was only at evening he had leisure to indulge in the tenderness of domestic feeling. He had never given up the hope that I might recover my sight. When I was very small there was an operation performed upon my eyes, but it was by an unskilful oculist, and unsuccessful. After this I had an unspeakable dread of any future attempt,—the slightest allusion to the subject threw me into such nervous agitation, my father at last forbore to mention it. "Let me live and die under this shade," I would say, "like the flower that blooms in the cleft of the rock. The sunshine and the dew are not for me." Time glided away. In one year more Henry would complete his collegiate course. I was in the morning of womanhood, but my helpless condition preserved to me all the privileges and indulgences of the child. It was at this era—why did I here dash aside my pen, and press my hands upon my temples to still the throbbings of a thousand pulses, starting simultaneously into motion? Why cannot we always be children? Why was I not suffered to remain blind?—A young physician came into the neighbourhood, who had already acquired some fame as an oculist. He visited in our family—he became almost identified with our household. Philanthropy guided him in his choice of a profession. He knew himself gifted with extraordinary talents, and that he had it in his power to mitigate the woes of mankind. But though the votary of duty, he was a worshipper at the shrine of intellect and taste. He loved poetry, and, next to music, it was my passion. He read to me the melodious strains of the sons of song, in a voice more eloquent, in its low depth of sweetness, than the minstrels whose harmony he breathed. When I touched the keys of the piano, his voice was raised, in unison with mine. If I wandered in the garden, his hand was ever ready to guide, and his arm to sustain me. He brought me the wild-flower of the field, and the exotic of the green-house, and, as he described their hues and outlines, I scarcely regretted the want of vision. Here, in this book, I have pressed each faded gift. I remember the very words he uttered when he gave me this cluster.— "See," said he, "nay, *feel* this upright stem, so lofty, till bending from the weight of the flower it bears. It is a lily— I plucked it from the margin of a stream, in which it seemed gazing on its white, waxen leaves. Touch gently the briars of this wild rose. Thus heaven guards the innocence and beauty that gladdens the eyes of the wayfaring man. Cecilia, would you not like to look upon these flowers?" "Yes, but far rather on the faces of those I love—my father's—my brother's. Man is made in the image of his Maker, and his face must be divine." "Oh!" added I, in the secrecy of my own soul, "how divine must be the features of that friend, who has unfolded to me such unspeakable treasures of genius and feeling, whose companionship seems a foretaste of the felicities of heaven." It was then, for the first time, he dared to suggest to me a hope that my blindness was not incurable. He told me he had been devoting all his leisure to this one subject, and that he was sure he had mastered every difficulty; that though mine was a peculiar case, and had once baffled the efforts of the optician, he dared to assure himself of complete success. "And if I fail," said he, "if through my means no light should visit your darkened orbs, then," continued he, with an expression of feeling that seemed wholly irrepressible, "suffer me to be a light to your eyes and a lamp to your feet. But if it should be my lot to bestow upon you the most glorious of the gifts of God, to meet from you one glance of gratitude and love, were a recompense I would purchase with life itself." Did I dream? or were these words breathed to me? —me, the helpless, blind girl! to receive the unmeasured devotion of one of the most gifted and interesting of created beings. I had thought that he pitied me, that he felt for me the kindness of a brother, that he found in me some congenial tastes—but that he loved me so entirely, it was a confession as unlooked for as overpowering. My heart ached, from the oppression of its joy. Let not the cold-hearted and vain smile, when I repeat the broken accents of gratitude, trust, and love, that fell from my lips. My helplessness sanctified the offer, and I received his pledge of faith as a holy thing, to be kept holy through time and eternity.

    *   *   *   *   *   *   *   *   *

Never shall I forget that moment, when the first ray of light penetrated the long midnight that had shrouded my vision. It was in a darkened apartment. My father, one female friend, and Clinton, the beloved physician—these were around me. Faint, dim, and uncertain, as the first gray of the dawn, was that ray, but it was the herald of coming light, and hailed as a day-spring from on high. A bandage was immediately drawn over my brow, but during the weeks in which I was condemned to remain in darkness, the memory of that dim radiance was ever glimmering round me.   There was a figure kneeling, with clasped hands and upraised head, pale and venerable—I knew it was my father's—for the same figure folded me to his heart the next moment, and wept like an infant.   There was one with soft flowing outline, and loose robes, by my side,—and bending over me, with eyes gazing down into the mysteries of my being, shadowy but glorious, was he, who received the firs glance of the being he had awakened to a new creation Slowly, gradually was I allowed to emerge from my eclipse, but when I was at last led from my darkened chamber, when I looked abroad on the face of nature, clothed as she was in the magnificent garniture of summer, when I saw the heavens unrolled in their majesty, the sun travelling in the greatness of his strength, the flowers glowing in the beams that enamelled them, I closed my eyes, almost fainting from the excessive glory.   I will not attempt to describe my sensations when I first distinctly saw the lineaments of my lover.   Creation contained nothing so lovely to my sight.   To see the soul, the thinking, feeling, immortal soul, flashing with enthusiasm, or darkening with tenderness, looking forth from his eyes, and feel my own mingling with his!   No one but those who have once been blind, and now see, can imagine the intensity of my emotions.   Next to my Creator, I felt my homage was due to him, and surely it is not impious to apply to him the sublime language of Scripture—" He said, let there be light, and there was light."

Our mansion was transformed.   My father gathered all his friends around him to participate in his joy.   My brother was summoned home.   There seemed one continual jubilee.   I turned coldly, however, from all these festivities, occupied almost exclusively with one feeling.   I could not feign an interest in others I did not feel.   I began even at this early period to experience the first symptoms of that passion, which has since consumed me.   Clinton, though still, as ever, the kind, devoted, and watchful guardian, hovering round my steps, as if to shield me from every danger, Clinton, I saw, shared in the pleasures of sociality, and returned the smiles that kindled wherever he moved.   He was a universal favourite in society, and knew how to adapt himself to others, not from a vague desire of popularity, but from a benevolence, a sunny glow of feeling, shedding light and warmth all around. Even then there were moments when I regretted my blindness, and wished I had never seen those smiles and glances, which

I would fain rivet for ever on myself. Henry, my brother,
once whispered to me, as I was turning, in a languid manner,
the leaves of a music book, not caring to play because Clinton
was not bending over my chair, "My dear Cecilia, do not let
Clinton see too glaringly his power over you. There is scarcely
man in the world who can be trusted with unlimited power.
We are ungrateful creatures, my sweet sister, and you do not
know us half as well as we know each other. You ought to
love Clinton, for he merits it, but be mistress of yourself. Do
not love him too well for *his* peace and your *own*." Alas!
poor Henry—how little have I heeded your brotherly admonitions? But when did passion ever listen to the counsels of
reason—when will it? When the cygnet's down proves a
barrier to the tempest's breath. We were married. I became
the inmate of a home, fashioned after the model of my own
taste. Everything was arranged with a view to my happiness.
The curtains and decorations of the house were all of the softest
green, for the repose of my still feeble eyes. Oh! thou benefactor of my life—friend, lover, husband, would that I could
go back to the hour when we plighted our wedded vows, and
live over the past, convinced, though too late, how deeply I
have wronged thee—confiding implicitly in thy love and truth,
we might live together the life of angels! And we were happy
for a while. We withdrew as much as possible from the gay
world. He saw that I loved retirement, and he consulted my
feelings as far as was consistent with the duties of his profession. I might have been convinced by this of the injustice of
my suspicions. I might have known that he loved me better
than all the world beside. During the day he was but
seldom with me, as his practice was extensive, and often called
him to a distance from home, but the evening was mine, and
it seemed my peculiar province, for I shrunk from the full
blaze of sunlight. The brightness was too intense, but when
the moon was gliding over the firmament, in her sweet, ap-
proachable loveliness, and the soft glitter of the stars was
around, I could lift my undazzled eyes, and marvel at the
wonderful works of God. Clinton was a devout astronomer—
he taught me the name of every planet that burned—of every
star known to science. He was rich in the wisdom of ancient
days, and his lips distilled instruction as naturally and constantly as the girl in the fairy tale dropped the gems of the
Orient. I have made mention of a female friend—she was
the daughter of a deceased friend of my father, and, as such,

came under his especial guardianship. Since my marriage she had remained with him, to cheer his loneliness, but her health becoming very delicate, he sent her to be my guest, that she might receive medical aid from my husband. She was not a decided invalid, but her mother had died of a consumption, and it was feared she had a hereditary tendency to that disease. Alice was a pale, delicate-looking girl, with sometimes a hectic flush on her cheek, a frail, drooping form, and extremely pensive cast of countenance. The dread of this constitutional malady hung over her like a death-cloud, and aggravated symptoms slight in themselves. Though there was nothing very attractive in the appearance of this poor girl, she was calculated to excite pity and sympathy, and surely she had every claim to mine. I did pity her, and sought, by every attention and kindness, to enliven her despondency, and rouse her to hope and vivacity. But I soon found that my father had encroached sadly on my domestic happiness by giving this charge to my husband. Air, exercise, and gentle recreation, were the remedies prescribed by the physician, and it was his duty to promote these by every means in his power. She often accompanied him on horseback in his rides, a pleasure from which I was completely debarred, for, in my blindness, I was incapacitated, and the timidity which originated from my situation remained after the cause was removed. It was some time before I was willing to acknowledge to myself the pain which this arrangement gave me. I felt as if my dearest privileges were invaded. I had been so accustomed, from infancy, to be the sole object of every attention, these daily offices bestowed upon another, though dictated by kindness and humanity, were intolerable to me. Had I seen the congregated world around her, offering every homage, it would not have given me one envious pang — but Clinton, my husband, he was more precious to me than ten thousand worlds. She leaned too exclusively on his guardian care. I tried to subdue my feelings —I tried to assume an appearance of indifference. My manners gradually became cold and constrained, and instead of greeting my husband with the joyous smile of welcome, on his return, I would avert from his the eyes which had received from him their living rays. Frank and unsuspicious himself, he did not seem to divine the cause of my altered demeanour. When he asked me why I was so silent, or so sad, I pleaded indisposition, lassitude—anything but the truth. I blamed him for his want of penetration, for I felt as if my soul were

bare, and that the eye of affection could read the tidings revealed by my changing cheek and troubled brow.   In justice
to myself, let me say, that Alice, by her manner, justified my
emotions.

Enlightened by the sentiment in my own bosom, I could
not but mark that the hectic flush always became brighter
when Clinton approached, that her glance, kindling as it moved
followed his steps with a kind of idolatry.   Then she hung
upon his words with an attention so flattering.   Was she reading, reclining on the sofa, apparently languid and uninterested,
the moment he spoke she would close her book, or lean forward, as if fearful of losing the faintest sound of that voice,
which was the music of my life.   I could have borne this for
a day, a week, a month—but to be doomed to endure it for an
indefinite term, perhaps for life, it was unendurable.   A hundred times I was on the point of going to my father, and, telling him the secret of my unhappiness, entreat him to recall
my too encroaching guest, but shame and pride restrained me.
Chilled and wounded by my coldness, my husband gradually
learned to copy it, and no longer sought the smiles and caresses
my foolish, too exciting heart, deemed he no longer valued.
Oh! blissful days of early confidence and love! were ye foi
ever flown?   Was no beam of tenderness permitted to penetrate the cold frost-work of ceremony deepening between us?
It is in vain to cherish love with the memory of what has
been.   It must be fed with daily living offerings, or the vestal
fire will wax dim and perish—then fearful is the penalty that
ensues.   The doom denounced upon the virgins of the temple,
when they suffered the holy flame to become extinct, was less
terrible.   Alice, when the mildness of the weather allowed,
almost made her home in the garden.   She must have felt
that I shrunk from her society, and I knew she could not love
the wife of Clinton.   She carried her books and pencil there
—she watched the opening blossoms, and gathered the sweet-
est, to make her offering at the shrine she loved.   My husband
was evidently pleased with these attentions, flowing, as he
thought, from a gentle and grateful heart, and his glance and
voice grew softer when he turned to address the invalid.

Once during the absence of Alice I went into her chamber
for a book I had lent her, which contained a passage I wished
to recall.   I took up several others, which lay upon the table.
There was one which belonged to my husband, and in it was
a piece of folded paper, embalmed with flowers, like some holy

relic.· It was not sealed—it was open—it was a medical prescription, written by Clinton, thus tenderly, romantically preserved. On another half-torn sheet were some broken lines,
breathing passion and despair. They were in the handwriting
of Alice, and apparently original, without address or signature,
but it was easy for my excited imagination to supply them.
Poor victim of passion—by the side of this record of all my
fears was the composing draught, prepared to check the con-
sumptive cough—the elixir to sustain the failing principles of
vitality. How is it that we dare to kindle an unhallowed
flame, even on the ashes of decaying mortality? I left the
chamber, and retired to my own. I knew not in what manner
to act. I endeavoured to reflect on what I ought to do. Alice
and myself could not live long under the same roof, yet how
could I bid her depart, or betray her to my husband? I could
not believe such feelings could be excited in her without sufficient encouragement. I laid myself down on the bed, and
wished I might never rise again. I closed my eyes, and
prayed that the dark fillet of night might rest on them again
and forevermore. My cheeks burned as with consuming fire,
but it was in my heart. When Clinton returned, not finding
me in the drawing-room, he sought me in my own chamber.
He seemed really alarmed at my situation. He forgot all his
former constraint, and hung over me with a tenderness and
anxiety that might have proved to me how dear I was. He
sat by me, holding my burning hand, and uttering every endearing expression affection could suggest. Melted by his
caresses, I yearned to unbosom to him my whole heart—my
pride, my jealousy was subdued. I endeavoured to speak,
but the words died on my tongue. Confused images flitted
across my brain—then came a dreary blank. For weeks I lay
on that bed of sickness, unconscious of everything around me.
My recovery was for a long time doubtful—but when I at last
opened my languid eyes, they rested on the face of my husband, who had kept his unwearied vigils by my pillow,
and still he held my feeble hand in his, as if he had never
unloosed his clasp. He looked pale and wan, but a ray of
divine joy flashed from his eye as he met my glance of recog-
nition.

Humbled and chastened by this visitation from heaven, renovated by the warm and gracious influences exerted for my
restoration, animated by new-born hope, I rose from my sick-
bed. The vulture had unloosened its fangs, and the dove once

more returned to its nest. I could even pity the misguided girl who had caused me so much unhappiness. I treated her with a kindness, of late very unwonted—but she evidently shunned my companionship, and in proportion as my spirits rose from the weight that had crushed them to the dust, hers became depressed and fitful. Let me hurry on—I linger too long on feelings. Few events have marked my brief history, yet some have left traces that all the waves of time can never wash out.

It was Sunday—it was the first time I had attended church since my illness. My husband accompanied me, while Alice, as usual, remained at home. The preacher was eloquent—the music sweet and solemn—the aspirations of faith warm and kindling. I had never before felt such a glow of gratitude and trust; and while my mind was in this state of devout abstraction, Clinton whispered to me that he was obliged to withdraw a short time, to visit a patient who was dangerously sick—"but I will return," said he, "to accompany you home." My thoughts were brought back to earth by this interruption, and wandered from the evangelical eloquence of the pulpit. The services were unusually long, and my head began to ache from the effort of listening. I experienced the lingering effects of sickness, and feeling that dimness of sight come over me, which was a never-failing symptom of a malady of the brain, I left the church, and returned home, without waiting for the coming of my husband. When I crossed the threshold, my spirit was free from a shadow of suspicion. I had been in an exalted mood—I felt as if I had been sitting under the outspread wings of the cherubim, and had brought away with me some faint reflection of the celestial glory. I was conscious of being in a high state of nervous excitement. The reaction produced by the unexpected scene that presented itself, was, in consequence, more terrible. There, on a sofa, half supported in the arms of my husband, whose hand she was grasping with a kind of convulsive energy, her hair unbound and wet, and exhaling the odorous essence with which it had been just bathed, sat Alice, and the words that passed her lips, as I entered, at first unperceived by them, were these—"Never, never—she hates me—she must ever hate me." I stood transfixed—the expression of my countenance must have been awful, for they looked as if confronted by an avenging spirit. Alice actually shrieked, and her pale features writhed, as the scroll when the scorching blaze comes near it.

My resolution was instantaneous. I waited not for explanations—the scene to my mind admitted none. The sudden withdrawal of my husband from church, upon the pretence of an errand of duty, the singular agitation of Alice—all that I saw and heard, filled me with the most maddening emotions—all the ties of wedded love seemed broken and withered, at once, like the withes that bound the awakening giant. "Clinton," exclaimed I, "you have deceived me—but it is for the last time." Before he could reply, or arrest my motions, I was gone. The carriage was still at the door. "Drive me to my father's, directly," was all I could utter, and it was done.

Swiftly the carriage rolled on—I thought I heard my name borne after me on the wind, but I looked not behind. I felt strong in the conviction of my wrongs. It would have been weakness to have wept. My scorn of such duplicity lifted me above mere sorrow. It was in the gloom of twilight when I reached my father's door. I rushed into the drawing-room, and found myself in the arms of my brother. "Cecilia, my sister! what brings you here?" He was alarmed at my sudden entrance, and through the dusky shade he could discover the wild flashing of my eyes, the disorder of my whole appearance. The presence of human sympathy softened the sternness of my despair. Tears gushed violently forth. I tried to explain to him my wretchedness and its cause, but could only exclaim, "Clinton, Alice, cruel, deliberate deceivers!" Henry bit his lip, and ground his teeth till their ivory was tinged with blood, but he made no comments. He spoke then with his usual calmness, and urged me to retire to my chamber, and compose myself before my father's return. He almost carried me there in his arms, soothing and comforting me. He called for an attendant, again whispered the duty and necessity of self-control, then left me, promising a speedy return. I watched for the footsteps of Henry, but hour after hour passed away, and he returned not. I asked the servants where he had gone? They knew not. I asked myself, and something told me, in an awful voice—"Gone to avenge thee." The moment this idea flashed into my mind, I felt as if I were a murderess. I would convince myself of the truth. I knew my brother's chamber—thither I ran, and drawing back the bed curtains, looked for the silver mounted pistols that always hung over the bed's head. They were gone—and a coat dashed hastily on the counterpane, a pocket-book fallen on the carpet, all denoted a hurried departure on some fatal errand. The agony I had previously suffered was light to what pierced me now. To follow him was my only impulse. I rushed out of the house—it was a late hour in the evening—there was no moon in the sky, and I felt the dampness of the falling dew, as I flew, with uncovered head, like an unblessed spirit, through the darkness. My brain began to be thronged with wild images. It seemed to me, legions of dark forms were impeding my steps. "Oh! let me pass," cried I, "it is my husband and brother I have slain. Let me pass," continued I, shrieking, for an arm of flesh and blood was thrown around me, and held me struggling. "Gracious heavens, it is the voice of my Cecilia!" It was my father that spoke. I remember that I recognised him, and that was all. My cries were changed to cries of madness. I was borne back raving. The malady that had so recently brought me to the door of the grave, had renewed its attack with increased malignancy. My brain had been too much weakened to bear the tension of its agony. For long months I was confined within my chamber walls, sometimes tossing in delirious anguish, at others lying in marble unconsciousness, an image of the death they prayed might soon release me from my sufferings. They prayed that I might die, rather than be doomed to a living death. But I lived—lived to know the ruin I had wrought.

My father was a man of majestic person, and time had scarcely touched his raven locks. His hair was now profusely silvered, and there were lines on his brow which age never furrowed. It was long before I learned all that had transpired during this fearful chasm in my existence, but gradually the truth was revealed. All that I was at first told, was, that my husband and brother lived—then, when it was supposed I had sufficient strength to bear the agitation, this letter from my husband was given me.

"Cecilia, how shall I address you? I will not reproach you, for you have had too bitter a lesson. I would fain have seen you before my departure, but you decline the interview, and perhaps it is well. Should I live to return—Oh! Cecilia, what wretchedness have you brought upon us all! If your alienated heart does not turn from any memento of me, you will read these lines, and I know you will believe them. I have been, as it were, to the very threshold of the presence-chamber of the King of Kings, and am just emerging from the shadows of approaching death. This is the first effort of my feeble hand. Most rash and misjudging woman, what have you done? How madly have I doted on you, how blindly have I worshipped! yet all the devotion of my life, my truth, love and integrity, weighed nothing in the balance with one moment's mystery. I leave my viudication to Alice. She will not deceive you. She will tell you that never did the heart of man throb with a more undivided passion for another than mine for you. She will tell you—but what avails it? You have cast me from you, unvalued and untrusted. Your poor, unhappy brother! his avenging hand sought my life— the life of him who he believed had betrayed his sister's happiness, the wretch almost unworthy of a brave man's resentment. In wresting the weapon from his frenzied grasp, I received an almost deadly wound. His wrath was slaked in my blood. He believes me innocent. He has been to me more than a brother. He will accompany me to another clime, whither I am going, to try the effect of more genial air on my shattered frame. Would to God we could have met before we parted—perhaps for ever. Your father says you have been ill, that you fear the effect of the meeting on both. You have been ill—my ever adored, still tenderly beloved Cecilia, I write not to reproach you. Bitter is the penalty paid for one moment of passion. Had I ever swerved in my affection for you, even in thought, I should deserve all I have suffered. I recall your sadness, your coldness, and averted looks. I now know the cause, and mourn over it. Why did you not confide in me? We might yet have been happy—but the will of God be done. The vessel waits that is to bear us to a transatlantic clime—farewell. Should I return, bearing with me some portion of my former vigour, should your confidence in my love be restored, then, perchance, through the mercy of heaven, two chastened and humble hearts may once more be united on earth. If I am never permitted to revisit my native soil, if I die in a foreign land, know, that, faithful to you to my latest hour, my last thought, prayer, and sigh, will be yours."

* * * * * * * * *

And he was gone—gone—sick, wounded, perhaps dying, he was gone to another land, and the blood that was drained from him on my soul. My father forbade him to see me—he was too feeble to bear the shock of beholding me in the condition I then was. My real situation was concealed from him. The only means of making the prohibition effectual, was to word it as proceeding from myself. Thus, he believed me cold and selfish to the last. My father talked to me of better days, of the hope of my husband's speedy restoration, and of our future reunion. I could only listen and weep. I dared not murmur. I felt too deeply the justice of the judgment the Almighty had passed against me. I had one ordeal yet to pass—an interview with Alice. She also was under my father's roof, confined by increasing debility to her own apartment. As soon as my strength allowed, I made it a religious duty to visit the poor invalid. I was shocked to see the ravages of her malady. Her eye of glassy brightness turned on me with such a look of woe and remorse, it cut me to the heart. I took the pale thin hand she extended towards me, and burst into tears. Yes! I saw it but too clearly. Here was another victim. The steps of the destroyer were fearfully accelerated. She had had a profuse hemorrhage from the lungs, and her voice was so weak and husky, it was with difficulty I could understand her. She drew me down near to her pillow, and, placing my hand on her heart, said, in a careful whisper—" Remorse, Cecilia, it is here. It is this which gives the sting to death." She then drew from beneath her pillow a paper that she had written for me, which she begged me to read when I was alone. I did read it. It was the transcript of a warm, romantic heart, erring and misguided, yet even in its aberrations discovering an innate love for virtue and truth. Her whole soul was bared before me—all her love, imprudence, and remorse. She described my husband as an angel of light and purity, soaring high above the clouds of passion that gathered darkly around herself. She spoke of that scene, followed by such irremediable woe. " Even now," continued Alice, " wasting as I am on the bed of death, with the shadows of earthly feeling dimly floating round me, knowing that I shall soon turn to cold, impassive clay, the memory of that hour presses with scorching weight on my brain. I must have been mad. Surely I had not the control of my reason. I had taken the previous night an unusual quantity of opium, which, instead of composing me to sleep, had excited my nerves, and strung them as with fire. Your husband came in only a short time before your sudden entrance, evidently on some errand; and though he kindly paused to speak to me, his looks expressed haste to depart. Just as he was about to leave the room, I was attacked with one of those spasms you have sometimes witnessed. He came to my relief—he administered every restorative. I know not all I uttered, but when I recovered I remember many wild expressions that escaped my lips. It seemed to me that I was going to die, and while his arms thus kindly supported me, I felt as if it would be joy to die. With this conviction, was it so black a crime to breathe forth the love that had so long pervaded my frail and lonely existence? Cecilia, he recoiled from me with horror. He proclaimed his inviolable love and devotion for you—his glance was stern and upbraiding. Then seeing me sinking in despair, the kindness of his nature triumphed, and he sought to calm my over-wrought and troubled spirit. He expressed the affection of a brother, the pity of a friend, the admonitions of a Christian. " Above all," said he, " make a friend of Cecilia. She will always cherish you with a sister's love." " Never !" I exclaim-ed, " she hates me, she must ever hate me." The vision of an injured wife arrested my unhallowed accents. You know the dreadful tragedy that followed. Never since that hour have I had one moment's calm. Conscience, with her thousand scorpions, lashes me—whether sleeping or waking there is no rest. 'There is no peace,' saith my God, to the wicked.' Yet mine was not deliberate guilt. Had I only wrecked my own happiness !—but the wide desolation, the irretrievable ruin ! I shudder, I weep, I lift my feeble hands to that Power whose laws I have transgressed, and pray for pardon. To you, whose home of love I have laid waste, dare I turn my fading eyes, and hope for forgiveness? To him whom I have driven from his native land, shorn of the brightness of his manhood—Oh ! sinful dust and ashes"——here the unhappy writer broke off—the blank was stained with tears. Probably in that broken sentence the embers of passion flashed out their last fires, through the " dust and ashes" of withering mortality. Poor Alice ! may'st thou be forgiven by a merciful Creator as freely as thou art by me. Gentle be thy passage through the valley of the shadow of death, to that country where no storms desolate the heart, where passion and penitence are unknown. As for me—why and for what do I live ? For hope or des-pair ? I pray for tidings from the beloved exiles, yet dread to receive them. If the night gale sweeps with hasty gust against the window, I tremble lest they be exposed to the stormy deep. When I gaze on the moon and stars, I ask my-self if they are lighting the wanderers on their homeward way, and sometimes gather hope from their heavenly bright-ness.

The manuscript of Cecilia here abruptly closes. It has

106

fallen to the lot of one who afterwards became the devoted
friend of Clinton, to relate the sequel of their melancholy
history.

"It was in the spring of the year 18——, I was sitting on
the deck, watching the rapid motion of the boat, as it glided
over the waves, thinking earnestly of the place of my destina-
tion, when I first beheld Cecilia, the wife of Clinton. I was a
stranger on board, and gazed around me with that indefinite
expression, which marks the stranger to the experienced eye.
At length my glance was riveted by the appearance of a lady,
leaning on the arm of a gray-haired gentleman, slowly prome-
nading the deck.   They passed and repassed me, while I continued to lean over the railing, fearing, by a change of position,
to disturb the silent strangers.   There was something in the
figure of the lady inexpressibly interesting.   She wore a
mourning-dress, and her eyes were covered with a green shade.
Notwithstanding her face was thus partially obscured, the
most exquisite beauty of outline and colouring was visible I
ever saw in any human countenance.   She wore no bonnet or
veil, for the sun was verging towards the west, and its rays
stole soft and mellow over the golden waters.   Fair and meek
as the virgin mother's was the brow that rose above the silken
screen, defined with beauteous distinctness by dark, divided
hair, whose luxuriance was confined by a golden band.   At
length they seated themselves very near me, and began to
converse in a low tone.   There was a melancholy sweetness in
her accents, and I was sure they were speaking of some sor-
rowful theme.   We were now entering the —— bay, and the
boat rocked and laboured as she plunged through the increased
volume of the waters.   Now, just visible on the glowing horizon, was the topmast of a vessel.   On she came, with sails
full spread, her canvas swelling in the breeze, her majestic
outline softened by the sunset hues.   The gentleman pointed
out the object to his companion, who lifted the shade from
her brow, revealing as she did so, eyes of such melting soft
ness, I wondered I had thought her lovely before.   She pressed
the arm of the gentleman, and gazed eagerly on the vessel
which now bore down 'majestically near.'   She rose, she bent
forward with earnest gestures, her face kindled, and sparkled
like the waters themselves.   The ship approached so near we
could discern figures on the deck.   The boat had diverged
from her path to give place to the nobler craft.   She was sailing with great rapidity, and the noise of the engine and the

dashing of the waves drowned the sound of the voices near me. I began to feel a strange interest in the vessel on which the eyes of the strangers were so earnestly riveted. Amid the' figures that walked her deck, I distinguished one, which was aloof from the others, of a more lofty bearing—a cloak was gathered round him, and from this circumstance, together with his extremely pallid complexion, I judged him to be an in valid. From the rapid motion of both vessels, it was but ? glance I obtained, after we were near enough to trace these lineaments. At this moment the lady sprang upon the bench beneath the railing—she stretched forth her arms, with a startling cry. I saw her for an instant, bending far over the edge of the boat. I rose and rushed towards her to warn her of her danger, but a plunging sound in the water, that closed darkly over her sinking form, froze my veins with horror. 'Oh! my God!' exclaimed the father, 'save her! My daugh- ter! Oh, my daughter!' then fell back, almost paralyzed, on the seat. To throw off my coat and plunge in after the ill- fated lady, in whom I had become so painfully interested, was an instantaneous deed. Alas! all my efforts were unavailing. The current was so powerful, I found it in vain to struggle with its force. I relaxed not, however, till my failing strength warned me that I was seeking a grave for myself, without being able to rescue the victim for whom I had willingly periled my life.

" I will not attempt to describe the grief of the half-distracted father. I never left him till he reached his own home. What a scene of agony awaited him there! The husband and brother, so long absent, were returned, yearning to behold once more that beloved being, whose involuntary sin had been so fearfully expiated. It was Clinton whom I had seen on the vessel's deck. As he afterwards told me, the dazzle of the rays on the water, in that direction, had prevented him from dis- tinguishing the features for ever engraven on his heart. The hoarse sound of the waves swallowed her drowning shriek— onward they bore him, and he saw not the fond arms tha would have embraced him, even over that watery chasm. ⊥ have witnessed many a scene of sorrow, but never saw I one like this. From the peculiar circumstances that brought us together, I became almost identified with this unhappy family. Clinton was the most interesting man I ever saw. He was a confirmed invalid, never having recovered from the effects of his wound I never saw a smile upon his face, nor could I ever smile in his presence. He seldom spoke, and never but once did he mention the name of Cecilia. It was one night when he was unusually ill, and I was sitting alone with him in his chamber. He gave me the manuscript for perusal which is here transcribed, an act of confidence he considered due to me, who would have been her saviour. Through the watches of that night he poured into my ear the hoarded agonies of his grief. Never before did I know how deep human sorrow could be, or how holy was that love which clings to the memory of the dead.

"Alice dwelt in 'the dark and narrow house.' She was spared the knowledge of the fatal catastrophe, for she died before her victim. Yes—*her victim!* Had she guarded against the first inroads of a forbidden passion, there might have been 'beauty for ashes, the oil of joy for mourning, and the garment of praise for the spirit of heaviness.' The angel form that lies low, wrapped in the winding-sheet of the waves, might now be moving in the light of loveliness, love, and joy. But who shall dare to arraign the doings of the Almighty?"

THE PARLOUR SERPENT.

Mrs. Wentworth and Miss Hart entered the breakfast-room together, the latter speaking earnestly and in a low confidential tone to the other, whose countenance was slightly discomposed.

"There is nothing that provokes me so much as to hear such remarks," said Miss Hart, "I have no patience to listen to them. Indeed, I think they are made as much to wound my feelings as anything else, for they all know the great affection I have for you."

"But you do not say what the remarks were, that gave you so much pain," answered Mrs. Wentworth. "I would much prefer that you would tell me plainly, than speak in such vague hints. You will not make me angry, for I am entirely indifferent to the opinion of the world."

Now there was not a woman in the world more sensitively alive to censure than Mrs. Wentworth, and in proportion to her sensitiveness, was her anxiety to know the observations of others.

"If you had overheard Miss Bentley and Miss Wheeler talking of you last night as I did," continued Miss Hart, "you would not have believed your own ears. They said they thought it was ridiculous in you to make such a nun of yourself, because Captain Wentworth was absent, and to dress so plain and look so moping. One of them said, you did not dar to visit or receive visiters while he was away, for that you were as much afraid of him as if you were his slave, and that he had made you promise not to stir out of the house, or to invite any company while he was gone."

"Ridiculous!—nonsense!" exclaimed Mrs. Wentworth, "there never was such an absurd idea. Captain Wentworth never imposed such a restraint upon me, though I know he would rather I would live retired, when he cannot attend me himself in the gay world. It is not despotism, but affection, that prompts the wish, and I am sure I feel no pleasure in dressing, shining, and mingling in society, when he is exposed to danger, and perhaps death, on the far deep sea."

"I know all that, my dear Mrs. Wentworth," replied Miss Hart, insinuatingly, "and so I told them; but how little can a heartless and censorious world judge of the feelings of the refined and the sensitive! It seems to be a general impression that you fear your husband more than you love him, and that this fear keeps you in a kind of bondage to his will. If I were you, I would invite a large party and make it as brilliant as possible, and be myself as gay as possible, and then that will be giving the lie at once to their innuendoes."

"It is so mortifying to have such reports in circulation," said Mrs. Wentworth, her colour becoming more and more heightened and her voice more tremulous. "I don't care what they say at all, and yet I am half resolved to follow your advice, if it were only to vex them. I *will* do it, and let them know that I am not afraid to be mistress of my own house while its master is absent."

"That is exactly the right spirit," answered the delighted Miss Hart; "I am glad you take it in that way. I was afraid your feelings would be wounded, and that is the reason I was so unwilling to tell you."

But though Mrs. Wentworth boasted of her spirit and her indifference, her feelings were deeply wounded, and she sat at the breakfast-table, cutting her toast into the most minute pieces, without tasting any, while Miss Hart was regaling herself with an unimpaired appetite, and luxuriating in fancy on the delightful party, she had so skilfully brought into promised existence, at least. She had no idea of spending the time of her visit to Mrs. Wentworth, in dullness and seclusion, sympathizing in the anxieties of a fond and timid wife, and listening to a detail of domestic plans and enjoyments. She knew the weak side of her character, and mingling the gall she extracted from others, with the honey of her own flattery, and building her influence on their ruined reputations, imagined it firm and secure on such a crumbling foundation. It is unnecessary to dwell on the genealogy of Miss Hart. She was well known as Miss Hart, and yet it would be very difficult for anybody to tell precisely who Miss Hart was. She was a general visiter; one of those young ladies who are always ready to fill

up any sudden vacuum made in a family—a kind of bird of
passage, who, having no abiding place of her own, went
fluttering about, generally resting where she could find the
softest and most comfortable nest. She was what was called
excellent company, always had something new and interesting
to say about everybody; then she knew so many secrets, and
had the art of exciting a person's curiosity so keenly, and
making them dissatisfied with everybody but herself, it would
be impossible to follow all the windings, or discover all the
nooks and corners of her remarkable character. It was astonishing to see the influence she acquired over the minds of those
with whom she associated, male as well as female. She was
a showy, well-dressing, attractive-looking girl, with a great
deal of manner, a large, piercing, dark eye, and an uncommonly sweet and persuasive tone of voice. Mrs. Wentworth
became acquainted with her a very short time before Captain
Wentworth's departure, and esteemed it a most delightful
privilege to have such a pleasing companion to charm away
the lingering hours of his absence. Acting upon the suggestions of her friend, and following up the determination she had
so much applauded, she opened her doors to visitors, and
appeared in society with a gay dress and smiling countenance.

"What a change there is in Mrs. Wentworth!" observed
Miss Bentley to Miss Hart, as they met one morning at the
house of a mutual friend. "I never saw any one so transformed in my life. She looks and dresses like the most complete flirt I ever saw; I suspect Captain Wentworth has very
good reason to watch her as he does."

Miss Hart shrugged her shoulders and smiled significantly,
but did not say anything.

"It must be a very pleasant alteration to you," continued
Miss Bentley, "the house seems to be frequented by gentlemen from morning till night. I suppose you have the grace
to appropriate their visits to yourself."

"I have nothing to say about myself," answered Miss Hart,
"and I do not wish to speak of Mrs. Wentworth otherwise
than kindly. You know she is excessively kind to me, and
it would be ungrateful in me to condemn her conduct. To be
sure I must have my own thoughts on the subject. She is
certainly very imprudent, and too fond of admiration. But
I would not have you repeat what I have said, for the
world, for being in the family it would have such weight.

Be very careful what you say, and above all, don't mention *my* name."

Miss Bentley was very careful to repeat the remarks to every one she saw, with as many additions of her own as she pleased, and the unutterable language of the smile and the shrug was added too, to give force to the comments. Mrs. Wentworth, in the mean while, unconscious of the serpent she was nursing in her bosom, suffered herself to be borne along on the current on which she had thoughtlessly embarked, without the power to arrest her progress, or turn back into the quiet channel she had quitted. The arrival of her brother, a gay and handsome young man, gave additional animation to her household, and company flowed in still more continuously. Henry More, the brother of Mrs. Wentworth, was the favourite of every circle in which he moved. With an uncommon flow of spirits, a ready and graceful wit, a fluent and flattering tongue, he mingled in society unaffected by its contrasts, unwounded by its asperities, and unruffled by its contentions. He seemed to revel in the happy consciousness of being able to impart pleasure to all, and was equally willing to receive it. He was delighted to find a fine-looking, amiable girl, an inmate of his sister's dwelling, and immediately addressing her in his accustomed strain of sportive gallantry, found that she not only lent a willing ear, but was well skilled in the same language. Though Miss Hart was still young, she had outlived the romance and credulity of youth. She had a precocious experience and wisdom in the ways of this world. She had seen the affections of many a young man, with a disposition open and ingenuous as Henry's, won through the medium of their vanity, by women, too, who could not boast of attractions equal to her own. She believed that juxtaposition could work miracles, and as long as they were the inmates of the same house, participating in the same pleasures, engaged in the same pursuits, and often perusing the same book, she feared no rival. She rejoiced, too, in the close-drawing socialities of the winter fireside, and delighted when a friendly storm compelled them to find all their enjoyment within their own little circle. Mrs. Wentworth, who had once been cheerful and serene in clouds as well as sunshine, was now subject to fits of despondency and silence. It was only when excited by company, that her eyes were lighted up with animation, and her lips with smiles. She dreaded the reproaches of her husband on his return, for acting so contrary to his wishes, and when she heard the night-gust sweep by her windows, and thought of him exposed to the warring elements, perhaps even then clinging to the drifting wreck, or floating in a watery grave, and recollected the scenes of levity and folly in which she was now constantly acting a part, merely to avoid the censures of the very people she detested and despised, she sighed and wept, and wished she had followed her bosom counsellor, rather than the suggestions of the friend in whom she still confided, and on whose affection she relied with unwavering trust. It was strange, she could hear Miss Hart ridicule others, and join in the laugh; she could sit quietly and see her breathe the subtle venom of slander over the fairest characters, till they blackened and became polluted under her touch, and yet she felt herself as secure as if she were placed on the summit of Mont Blanc, in a region of inaccessible purity and splendour. So blinding is the influence of self-love, pampered by flattery, strengthened by indulgence, and unrestrained by religious principle.

One evening, and it chanced to be the evening of the Sabbath day, Henry sat unusually silent, and Miss Hart thought that his eyes were fixed upon her face with a very deep and peculiar expression—"No," he suddenly exclaimed, "I never saw such a countenance in my life."

"What do you see so remarkable in it?" asked she, laughing, delighted at what she supposed a spontaneous burst of admiration.

"I don't know; I can no more describe it, than one of those soft, fleecy clouds that roll melting away from the face of the moon. But it haunts me like a dream."

Miss Hart modestly cast down her eyes, then turned them towards the moon, which at that moment gleamed with pallid lustre through the window.

"Your imagination is so glowing," replied she, "that it invests, like the moonlight, every object with its own mellow and beautiful tints."

"Jane," continued he, without noticing the compliment to his imagination, and turning to his sister, who was reading intently, "Jane, you must have noticed her—you were at the same church."

"Noticed her!" repeated Miss Hart to herself, in utter dismay; "who can he mean?"

"Noticed who?" said Mrs. Wentworth, laying down her book, "I have not heard a syllable you have been saying."

" Why, that young lady dressed in black, with such a sweet, modest, celestial expression of face. She sat at the right hand of the pulpit, with another lady in mourning, who was very tall and pale."

" What coloured hair and eyes had she?" asked his sister.

" I could no more tell the colour of her eyes, than I could paint yon twinkling star, or her hair either. I only know that they shed a kind of glory over her countenance, and mantled her brow with the softest and most exquisite shades."

" I declare, Henry," cried Mrs. Wentworth, " you are the most extravagant being I ever knew. I don't know whether you are in jest or earnest."

" Oh ! you may be sure he is in earnest," said Miss Hart. I know whom he means very well. It is Miss Carroll. Lois Carroll, the grand-daughter of old Mr. Carroll, the former minister of —— church. The old lady with whom she sat is her aunt. They live somewhere in the suburbs of the city—but never go anywhere except to church. They say she is the most complete little methodist in the world."

" What do you mean by a methodist?" asked Henry abruptly —" an enthusiast?"

" One who never goes to the theatre, never attends the ballroom, thinks it a sin to laugh, and goes about among poor people to give them doctor's stuff, and read the Bible."

" Well," answered Henry, " I see nothing very appalling in this description. If ever I marry, I have no very great desire that my wife should frequent the theatre or the ballroom. She might admire artificial graces at the one and exhibit them in the other, but the loveliest traits of her sex must fade and wither in the heated atmosphere of both. And I am sure it is a divine office to go about ministering to the wants of the poor and healing the sick. As to the last item, I may not be a proper judge, but I do think a beautiful woman reading the Bible to the afflicted and dying, must be the most angelic object in the universe."

" Why, brother," said Mrs. Wentworth, " what a strange compound you are ! Such a rattle-brain as you, moralizing like a second Johnson !"

" I may be a wild rattle-brain, and sport like a thousand others in the waves of fashion, but there is something here, Jane," answered he, laying his hand half seriously, half sportively on his breast, " that tells me that I was created for immortality ; that, spendthrift of time, I am still bound for eternity. I have often pictured the future, in my musing hours, and imagined a woman's gentle hand was guiding me in the path that leads to heaven."

Mrs. Wentworth looked at her brother in astonishment. There was something in the solemnity of his expressions that alarmed her, coming from one so gay and apparently thoughtless. Miss Hart was alarmed too, but from a different cause. She thought it time to aim her shaft, and she knew in what course to direct it.

"This Miss Carroll," said she, "whom you admire so much, has lately lost her lover, to whom she was devotedly attached. He was her cousin, and they had been brought up together from childhood, and betrothed from that period. She nursed him during a long sickness, day and night, and many thought she would follow him to the grave, her grief was so great."

"Her lover!" exclaimed Henry, in a mock tragedy tone. "Then it is all over with me—I never would accept the second place in any maiden's heart, even if I could be enshrined there in heaven's crystal. Give me the rose before the sunbeams have exhaled the dew of the morning, or it wears no charms for me."

Miss Hart and Mrs. Wentworth laughed, rallied Henry upon his heroics, and the beautiful stranger was mentioned no more. Miss Hart congratulated herself upon the master stroke by which she had dispelled his enchantment, if indeed it existed at all. She had often heard Henry declare his resolution never to marry a woman who had acknowledged a previous affection, and she seized upon a vague report of Miss Carroll's being in mourning for a cousin who had recently died, and to whom she thought she might possibly be betrothed, and presented it as a positive truth. Finding that Henry's ideas of female perfection were very different from what she had imagined, she was not sorry when an opportunity offered of displaying those domestic virtues, which he so much extolled. One night, when Mrs. Wentworth was prepared to attend a private ball, she expressed her wish to remain at home, declaring tha she was weary of dissipation, and preferred reading and meditation. She expected Henry would steal away from the party, and join her in the course of the evening, but her real motive was a violent toothache, which she concealed that she might have the credit of a voluntary act. After Mrs. Wentworth's departure, she bound a handkerchief round her aching jaw, and having found relief from some powerful anodyne, she reclined back on the sofa and fell at last into a deep sleep. Th candles burned dim from their long, unsnuffed wicks, and threw a very dubious light through the spacious apartment. She was awakened by a tall, dark figure, bending over her, with outspread arms, as if about to embrace her, and starting up, her first thought was that it was Henry, who had stolen on her solitude, and was about to declare the love she had no doubt he secretly cherished for her. But the figure drew back, with a sudden recoil, when she rose, and uttered her name in a tone of disappointment.

"Captain Wentworth," exclaimed she, "is it you?"

"I beg your pardon," said he, extending his hand cordially towards her, "I thought for a moment it was my wife, my Jane, Mrs. Wentworth—where is she? Is she well? Why do I not see her here?"

"Oh! Captain Wentworth, she had no expectation of your coming so soon. She is perfectly well. She is gone to a quadrille party, and will probably not be at home for several hours —I will send for her directly."

"No, Miss Hart," said he, in a cold and altered voice, "no, I would not shorten her evening's amusement. A quadrille party—I thought she had no taste for such pleasures."

"She seems to enjoy them very much," replied Miss Hart, "and it is very natural she should. She is young and handsome, and very much admired, and in your absence she found her own home comparatively dull."

The captain rose, and walked the room with a sailor's manly stride. His brows were knit, his lips compressed, and his cheek flushed. She saw the iron of jealousy was entering his soul, and she went on mercilessly deepening the wound she had made.

"You will be delighted when you see Mrs. Wentworth— she looks so blooming and lovely. You have reason to be quite proud of your wife—she is the belle of every party and ball-room. I think it is well that you have returned." This she added, with an arch, innocent smile, though she knew every word she uttered penetrated like a dagger, where he was most vulnerable. "How thoughtless I am!" she exclaimed; "you must be weary and hungry—I will order your supper."

"No, no," said he, "I have no appetite—I will not trouble you. Don't disturb yourself on my account—I will amuse myself with a book till she returns."

He sat down and took up a book, but his eyes were fixed

moodily on the carpet, and his hands trembled as he unconsciously turned the leaves. Miss Hart suffered occasional
agony from her tooth, the more as she had taken off the disfiguring bandage, but she would not retire, anticipating with
a kind of savage delight, the unpleasant scene that would ensue
on Mrs. Wentworth's return. The clock struck twelve before
the carriage stopped at the door. Mrs. Wentworth came
lightly into the room, unaccompanied by her brother, her cloak
falling from her shoulders, her head uncovered, most fashionably and elegantly dressed. She did not see her husband
when she first entered, and throwing her cloak on a chair,
exclaimed, "Oh! Miss Hart, I'm so sorry you were not there,
we had such a delightful party—the pleasantest of the whole
season." Her eye at this moment fell upon her husband,
who had risen upon her entrance, but stood back in the shade,
without making one step to meet her. With a scream of surprise, joy, and perhaps terror too, she rushed towards him, and
threw her arms around him. He suffered her clinging arms to
remain round his neck for a moment while he remained as passive as the rock on the seabeat shore when the white foam
wreathes and curls over its surface, then drawing back, he looked
her steadfastly in the face, with a glance that made her own to
quail, and her lip and cheek blanch. She looked down upon
her jewelled neck and airy robes, and wished herself clothed
in sackcloth and ashes. She began to stammer forth some
excuse for her absence, something about his unexpected
return, but the sentence died on her lips. The very blood
seemed to congeal in her heart, under the influence of his
freezing glance.

"Don't say anything, Jane," said he, sternly. "It is
better as it is—I had deluded myself with the idea, that in all
my dangers and hardships, to which I have exposed myself
chiefly for your sake, I had a fond and faithful wife, who pined
at my absence and yearned for my return. I was not aware
of the new character you had assumed. No," continued he
impetuously, entirely forgetful of the presence of Miss Hart
"I was not prepared for a welcome like this. I expected to
have met a wife—not a flirt, a belle, a vain, false-hearted,
deceitful woman." Thus saying, he suddenly left the room,
closing the door with a force that made every article of the
furniture tremble. Mrs. Wentworth, bursting into hysterical
sobs, was about to rush after him, but Miss Hart held her
back —"Don't be a fool," said she; "he'll get over it directly

—you've done nothing at which he ought to be angry; I had no idea he was such a tyrant."

"He was always kind to me before," sobbed Mrs. Wentworth. "He thinks my heart is weaned from him. Now, I wish I had disregarded the sneer of the world! It can never repay me for the loss of his love."

"My dear Mrs. Wentworth," said Miss Hart, putting her arms soothingly round her, "I feel for you deeply, but I hope you will not reproach yourself unnecessarily, or suffer your husband to suppose you condemn your own conduct. If you do, he will tyrannize over you, through life—what possible harm could there be in your going to a private party with your own brother, when you did not look for his return? You have taken no more liberty than every married lady in the city would have done, and a husband who really loved his wife, would be pleased and gratified that she should be an object of attention and admiration to others. Come, dry up your tears, and exert the pride and spirit every woman of delicacy and sense should exercise on such occasions."

Mrs. Wentworth listened, and the natural pride and waywardness of the human heart strengthening the counsels of her treacherous companion, her sorrow and contrition became merged in resentment. She resolved to return coldness for coldness and scorn for scorn, to seek no reconciliation, nor even to grant it, until he humbly sued for her forgiveness. The husband and wife met at the breakfast-table without speaking. Henry was unusually taciturn, and the whole burthen of keeping up the conversation rested on Miss Hart, who endeavoured to entertain and enliven the whole. Captain Wentworth, who had all the frankness and politeness of a sailor, unbent his stern brow when he addressed her, and it was in so kind a voice, that the tears started into his wife's eyes at the sound. He had no words, no glance for her, from whom he had been parted so long, and whom he had once loved so tenderly. Henry, who had been absorbed in his own reflections, and who had not been present at their first meeting, now noticed the silence of his sister, and the gloom of her husband, and looking from one to the other, first in astonishment, and then in mirth, he exclaimed, "Well, I believe I shall remain a bachelor, if this is a specimen of a matrimonial meeting. Jane looks as if she were doing penance for the sins of her whole life, and Captain Wentworth as if he were about to give a broadside's thunder. What has happened?

Miss Hart resembles a beam of sunshine between two clouds."

Had Henry been aware of the real state of things, he would never have indulged his mirth at the expense of his sister's feelings. He had no suspicion that the clouds to which he alluded, arose from estrangement from each other, and when Mrs. Wentworth burst into tears and left the table, and Captain Wentworth set back his chair so suddenly as to upset the teaboard and produce a terrible crash among the china, the smile forsook his lips, and, turning to the captain in rather an authoritative manner, he demanded an explanation.

"Ask your sister," answered the captain, "and she may give it—as for me, sir, my feelings are not to be made a subject of unfeeling merriment. They have been already too keenly tortured, and should at least be sacred from your jest. But one thing let me tell you, sir, if you had had more regard to your sister's reputation, than to have escorted her to scenes of folly and corruption during her husband's absence, you might perhaps have spared me the misery I now endure."

"Do you threaten me, Captain Wentworth?" said Henry, advancing nearer to him with a flushed brow and raised tone. Miss Hart here interposed, and begged and entreated, and laid her hand on Henry's arm, and looked softly and imploringly at Captain Wentworth, who snatched up his hat and left the room, leaving Henry angry, distressed, and bewildered. Miss Hart explained the whole as the most causeless and ridiculous jealousy, which would soon pass away and was not worth noticing, and urged him to treat the matter as unworthy of indignation. She feared she had carried matters a little too far; she had no wish that they should fight, and Henry, perhaps, fall a victim to excited passions. She was anxious to allay the storm she had raised, and she succeeded in preventing the outbreakings of wrath, but she could not restore the happiness she had destroyed, the domestic peace she had disturbed, the love and confidence she had so wantonly invaded. Nor did she desire it. Incapable herself of feeling happiness from the evil passions that reigned in her bosom, she looked upon the bliss of others as a personal injury to herself; and where the flowers were fairest and the hopes the brightest, she loved to trample and shed her blasting influence. As the serpent goes trailing its dark length through the long grasses and sweet blossoms that veil its path, silent and deadly, she glided amid the sacred shades of domestic life, darting in ambush her venomed sting, and winding her coil in the very bosoms that warmed and caressed her. She now flitted about, describing what she called the best and most ridiculous scene imaginable; and the names of Captain Wentworth and his wife were bandied from lip to lip, one speaking of *him* as a tyrant, a bear, a domestic tiger—another of *her* as a heartless devotee of fashion, or a contemner of the laws of God and man. Most truly has it been said in holy writ, that the tongue of the slanderer is set on fire of hell, nor can the waters of the multitudinous sea quench its baleful flames. One evening Henry was returning at a late hour from the country, and passing a mansion in the outskirts of the city, whose shaded walls and modest situation called up ideas of domestic comfort and retirement; he thought it might be the residence of Miss Carroll, for, notwithstanding Miss Hart's damper, he had not forgotten her. He passed the house very slowly, gazing at one illuminated window, over which a white muslin curtain softly floated, and wishing he could catch another glimpse of a countenance that haunted him, as he said, like a dream. All was still, and he passed on, through a narrow alley that shortened his way. At the end of the alley was a small, low dwelling, where a light still glimmered, and the door being partially open, he heard groans and wailing sounds, indicating distress within. He approached the door, thinking he might render relief or assistance, and stood at the threshold, gazing on the unexpected scene presented to his view. On a low seat, not far from the door, sat a young lady, in a loose white robe, thrown around her in evident haste and disorder, her hair partly knotted up behind and partly falling in golden waves on her shoulders, holding in her lap a child of about three years old, from whose bandaged head the blood slowly oozed and dripped down on her snowy dress—one hand was placed tenderly under the wounded head, the other gently wiped away the stains from its bloody brow. A woman, whose emaciated features and sunken eyes spoke the ravages of consumption, sat leaning against the wall, gazing with a ghastly expression on the little sufferer, whose pains she had no power to relieve, and a little boy about ten years of age stood near her, weeping bitterly. Here was a scene of poverty, and sickness, and distress that baffled description, and in the midst appeared the outlines of that fair figure, like a descended angel of mercy, sent down to console the sorrows of humanity.

"This was a dreadful accident," said the young lady,

"dreadful," raising her head as she spoke, and shading back her hair, revealing at the same time the heavenly countenance which had once before beamed on Henry's gaze. It was Lois Carroll, true to the character Miss Hart had sarcastically given her, a ministering spirit of compassion and benevolence.

"She will die," said the poor mother, "she'll never get over such a blow as that. She fell with such force, and struck her head on such a dangerous part too. Well, why should I wish her to live, when I must leave her behind so soon?"

"The doctor said there was some hope," answered the fair Lois, in a sweet, soothing voice, "and if it is God's will that she should recover, you ought to bless Him for it, and trust Him who feedeth the young ravens when they cry to Him for food. Lie down and compose yourself to rest. I will remain here through the night, and nurse the poor little patient. If she is kept very quiet, I think she will be better in the morning."

"How kind, how good you are!" said the mother, wiping the tear from her wasted cheek, "what should I do without you? But I never can think of your sitting up the whole night for us."

"And why not for you?" asked Lois, earnestly. "Can I ever repay your kindness to poor Charles, when he was sick, and you sat up, night after night, and refused to leave him? And now, when you are sick and helpless, would you deprive me of the opportunity of doing for you, what you have done for one so dear to me?"

A pang shot through Henry's heart. This poor *Charles* must have been the lover for whom she mourned, and at the mention of his name, he felt as if wakening from a dream. The love that bound the living to the dead, was a bond his hand would never attempt to loosen, and turning away with a sigh, he thought it would be sacrilege to linger there longer. Still he looked back to catch one more glimpse of a face where all the beatitudes dwelt. He had beheld the daughters of beauty, with all the charms of nature aided by the fascinations of art and fashion, but never had he witnessed anything so lovely as this young girl, in her simplicity, purity, and gentleness, unconscious that any eye was upon her, but the poor widow's and weeping orphan's. He had seen a fair belle in ill-humour for an hour, because a slight accident had soiled a new dress, or defaced a new ornament, but Lois sat in her blood-spotted robes, regardless of the stains, intent only on the object of her tenderness, and that a miserable child.

"Surely," thought he, as he pursued his way homeward, "there must be a divine influence operating on the heart, when a character like this is formed. Even were her affections free and not wedded to the dead, I should no more dare to love such a being, so spiritual, so holy, so little of the earth, earthy, than one of those pure spirits that live in the realms of ether. *I!* what has my life hitherto been? Nothing but a tissue of recklessness, folly, and madness. I have been trying to quench the heaven-born spark within me, but it still burns, and will continue to burn, while the throne of the Everlasting endures."

Henry felt more, reflected more that night, than he had done for five years before. He rose in the morning with a fixed resolve, to make that night an era in his existence. During the day the poor widow's heart was made to "sing for joy," for a supply was received from an unknown hand, so bounteous and unlooked for, she welcomed it as a gift from heaven. And so it was, for heaven inspired and also blessed the act.

Miss Hart began to be uneasy at Henry's deportment, and she had no reason to think she advanced in his good graces, and she had a vague fear of that Lois Carroll, whom she trusted she had robbed of all power to fascinate his imagination.

"By the way," said she to him, one day, as if struck by a sudden thought, "have you seen that pretty Miss Carroll since the evening you were speaking of her?"

"Yes," answered Henry, colouring very high, "I have met her several times—why do you ask?"

"No matter," said she, petrified at this information; "I saw a lady yesterday, who knows her intimately, and her conversation reminded me of ours on the same subject."

"What does the lady say of her character?" asked Henry.

"What every one else does, who knows her—that she is the greatest hypocrite that ever breathed. Perfectly selfish, self-righteous, and uncharitable. She says, notwithstanding her sweet countenance, she has a very bad temper, and that no one is willing to live in the same house with her."

"You told me formerly," said Henry, "that she was *over* charitable and kind, constantly engaged in labours of love."

"Oh, yes!" answered she, with perfect self-possession; 'there is no end to the parade she makes about her *good works*, as she calls them, but it is for ostentation, and to obtain the reputation of a saint, that she does them."

"But," said Henry, very warmly, "supposing she exercised this same heavenly charity when she believed no eye beheld her, but the poor whom she relieved, and the sick whom sh healed, and the God whom she adores; would you call tha ostentation?"

"Oh, my dear Mr. More," cried Miss Hart, with a musical laugh, "you do not know half the arts of the sex. There is a young minister and young physician too, in the neighbour-hood, who know all her secret movements, and hear her praises from morning till night—they say they are both in love with her, but as her cousin hasn't been dead long, she thinks it proper to be very demure—I must say frankly and honestly, I have no faith in these female *Tartuffes*."

"Nor I neither," added Henry, with so peculiar a manner, that Miss Hart started and looked inquisitively at him, with her dark, dilated eyes. She feared she had hazarded too much, and immediately observed,

"Perhaps, in my abhorrence of duplicity and hypocrisy, I run into the opposite extreme, and express my sentiments too openly. You think me severe, but I can have no possible motive to depreciate Miss Carroll, but as she herself stretches every one on the bed of Procrustes, I feel at liberty to speak my opinion of her character, not mine only, but that of the whole world."

Henry made some evasive reply, and turned the conversa-tion to another topic, leaving Miss Hart lost in a labyrinth of conjecture, as to the impression she had made on his mind—where and when had he met Lois Carroll, and why was he so reserved upon a theme, upon which he had once been so elo-quent?

She sat for half an hour after Henry left her, pondering on these things, and looking at one figure in the carpet, as if her eyes grew upon the spot, when her thoughts were turned into another channel by the entrance of Captain Went-worth.

She believed that she stood very high in his favour, for he was extremely polite to her, and showed her so much deference and attention, that she had no doubt that if Mrs. Wentworth were out of the way, he would be at no loss whom to choose as a successor. Her prospects with Henry grew more and more dubious—she thought, upon the whole, the captain the finer-looking and most agreeable man of the two. There was no knowing but he might separate from his wife, and as they seemed divorced in heart, she thought it would be much better than to remain together so cold and distant to each other. There was nothing she feared so much as a reconciliation; and as long as she could prevent Mrs. Wentworth from manifesting any symptoms of submission and sorrow, she was sure her husband's pride would be unyielding. She had a scheme on hand at present, which would promote her own gratification, and widen the breach between them.

There was a celebrated actor in the city, whom she was very desirous of seeing, and of whom Captain Wentworth had a particular dislike; he disliked the theatre and everything connected with it, and Miss Hart had vainly endeavoured to persuade Mrs. Wentworth to go with her brother, in open defiance of her husband. Henry manifested no disposition himself, and never would understand the oblique hints she gave him; she was determined to make a bold attack upon the captain himself.

"Captain Wentworth," said she, carelessly looking over the morning paper, "don't you mean to take Mrs. Wentworth to see this superb actor? she is dying to see him, and yet does not like to ask you."

"She's at perfect liberty to go as often as she pleases," replied the captain coldly—"I've no wish to control her inclinations."

"But she will not go, of course, unless you accompany her," replied Miss Hart, "not even with her brother."

"Did she commission you to make this request?"

"Not precisely; but knowing her wishes, I could not forbear doing it, even at the risk of your displeasure."

"If her heart is in such scenes, there can be no possible gratification to confine her body within the precincts of home."

The captain walked several times up and down the room, as was his custom when agitated, then abruptly asked Miss Hart if she wished to go herself.

She wished it, she said, merely to avoid singularity, as everybody else went; but had it not been for Mrs. Wentworth, she would never have mentioned it.

The captain declared that if she had the slightest desire,

it was a command to him, and the tickets were accordingly purchased.

Late in the afternoon, Captain Wentworth sat in the dining-room, reading. As the sun drew near the horizon, and the light grew fainter, he sat down in a recess by a window, and the curtain falling down, completely concealed him. In this position he remained while the twilight darkened around him, and no longer able to read, he gave himself up to those dark and gloomy reflections which had lately filled his mind. He thought of the hours when, tossed upon the foaming billows, he had turned in heart towards his home,

> "And she, the dim and melancholy star,
> Whose ray of beauty reached him from afar,"

rose upon the clouds of memory, with soft and gilding lustre. Now he was safely anchored in the haven of his hopes and wishes, but his soul was drifted by storms, wilder than any that swept the boisterous seas. The very effort of preserving outward calmness, only made the tempest fiercer within. This new instance of his wife's unconquerable levity and heartless-ness, filled him with despair. He believed her too much demoralized by vanity and love of pleasure, ever to return to her duty and allegiance as a wife.

While indulging these bitter feelings, Miss Hart and Mrs. Wentworth entered the dining-room, unaware of his presence. Miss Hart, as usual, was speaking in an earnest, confidential tone, as if she feared some one was listening to her counsels.

"I beg, I entreat," said she, "that you would rally your spirits, and not let the world see that you are cast down by his ill treatment. All the fashionable people will be there to-night, and you must remember that many eyes will be upon you; and pray don't wear that horrid unbecoming dress, it makes a perfect fright of you, muffling you up to the chin."

"It is no matter," replied Mrs. Wentworth, despondingly, 'I don't care how I look—the only eyes I ever really wished to charm, now turn from me in disgust; I'm weary of acting the part of a hypocrite, of smiling and chattering, and talking nonsense, when I feel as if my heart were breaking. Oh! that I had not weakly yielded my better reason to that fear of the world's censure, which has been the ruin of my happiness."

"I would never suffer my happiness to be affected one way or

the other," cried Miss Hart, "by a man who showed so little
tenderness or delicacy towards me. I wonder your affection
is not chilled, nay utterly destroyed by his harshness and
despotism."

" Oh ! you little know the strength or depth of a woman's
love, if you deem it so soon uprooted. My heart yearns to be
admitted once more into the foldings of his—a hundred times
liave I been tempted to throw myself into his arms, implore his
forgiveness, and entreat him to commence a new life of confidence and love."

Miss Hart began to laugh at this romantic speech, but the
laugh froze on her lips when she saw the window-curtains suddenly part, and Captain Wentworth rushing forward, clasp his
astonished wife in his arms, exclaiming " Jane, dear Jane, that
life is begun !" He could not utter another word.

When, after a few moments of intense emotion, he raised
his head, tears which were no stain upon his manhood, were
glistening on his dark cheek. Miss Hart looked on with feelings similar to those which we may suppose animate the spirits
of darkness, when they witness the restoration of man to the
forfeited favour of his Maker. There was wormwood and bitterness in her heart, but her undaunted spirit still saw a way
of extrication from all her difficulties.

" Really, Captain Wentworth," exclaimed she, laughing violently, " the next time you hide yourself behind a curtain, you
must draw your boots under ; I saw the cloven foot peeping
out, and spoke of you as I did, just to see what Mrs. Wentworth would say, and I thought very likely it would have a
happy result—I am sure this is a finer scene than any we shall
see at the theatre."

" That you have deceived me, Miss Hart," answered the
captain, " I acknowledge to my shame, but my eyes are now
opened. My situation was accidental ; no, I should say providential, for I have made discoveries, for which I can never
be sufficiently grateful. Jane, I have been harsh and unjustly
suspicious, I know, and richly deserve all I have suffered ; but
from the first hour of my return, this treacherous friend of
yours, discovering the weakness of my character, has fanned
the flame of jealousy, and fed the fires that were consuming
me. I despise myself for being her dupe."

" Oh ! Miss Hart," cried Mrs. Wentworth, " how could you
be so cruel ? you whom I so trusted, and thought my best and
truest friend !"

" I have said nothing but the truth to either," cried Miss
Hart boldly, seeing all subterfuge was now vain, "and
you had better profit by it. Everybody has a weak side, and
if they leave it unguarded and open to the attacks of the enemy,
they have no one to blame but themselves. I never made you
jealous, Captain Wentworth, nor your wife credulous; and, as
I leave you wiser than I found you, I think you both ought to
be very much obliged to me."

Thus saying, with an unblushing countenance, she left the
apartment, and recollecting the next morning that a certain
lady had given her a most pressing invitation to visit her, she
departed, and no one said " God bless her."

Henry, who had seen full as much as he desired of her,
hardly knew which rejoiced him more, her departure or his
sister's happiness. Indeed the last seemed the consequence
of the first, for never was there such a transformation in a
household. There was blue sky for stormy clouds—spring
gales for chill east winds—love and joy for distrust and sorrow.

Henry had seen the physician and minister whom Miss Hart
had mentioned as the lovers of Lois Carroll. The *young physician* happened to be a bald, broad-faced man, with a long
nose, which turned up at the end, as if looking at his forehead,
and the *young* minister, a man whose hair was frosted with
the snow of sixty winters, and on whose evangelical countenance disease had written deeper lines than those of age.
Charles, too, the lover-cousin, proved to be an only brother,
whose lingering hours of disease she had soothed with a
Christian sister's holy ministration. Henry became a frequent,
and, as he had reason to believe, a welcome visiter, at the house.
He found Lois skilled in all the graceful accomplishments of
her sex—her mind was enriched with oriental and classical
literature, her memory stored with the brightest and purest
gems of genius and taste; yet, like the wise men of the East, who
brought their gold and frankincense and myrrh to the manger
of the babe of Bethlehem, she laid these precious offerings in
lowliness of spirit, at the feet of her Redeemer. All at once,
Henry perceived a cloud come over the confidence in which he
was established there. The good aunt was cold and distant;
Lois, though still gentle and kind, was silent and reserved,
and he thought he caught her melting blue eyes fixed upon
him more than once with a sad and pitying expression.

" What has occurred?" asked he with the frankness so

peculiar to him—when for a moment he was left alone with her "I am no longer a welcome guest."

"Forgive us," answered Lois, her face mantling with earnest blushes, "if we feel constrained to deny ourselves the pleasure we have derived from your society. As long as we believed you the friend of religion, though not her acknowledged votary, our hearts acknowledged a sympathy with yours, and indulged a hope that you would ere long go goal for goal with us for the same immortal prize. But an infidel, Mr. More! Oh! my soul!" continued she, clasping her hands fervently together, and looking upward, "come not thou into his secret!"

"An infidel!" cried Henry, "and do you believe me such, and condemn me as such, unheard, without granting me an opportunity of vindication?"

"We would not have admitted the belief from an authority less respectable. The intelligence came from one who had been an inmate of your family, and expressed for you the warmest friendship. We were told that you ridicule our faith, make the Bible a scorn and mockery, and expose us as individuals to contempt and derision."

"It must have been that serpent of a Miss Hart!" exclaimed Henry, trembling with passion; "that scorpion, that fiend in woman's form, whose path may be traced by the slime and the poison she leaves behind! The lips which could brand *you*, Lois, as a hypocrite, would not leave my name unblackened. My sister received her into her household, and her domestic happiness came near being the wreck of her malignant arts— I could give you any proof you may ask of her falsehood and turpitude."

"I ask none," cried Lois, with an irradiated countenance, "I believe your assurance, and rejoice in it. I cannot describe the pain, the grief I felt that one so kind to others, could be so cruel to himself."

Lois, in the godly simplicity of her heart, knew not of the warmth with which she spoke, or of the vivid expression that lighted up her eyes. Henry thought if ever there was a moment when he could dare to address her as a being born to love, and to be loved with human tenderness, it was the present. He began with faltering lips, but in the intensity of his feelings he soon forgot everything, but the object for which he was pleading, with an ardour and a vehemence that made the unsophisticated Lois tremble. She trembled and wept

Her heart melted before his impassioned declaration, but she feared to yield immediately to its dictates.

Their course of life had hitherto been so different, their early associations, their pursuits and habits—she dreaded lest he should mistake the fervour of his attachment for her, for the warmth of religious sentiment, and that the temptations of the world would resume their influence over his heart. "Let us still be friends," said she, smiling through her tears, "till time has more fully unfolded our characters to each other. We are as yet but acquaintances of a day, as it were, and if we hope to pass an eternity together, we should pause a little before we become fellow-travellers in our pilgrimage. The love of a Christian," continued she, a holy enthusiasm illuminating her face, "cannot be limited to the transient union of this world—it soars far, far beyond it, illimitable as space, and everlasting as the soul's existence." Henry felt, while listening to this burst of hallowed feeling, that to possess the love of Lois Carroll here, without a hope of reunion beyond the grave, would be a dark and cheerless destiny, compared to the glorious hopes that now animated his being.

It was about two years after this, Miss Hart took passage in the stage, and started for the habitation of some obscure relative who lived in a distant town. She had gone from family to family, indulging her odious propensity, flattering the present, and slandering the absent, till, her character becoming fully known, all doors were closed against her, and she was compelled to seek a home, among kindred she was ashamed to acknowledge. "Whose beautiful country-seats are those?" asked a fellow-passenger, pointing to two elegant mansions, that stood side by side as if claiming consanguinity with each other. "The first belongs to Captain Wentworth, and the other to Mr. Henry More, his brother-in-law," answered Miss Hart, putting her head from the window, as they passed— "you must have heard of them." "No," said the stranger; "is there anything remarkable connected with them?" "Nothing," replied she, with one of her significant shrugs, "only the captain is one of your dark Spanish Knights, who lock up their wives, and fight everybody who looks at them; and his lady likes every other gentleman better than her husband— and they could not agree, and the whole city were talking about them, so he took her into the country, and makes her fast and pray, and do penance for her sins. The other gentleman, Mr. More, married a low, ignorant girl, who had never been accus-

tomed to good society; so, being ashamed to introduce her
among his friends, he immured himself in the country also.
They say he is so wretched in his choice, he has turned a fana-
tic, and there is some danger of his losing his reason." At
this moment one of the horses took fright, and springing from
the road, the stage was upset, with a terrible crash. Miss
Hart, whose head was projecting from the window, was the
only one who was seriously injured. She was dreadfully bruised
and mangled, and carried insensible into Captain Wentworth's
house. The stranger, whose curiosity was excited by the
description he had just heard, and seeing the inhabitants of
both dwellings were gathering together in consequence of the
accident, assisted in carrying her, and lingered as long as he
could find a reasonable excuse for doing so. " I believe that
young woman's jaw is broken," said he, when he rejoined his
fellow-passengers; "and it is a judgment upon her—I know
there is not a word of truth in what she has been saying. If
ever domestic happiness, as well as benevolence, dwelt on
earth, I verily believe it is in those two families."

It was long before Miss Hart recovered her consciousness,
and when she did, and endeavoured to speak, she felt such an
excruciating pain in her jaw, as prevented her utterance. It
seemed a remarkable instance of the retribution of Providence,
that she should be afflicted in the very part which she had
made an instrument of so much evil to others. Her jawbone
was indeed broken, and there she lay, writhing in agony, incapable of speech, indebted to the beings she hated because she
had injured, for the cares that prolonged her miserable existence. She could not speak, but she could see and hear, and
her senses seemed sharpened by the bondage of her tongue.
Mrs. Wentworth, and Lois too, hovered round her, with gentle
steps and pitying looks, and the tenderest alleviations; and
for this she might have been prepared. But when, through
the shades of evening, she heard the deep voice of the once
haughty and ungovernable Captain Wentworth, breathing forth
humble and heartfelt prayers, while his wife knelt meek and
lowly by his side, when she heard the gay and gallant Henry
More, reading with reverence God's holy word, and joining
with Lois in hymns to the Redeemer's praise, she rolled her
eyes in wild amazement, and her dark spirit was troubled within her. "There seems a reality in this," thought she. "The
worldling become the saint, and the lion transformed into the
lamb! How happy they look, while I—poor, wretched, man-

gled creature that I am !" Paroxysms of agony followed these reflections, for which there seemed no mitigation.

She lingered for a long time speechless and in great suffering, but at length recovered with a frightful distortion in the lower part of the face. When she first beheld herself in a mirror, the shock was so great as to produce delirium, and when that subsided, a gloom and despair succeeded, from which they vainly endeavoured to rouse her by the soothings of sympathy and the consolations of religion. She felt that, like Cain, she must carry about an indelible brand upon her face, and cried like him, in bitterness of spirit, " My punishment is greater than I can bear." It was intolerable to her to look upon the fair, serene countenances of Mrs. Wentworth and Lois, and to see too the eyes of their husbands follow them with such love and delight, and then to draw the contrast between them and her own disfigured beauty and desolate lot. She expressed a wish to be sent to her relatives, and the wish was not opposed. She . received from them a grudging welcome, for they had felt her sting, and feared that serpent tongue of slander, whose ancestral venom is derived from the arch reptile that lurked in the bowers of Eden.

Woe to the slanderer !—To use the language of the wise man, " her end is bitter as wormwood, and sharp as a twoedged sword—Her feet go down to death, her steps take hold on hell !"

THE SHAKER GIRL.

It was on a Sunday morning, when Roland Gray entered the village of ———. Though his mind was intent on the object of his journey, he could not but admire the singular neatness and uniformity of the houses, the velvet smoothness of the grass on the wayside, and the even surtace of the street, from which every pebble seemed to have been removed. An air of perfect tranquillity reigned over the whole—not a being was seen moving abroad, not a human face beaming through the windows; yet far as the eye could reach, it roamed over a vast, cultivated plain, covered with all the animated hues of vegetation, giving evidence that the spirit of life was there, or had been recently active. "Surely," thought Roland, "I have entered one of those cities, described in the Arabian Nights, where some magician has suddenly converted the inhabitants into stone. I will dismount and explore some of these buildings—perchance I shall find some man, who is only half marble, who can explain this enchantment of silence." He had scarcely dismounted, and fastened his horse to a part of the snow-white railing which guarded every avenue to the dwellings, when he saw a most singular figure emerging from one, and approaching the spot where he stood. It was a boy of about twelve years old, clad in the ancient costume of our forefathers—with large breeches, fastened at the knees with square shining buckles—a coat, whose skirts were of surprising breadth, and a low-crowned hat, whose enormous brim shaded his round and ruddy visage. Roland could not forbear smiling at this extraordinary figure, but habitual politeness checked his mirth. He inquired the name of the village, and found to his surprise he was in the midst of one of those Shaker establishments, of whose existence, and of whose singular doctrines, he was well aware, but which, his own home being remote, he had never had an opportunity of witnessing. Delighted with the circumstance, for the love of novelty and excitement was predominant in his character, he determined to avail himself of it to its fullest extent. An old man, dressed in the same obsolete fashion, came up the path and accosted him:

"Are you a traveller," said he, "and seeking refreshments? If so, I am sorry you have chosen this day, but nevertheless we never refuse to perform the rites of hospitality."

Roland confessed he had no claims upon their hospitality, having partaken of a hearty breakfast two hours before in a town not far distant, and he wondered within himself why they had not mentioned the vicinity of this interesting establishment; forgetting that to those who live within the reach of any object of curiosity, it loses its interest. It is said there are some, who live where the echo of Niagara's eternal thunders are ringing in their ears, who have never gazed upon its foam. "If you come to witness our manner of worship, young man," said the elder, "and come in a sober, godly spirit, I give you welcome. The world's people often visit us, some, I am sorry to say, to scoff and to jest; but you have an honest, comely countenance, and I trust are led by better motives."

Roland was no hypocrite, but the good Shaker opened for him so fair a door of excuse for his intrusion, he was unwilling to deny that he was moved by a laudable desire to behold their peculiar form of worship. Pleased by the sunny openness of his countenance, the elder led the way to the house set apart for the service of the Most High, exhorting him at the same time to renounce the pomps and vanities of the world, and unite with them in that *oneness* of spirit, which distinguished their society from the children of mankind. No lofty spire marked out the temple of the Lord, nor did its form differ from that of a common dwelling-place. They entered a spacious hall, the floor of which presented such a dazzling expanse of white, the foot of the traveller hesitated before pressing its polished surface. The walls were of the same shining whiteness, chilling the eye by their cold uniformity— and benches arranged with the most exact precision on each side of the building, marked the boundaries of either sex Roland seated himself at some distance from the prescribed limits, and waited with proper solemnity the entrance of the worshippers. He observed that the men invariably entered at one door, the women at another, and that they had as little intercourse as if they belonged to different worlds. The men were all clothed in the ancient costume we have just described, and the women were dressed in garments as peculiar and unbecoming. A shirt of the purest white, short gown of the same texture, a 'kerchief folded in stiff unbending plaits, a mob cap of linen fastened close around the face, from which every tress of hair was combed carefully back, constituted their chill and ghost-like attire. As one by one these pallid figures glided in, and took their appointed seat, Roland felt as if he were gazing on the phantasmagoria of a dream, so pale and unearthly did they seem. The countenances of the males were generally suffused with a ruddy glow, but cold and colourless as marble were the cheeks of that sex he had been wont to see adorned with the roses of beauty and health. They arose and arranged themselves in a triangular form, while several of the aged stood in the centre, commencing the worship by a hymn of praise. Their voices were harsh and broken, but the devotion of their manner sanctified the strains, and, Roland felt not, as he feared he should, a disposition for mirth. But when they gradually formed into a procession, marching two and two in a regular line, all joining in the wild and dissonant notes, then warming as they continued, changing the solemn march into the liveliest dance, clapping their hands simultaneously and shouting till the cold white walls resounded with the strange hosannas; all the while, those hueless, passionless faces gleaming by him, so still and ghastly mid their shroud-like garments, his brain began to reel, and he almost imagined himself attending the orgies of the dead, of resuscitated bodies, with the motions of life, but without the living soul. . Still, over the whole group there was a pervading solemnity and devotion, an apparent abandonment of the whole world—an anticipation of the loneliness and lifelessness of the tomb, that redeemed it from ridicule, and inspired emotions kindred to awe. This awe, however, soon melted away in pity at such delusion, and this sensation became at length converted into admiration for an object, at first unnoticed in the general uniformity of the scene, but which grew upon his eye, like the outline of the landscape through the morning mist. There was one young girl moving in this throng of worshippers, whose superior bearing could not long elude the stranger's scrutiny. Her age might be fourteen or fifteen, perhaps younger; it was difficult to decide through the muffling folds of a dress which levelled every distinction of form and comeliness. As she passed and repassed him, in the evolutions of their dance, he caught occasional glimpses of a face, which, though pale, betrayed the flitting colour through the transparent skin; and once or twice the soft, thoughtful gray eyes were turned towards him, with a wistful and earnest expression, as if claiming sympathy and kindness from some congenial being. Fixing his gaze upon the spot where he first beheld her, he watched her returning figure with an intensity that at last became visible to the object of it, for the pale rose of her cheek grew deeper and deeper, and her beautiful gray eyes were bent upon the floor. Roland leaned from the window near which he was seated, to see if it was actually the same world he had inhabited that morning, so strangely were his senses affected by the shrill music, growing louder and louder, the shuffling, gliding motions, increasing in velocity, and this sweet apparition so unexpectedly mingling in such an incongruous scene. The breath of summer redolent with a thousand perfumes stole over his brow—the blue sky was arching over his head; never had creation seemed more lovely or glowing; yet the worshippers within deemed they were offering an acceptable sacrifice on the altar of God, the sacrifice of those social affections, which find such beautiful emblems in the works of nature. Roland became so lost in these reflections, he hardly noticed the closing of the exercise, or heard the monotonous tones of one of the elders, who was exhorting in the peculiar dialect of his sect. When the services were concluded, he left the hall, still watching the motions of the gray-eyed damsel, in the bold resolution of accosting her, and discovering if she were a willing devotee. As she walked along with a light step, in spite of her clumsy high-heeled shoes, by the side of an ancient dame, Roland, unconscious of the extreme audacity of the act, and hardly knowing himself in what manner to address her, crossed her path, and was in the very act of apologizing for the intrusion, when his arm was seized with a sturdy grasp, and he saw the old Shaker who had introduced him into the assembly, standing by his side. "Young man," said he, in a stern voice—"do you come here, a wolf in sheep's clothing, in the very midst of the flock? what is your business with this child, whom our rules forbid you to address?" Roland felt at first very indignant, but a moment's reflection convinced him he had erred, and transgressed their rigid rules. He felt too that he had placed himself in rather a ridiculous situation, and he stood before the rebuking elder with a blush of ingenuous shame, that completely disarmed his wrath. " You are young, very young," said the old man—"and I forgive you—you have been brought up in the midst of the vanities of the world, and I pity you; yet my heart cleaves to you, young man, and when you become weary of those vanities, as you shortly will, come to us, and you will find that peace which the world can neither give nor take away."

He shook hands with Roland after he had spoken, who acknowledged his offence, thanked him for his counsel and kindness, and, mounting his horse, left him with a sentiment of unfeigned respect; so true it is, that sincerity of faith gives dignity to the professor of many a creed revolting to human reason. Roland looked back upon the beautiful village, and wondered at what he had just witnessed. He felt a strong disposition to linger, that he might discover something more of the peculiarities of this singular and isolated people. Had he known their incorruptible honesty, their unwearied industry, their trusting hospitality, their kindness and charity—had he seen the pale sisterhood extending their cherishing cares to the children of orphanage and want, he would have been convinced that warm streams of living tenderness were flowing beneath the cold forms of their austere religion.

Roland Gray was very young, and had seen but little of the world. He had led the secluded life of a student, and, but lately freed from collegiate restraints, he had been trying his wings, preparatory to a bolder flight across the Atlantic. He was now on the way to his sister, who, with himself, was placed under the guardianship of the excellent Mr. Worthington, for they were orphans, left with an independent fortune, but singularly destitute of kindred, being the last of their race. An invalid gentleman, one of his father's early friends, was about to travel in foreign climes to try the benefit of a milder atmosphere, and he urged Roland to be his companion. Such a proposal was accepted with gratitude, and Roland, with buoyant spirits, returned to his sister, to bid her farewell, before launching on the " deep blue sea." Lucy Gray was older than her brother, and from childhood had exercised over him the influence with which a few additional years, joined to a strength of mind far beyond her years, invested her. He was the object no less of her love than her pride. She looked upon him as the last representative of a family, honoured among the most honourable, and destined to transmit to posterity his ancestral name, with unblemished and still more exalted lustre. She resolved he should ennoble himself by marriage, and would have scorned, as degrading, the thought that love might make the youth a rebel to her will. She believed the affections entirely under the control of the reason, and looked upon the passions as vassals to be dragged at its chariot wheels. Lucy was not loved by her friends, but she was respected and esteemed for the firmness of her principles, and the strength of her mind. But Roland loved as much as he revered her. His heart was a fountain of warm and generous affections, and it flowed out towards her, his only sister, in the fulness of a current, that found no other legitimate channel. Accustomed to yield his rash and ardent impulses to the direction of her cooler judgment, he looked up to her as the mentor of his follies, rather than as the companion of his youthful amusements, and now, after an absence of several months, partly from pleasure and partly from business, he looked forward to meeting her with something of the feelings of a son, blended with the affection of a brother. His arrival at Mr. Worthington's was hailed with a burst of joy, for Roland had a face of sunshine and a voice of melody, that shed light and music wherever he went. In relating his adventures, he failed not to give due interest to his interview with the Shakers, and laughed over the Quixotism that exposed him to so stern a rebuke. The pretty little Shakeress did not lose any of her attractions in his romantic description, and he dwelt upon her dovelike eyes, melting beneath the snows of her antiquated cap, her sweet, appealing countenance and spiritual air, till Mr. Worthington's childless heart warmed within him, and Lucy listened with apprehensive pride lest her brother's excited imagination should convert this obscure unknown into a heroine of romance. It was but a transient alarm, for she knew that the waves of the Atlantic would soon roll between them, and Roland, surrounded by all the glorious associations of an elder world, would cast aside every light and ignoble fancy, and fit himself for the high station in society she felt he was born to fill.

*   *   *   *   *   *   *   *   *

After an absence of four years Roland Gray appeared once

more in the family circle of Mr. Worthington. His hair had assumed a darker shade, and his cheek a darker glow, but the same sunshiny spirit lighted up his brow and animated his lips; it was Roland Gray still, only the bloom of boyhood was lost in the sunniness of manhood. Lucy's handsome, but severe countenance was so irradiated with joy, it was almost dazzling from the effect of contrast: and as she sat by his side, and gazed in his face, she felt that all her affections and her hopes were so completely centered in him, they could be separated only with the breaking of her heart. Happy as Roland was in being reunited to his sister, his attention was not so engrossed as to forget the kindly greetings due to the other members of Mr. Worthington's household.

"I have an adopted daughter to introduce you to," said Mr. Worthington, drawing forward a young girl who, on the entrance of Roland, had retreated behind a stand of geraniums, and busied herself in picking off the faded leaves. Roland had become too familiar with beauty in foreign climes, to be surprised into admiration of a face however fair, but there was a sweetness, a modesty and simplicity diffused over the young face before him, that interested his feelings and disarmed his judgment. He could scarcely tell the colour of her eyes, for they were downcast, but there was something in the play of her features, that implied she sympathized in the pleasure his coming had excited. "Roland," continued Mr. Worthington, evidently delighted with the reception he had given his favourite, "this is my daughter Grace, whom Providence has kindly given to cheer a widowed and childless heart. You know I look upon you almost as my son, so you will find in her, I trust, another sister to love." Roland held out his hand with great alacrity to seal this new compact, but the pretty Grace drew back with an embarrassment he was unwilling to increase, seeing it was entirely unaffected; and there was something in Lucy's glance that told him she resented the idea of such a partnership in his affections. He could not but marvel where good old Mr. Worthington had found such a fairy gift, but believing the mystery would be explained in due time, he promised himself no slight gratification in studying a character, concealed under such a veil of bashfulness and reserve. The twilight hour found the brother and sister walking together towards their accustomed seat under the sycamore boughs, the scene of many of Lucy's former counsels, and Roland's high resolves. She wanted to be alone with him—to guard him against a thousand dangers and snares, visible only to her proud and jealous eye. "Oh! Roland," said she, taking his hand and looking earnestly in his face—"do you return unchanged?—may I still, as wont, presume to counsel, to direct, and to sustain?" "Unchanged in everything as regards my affection for you, my dear sister," replied he—"be still my mentor and my guide, for I fear, with all the worldly wisdom I have acquired, I am often the sam impulsive being you have so long tried in vain to bring under the square and compass of reason and right. Now, I feel at this moment an irresistible impulse to know who is this pretty God-send of Mr. Worthington's; did she drop down from the skies, or did she come on the wings of the wind?"

"I am glad you have opened the subject, Roland, for I brought you here to warn you of that girl's influence. Do not laugh, for, knowing you so well, I feel bound to prevent any imposition on your open, generous nature. I do not know who she is, probably some poor child of shame and desertion, whom Mr. Worthington discovered and educated, for it is but a year since he brought her from school, and introduced her as his adopted daughter. He made a long visit to his relatives, since you left us, and found her, I believe, in the family of his brother, in a dependent and perhaps menial situation. Charmed by her beauty and beguiled by her arts, the good man conceived the romantic design of educating her as his own, and now he is felicitating himself with another project, that of securing for this nameless foundling the heart and the fortune of Roland Gray." Roland had heard too much about gentle blood and honourable parentage, and been too much under the influence of his aristocratic sister, not to shrink from the supposition of such an union, but he protested against the word *arts*, which Lucy had used in reference to Grace, for she looked the most artless of human beings; and he accused her of injustice towards Mr. Worthington, who in his singleness of heart was incapable of making a project of any kind. "You must not think it strange," said Lucy, "that I, a woman should not be blinded by the beauty of one of my own sex, and I know I am superior to the weakness of envy. With an insight into character which has never deceived me, I know that girl to be vain, selfish, and calculating. Mr. Worthington may claim her as *his daughter*, but he shall never impose her on me, by the name of *sister*." Those who have witnessed the empire an elder sister of commanding mind and manners is

capable of obtaining over a younger brother's judgment, will
not be surprised that Roland learned to look upon Grace with
distrustful eyes, though he could not believe in the duplicity
Lucy ascribed to her character, and he invariably treated her
with that consideration due to the situation she held in Mr.
Worthington's family. It was impossible, however, to be do-
mesticated with her, to be seated at the same table, parties in
the same amusements, near each other in the evening circle,
and the moonlight walks, notwithstanding the unsleeping vigilance of Lucy, not to feel the reality of her loveliness, her simplicity and truth. There was something about her that haunted
him like a dream, and whenever she turned her eyes towards
him, he experienced a sudden thrill of recollection, as if he
had seen that fair face before. In the evening Mr. Worthington often challenged Lucy to a game of chess, for though not
a skilful performer, he was extravagantly fond of the game,
and Lucy had no rival in the art. She now regretted this accomplishment, as it threw her brother more immediately into
companionship with Grace, whose conversation, when unrestrained, was perfectly bewitching, from a mixture of bright
intelligence, quick sensibility, and profound ignorance of the
vices and customs of the world. It was evident she felt oppressed by Lucy's scrutinizing gaze, for when she was conscious of its withdrawal, her spirits rebounded with an unob-
trusive gayety, that harmonized admirably with the life and
vivacity of Roland's disposition.

One evening, as Lucy was absorbed in the crisis of the
game, Grace was busily plying her needle, making some garments for a poor woman, whose house and wardrobe were completely consumed by fire, the previous night; all the ladies in
the neighbourhood were contributing their part towards relieving her wants, and a very pretty little girl, with a basket half-
filled with her mother's offerings, was waiting till Grace had
put the last stitches into a cap, whose fashion seemed to fix the
particular attention of Roland. The child, who was a petted
favourite in the family, caught up the cap the moment it was
completed, and drawing it over the soft brown locks of Grace,
laughingly fastened the linen bands. Roland uttered so sudden
an exclamation, it made Lucy start from her seat, upsetting
bishop, knight, and royalty itself. The mystery was revealed,
the pretty little Shakeress stood before him. The close linen
border, under which every lock of hair was concealed, transformed at once the fashionable and elegant young lady into

the simple and humble Shaker girl. A scene, which the lapse
of years and the crowding events of a transatlantic tour had
effaced from his memory, returned vividly to his recollection.
He wondered he had not recognised her earlier, but the hue
of the soft gray eye was darkened, and its light more warm
and shifting, her complexion had a richer colouring, and
shadows of bright hair relieved the fairness of a brow where
ntelligence and sensibility now sat enthroned. Then her
figure—now revealed in all the graces of womanhood, was it
the same he had seen muffled in the stiff starched shirt and 'kerchief, moving on high-heeled shoes with large shining buckles?
Grace blushed deeply beneath his riveted gaze, and hastily
snatching the cap from her head, folded it with the other garments she had made into the basket, and bade the little girl
hasten to her mother. "What is the meaning of all this
bustle?" said Lucy, looking at Grace with so much asperity it
made her involuntarily draw closer to Mr. Worthington. "It
means," said Roland, delighted and excited by the discovery
he had made, and forgetting his sister's daily cautions—"it
means that I have found my pretty Shakeress at last. Ah!
Mr. Worthington, why did not you tell me that your adopted
daughter and my fair unknown were one?" Mr. Worthington
laughed, and taking the hand of Grace drew her upon his
knee. "Because the world is full of prejudice, and I did not
like to expose my girl to its influence. I always wanted to
tell *you*, but Grace insisted I should allow you to find it out
yourself, for she told me about the bold youth, who almost
stared her out of her devotion and her wits. Nay, Grace, I
owe him a thousand thanks, for had he not warmed my old
heart by a description of your loveliness, I never should have
gone so far out of my journey to visit your village, begged
you of the good people for my own, nor would I now have
such a sweet blossom to shed fragrance over my declining
years."

"And how," exclaimed Roland with irresistible curiosity,
"how came she amongst them?" Before Mr. Worthington
could reply, Grace clasped her hands earnestly together, and
cried, "I was a stranger, and they took me in; I was an orphan and they clothed me, sheltered and—" Previously much
agitated, Grace here entirely lost her self-command, and leaning her head on the shoulder of Mr. Worthington, she wept
audibly. Lucy actually trembled and turned pale. She saw
that her empire was tottering from its foundation. Accustomed

to interpret every change of her brother's countenance, she
read with terror the intense expression with which his eyes
were fixed on Grace. She was willing he should marry from
ambition, but not for love. She had never for a moment
admitted the idea that another should supplant her in his affections—a jealousy far more dark and vindictive than that
excited by love, the jealousy of power, took possession of her
soul, mingled with a bitter hatred towards the innocent cause
of these emotions. Through life she had bowed the will
of others to her own, and as long as no opposition roused
the strength of her passions, she maintained a character of
integrity and virtue, that bid defiance to scandal and reproach.
She did not know herself the evil of which she was capable,
but now the lion was unchained in her bosom, and chafed and
wrestled for its prey. Too politic to attempt checking too
suddenly the tide of feeling, yet too angry to hide her own
chagrin, she left the room, and meditated in what manner she
could best arrest the evil she dreaded. She failed not, however, to breathe a warning whisper into her brother's ear as
she passed out. Here Mr. Worthington entreated Grace to
tell Roland all she knew of herself, assuring her, in his simplicity, that no one, next to himself, felt so deep an interest in
her, as he did. Roland felt no disposition to contradict this
assertion, and joined his own entreaties so earnestly to Mr.
Worthington's, Grace hesitated not to relate her simple history. It could be comprised in a few words. She told of
her sad and almost desolate childhood, of her dwelling in a
little cottage deep in the woods, remote from neighbours or
friends; of a dark and cruel man she called father—here
Grace's voice grew low and husky—of a pale, sick, and dying
mother, who was found by a good Shaker, on the bed of death,
and who committed her orphan child to the care of the kind
Samaritan. The man who had deserted her mother, in the
extremity of her wants, never appeared to claim his child.
She was cherished in the bosom of that benevolent society,
where Roland first beheld her, grateful for their kindness,
though yearning after freedom and the fellowship of youth,
till Mr. Worthington came, and offered her the love and
guardianship of a father, if she would occupy a daughter's
place in his heart and home. Her father's name was Goldman, which she had willingly resigned for that of Worthington, for the memory she had of him, was like a dark and
terrible dream—fearful to remember. The dread that he might

appear some day to claim her, often made her shudder in the
midst of her happiness; but as so many years had passed
away, it was more natural to suppose he had expiated his
cruelty with his life.

Had Mr. Worthington conceived the project that Lucy had
suggested, and been aware at the same time of Roland's family
pride, it is not probable he would have induced her to reveal
to him the sad events of her childhood; and had Grace been
the artful being described, she would never have told with such
straightforward simplicity and deep sensibility of her father's
brutality and vices, nor expressed the startling fear, that he
might still assert the forfeited rights of nature, and tear her
from the arms of her benefactor.   Such thoughts as these
filled the breast of Roland, as Grace continued her affecting
recital, where truth was attested by her blushes and her tears.
She unclasped from her neck a golden chain, from which a
miniature was suspended, the sole relic of her mother.   The
chain was beautifully wrought, and indicated that however
abject was the condition to which the owner had been reduced,
she had once been accustomed to the decorations of wealth.
The miniature was that of a gentleman in the prime of life,
with a dark, but interesting countenance, and dignified bearing.
Grace knew not whether it was her father's picture, for she had
but a faint recollection of his features, and the Shaker who
discovered it around her mother's neck, after she was speechless in death, could give her no information.

Here was mystery and romance, innocence, beauty, and
youth; and Roland felt as if he would gladly twine them
together, and bind them around his heart, as all " he guessed
of heaven."   But while his imagination was weaving the gar-
land and revelling in its fragrance, the vision of

> " A sister's jealous care,
> A cruel sister she,"

rose before him, and the wreath faded and the blossoms fell.
With a stinging sensation of shame, he admitted the conviction, that he *feared* his sister.   He had long worn her fetters
unconsciously, but now, when for the first time they galled
and restrained him, his pride and his heart rebelled against
the hand that bound him in thraldom.   Grace retired that
night, with a thousand bright hopes hovering round her pillow
Roland then was her first benefactor.   It was he, who had
awakened the interest of Mr. Worthington, and directed him

to her retreat. He, the handsome and noble-looking youth, whose dark piercing eyes had kindled in her such yearnings after the world from which she was excluded, and who for four years had been the morning and evening star on the horizon of her memory. She knew something of this before, but she had never realized it so fully as now; for he had imself confirmed it, by words, which, though simple in themelves, were unutterably eloquent, accompanied by such looks —she blushed even in the darkness, as she caught herself involuntarily repeating, "and have I found my pretty Shakeress at last?" For two or three days, Roland avoided being alone with Lucy, but to his surprise, she did not seem to desire an opportunity to renew her warnings. On the contrary, she was more kind and affectionate towards Grace than she had ever been before, who, in the confidingness of innocence, relied on her unwonted testimonies of favour, as the harbingers of her dearest wishes. "Grace," said Lucy—they were alone and secure of interruption, for Mr. Worthington and Roland were both absent on business—"Grace, are you willing to tell me of what you are now thinking?" Grace started—she had fallen into an unconscious revery, and her work lay idly in her lap; her cheeks glowed painfully, but with that habitual reverence for truth which always distinguished her, she answered, "I was thinking of Roland." Unprepared for such perfect ingenuousness, Lucy hesitated a moment, and conscience upbraided her for the part she was about to act, but again fixing her keen eye on a countenance as transparent as crystal, she continued: "Has Roland ever told you that he loved you?" Grace crimsoned still more deeply from wounded modesty and shame, while she answered in a low voice, "Never!" "Then," said the inquisitor, drawing a relieving breath, "Grace, your task is easy, and I rejoice that he has made it so; you must not think of Roland, you must not love him, for he never can be to you anything more than he now is." Grace turned deadly pale, but she did not speak, and Lucy went on—"My brother was my father's only son, and is sole heir of a name long conspicuous for its honours. Our parents died when we were both young; but I, as the elder, became the guardian and guide. To me, on his death-bed, my father committed my young brother, charging me with the solemnity of that awful hour, to guard his honour from stain, and his name from degradation. My father was a proud and haughty man, and he has transmitted to his children a

portion of his own spirit. Grace, you have told me all the
circumstances of your life; you know there is mystery, but
you may not know in your extreme simplicity, that there may
be disgrace in your birth. The golden chain that wreathes
your neck, shows that your mother was not born to poverty.
Why then did she flee from her friends, to bury herself in
solitude with the dark and cruel man you called father; and
why are you an alien from your kindred? You ought to
know these truths, which the mistaken kindness of your
friends conceals from you, and I reveal them to you, that you
may not encourage hopes that never can be realized; to convince you, you can never be the wife of Roland. For myself,
hear me, Grace, to the end—if Roland could forget himself so
far as to think of such an union, I would for ever disown him
as a brother, and load with maledictions the being who had
brought such misery on us both." All the strong passions
at work in Lucy's bosom, sent their baleful lustre to her eyes,
and poor Grace shrunk from their beams as if they were withering her very heart. Brought up in the midst of that gentle
and subdued sisterhood, in whose uniform existence the passions seemed cradled into unbroken slumber, she had almost
forgotten their existence. The terrible dreams of her childhood were brought back to her. The curses of her father again
rung in her ears—the helpless cries of her mother. She
clasped her hands despairingly over her eyes—she knew she
had been poor and wretched; but benevolence and charity had
administered to her wants, and the very remembrance of poverty had faded from her mind; but disgrace—that there was
a disgrace attached to her that made it sinful in her to love
Roland Gray, that debarred her from an union with the
honourable and good—that was the thought that crushed her,
that chilled her blood, and turned her cheeks to marble and
her lips to ashes. Lucy paused, and attempted to soothe the
agony she had excited. Cold herself to the softer emotions,
she had no faith in the eternity of love. Grace, like a child
robbed of its plaything, now wept and refused to be comforted,
but she would soon smile animated by some new-born hope.
Thus Lucy tried to reason, while she held her chill grasp on
the heart of Grace, and bound her still more closely to her
will. "Promise me," said she, "that you will not reveal to
any one the conversation of this morning—Mr. Worthington
has deceived you, and you would not meanly appeal to the
compassion of Roland—promise this, and you shall find in me

a friend who will never forsake you in weal or woe. Deny it, and you will create an enemy whose power can make you tremble." Grace, with all her woman's pride rising to her relief, at the idea of appealing to the compassion of Roland, gave the desired promise, and still more—she voluntarily declared she would rather die than think of Roland, after what Lucy had just uttered. Lucy, satisfied with her promise, for he knew her truth, embraced her with commendations which fell heedlessly on poor Grace's paralyzed ears—she withdrew to her chamber, "for her whole head was pained and her whole heart sick;" and when Mr. Worthington and Roland returned, Grace was said to be unable, from indisposition, to join the circle, where she was wont to preside an angel of light and joy. The sympathy and sorrow excited by so common an event, reconciled Lucy more than anything else, to her selfishness and cruelty. But was she happy in the success of her operations ! She had planted thorns in the bosom of another —but were there none rankling in her own ! Could she, a daughter of this land of republicanism, shelter herself under the cold shadow of family pride, from the reproaches of her own conscience ? Ah ! no ! the heart is its own avenger, and for every drop of sorrow wilfully wrung from the eyes of another, shall be doomed to give only tears of blood.

Roland wondered at the change that had come over Grace, and sought by every means to ascertain the cause, but she seemed wrapped in a cloud of impenetrable reserve. She avoided him, but in so quiet a manner, it appeared to him more the result of sudden indifference or aversion, than unexplained resentment. The sunshine of her smile was gone, and an expression of calm apathy settled on her brow, where the alternations of feeling had lately flitted, like the lights and shadows of a moonlight landscape. Roland sometimes had a painful suspicion of his sister, but she had always been so open in all her actions, so undisguised in her least amiable traits, that notwithstanding all the prejudice she had manifested towards Grace, he believed her incapable of any mean or dark designings. Mr. Worthington was anxious and alarmed. He was sure some incipient and insidious disease was the cause of her pale and dispirited appearance. He was constantly feeling her pulse, and inquiring her symptoms, and insisting upon calling in a physician, till poor Grace, really glad to shelter herself from observation, under the pretext held out, acknowledged herself ill, and passively submitted to a course of medicine, which reduced her soon to a state of real debility and suffering. They applied blisters to her forehead to still its hot throbbings; they drew blood from her veins to reduce her feverish pulse, and Lucy sat by her bedside and administered to her unweariedly, and discussed the nature of her malady, and talked of its different stages; while all the time she knew it was herself who had coldly and deliberately dried up the fountain of hope and joy, and love, which had sent such roses to her cheek and sunbeams to her eye. She sometimes trembled in the darkness of night, at the possibility that Grace might die, under the regimen of this imaginary disease; and then a voice whispered in hollow murmurs, in her ears, "Thou shalt sleep no more, for thou hast murdered sleep." But in day's broad light a witness to Roland's abstraction, anxiety and gloom, she steeled her conscience, in reflecting on the necessity of the act. Let not Grace be condemned, as too weak and yielding, as too blind an instrument in the hands of another. Her education had been peculiar, and her natural disposition was extremely sensitive and timid. The first years of her life had been passed in terror and sorrow—terror for her father's cruelty, and sorrow for her mother's woe. Everything around her was tumultuous and fearful, and she learned to shudder at the awful manifestations of evil passions, before she knew them by name. Transplanted to a scene, where everything breathed of peace and silence, where industry, neatness, and order were heaven's first laws, where the voice of dissension was unheard, and the storms of passion unfelt, her spirit had been so hushed and subdued, her sensibilities so repressed, and her energies held down, she moved along her daily path a piece of beautiful and exquisite mechanism, but whose most powerful springs had never been touched. It is true she loved the kind and gentle Shakers, but it was with a tranquil feeling of gratitude and trust. The visit of Roland Gray acted as an electrical communication between her and the world to which he belonged. It seemed to her it must be inhabited by angels; and when Mr. Worthington came and induced her benefactor to resign her to his care, she welcomed the change as into the garden of Eden. In the seclusion of a school, her timidity still induced her to shrink within herself; in the companionship of Lucy, she felt awe-struck and abashed; but Roland came, and then she realized the paradise of her imagination. Everything around her was music and beauty and love—flowers sprang up in the waste places, water gushed from the rock, and melody filled the air. To be forbidden to think of him, to be commanded to wrench him from her heart, to be made to think of herself as a low and disgraced being— Grace would have shuddered at the idea of impiety, but when she laid her head on her pillow, willing to be thought sick, rather than wretched, she certainly wished to die. But the strength of youth, though prostrated, rebounded from the pressure. She was not doomed to the *curse of a granted prayer.* The Providence that had so long watched over her destiny, still kept its unseen but slumbering vigils. Grace remembered her old friends, the Shakers, and yearned once more for their still and passionless existence. She prayed Mr. Worthington to take her there so earnestly, he did not hesitate to grant her request, believing the journey would invigorate her constitution and change of scene animate her mind. She spoke not of remaining, and the wish was so natural and grateful, it could not excite surprise or censure.

"You see," said Lucy to her brother, the night before Grace's departure, "the influence of early habits. Perhaps all this time Grace has been pining after the Shakers. She has been suffering from a kind of calenture, and when she sees their green plain, and quiet village, she will be happy" "Impossible!" cried Roland, completely thrown off his guard by Lucy's sudden insinuation. "She is strange and unaccountable, but I never will believe anything so preposterous. She, that sweet, lovely, spiritual creature, to be immured again in their cold walls, and to wish it, and pine after it! By heavens! Lucy, if I could believe such a thing, I would go this moment and prevent the immolation. I will not deceive you; I do not care any longer for pride and empty sounding names, and birth and parentage. It is ridiculous to think of such things in this republican country. Grace is equal to the highest; for she claims her birthright from the Almighty himself, and carries on her brow the signet of heaven." "Stop, Roland, for heaven's sake, and hear me." "I will not stop," continued Roland, a spirit of determination flashing from his eyes she had never seen in them before; "shall I sacrifice my happiness to a shadow, a bubble? No! I have hesitated too long; I love Grace; I love her with all my heart and soul, and I will go this moment and tell her so." He laid his hand upon the latch, but Lucy sprang forward like lightning, and seized it in her own. "One moment, Roland, only one moment; I, your only sister, ask it." Roland saw she was very pale, and he felt her hand tremble as it grasped him. She was indeed his only sister, whom he had so much loved, and he felt he had met her prejudices with too much impetuosity; they might yield, perhaps, to softer measures. "What is it you would say, Lucy? you asked for one moment, and I have given you more." "Only promise to wait till her return; that is all I ask; I spoke in jest; you knew she would not remain; Mr. Worthington will never leave her. Promise me this, dear Roland, and I will not oppose my pride to your happiness." Lucy knew that she was uttering a falsehood, for she herself had confirmed Grace in her resolution to remain; but she had begun to weave the tangled web of deceit, and she wound herself deeper and deeper in its folds. All she wanted now was to gain time, and she then felt she should be safe. Roland promised, for delay was not sacrifice, and he was surprised and grateful for Lucy's concession.

"Grace," whispered Lucy, as she embraced and bid her farewell, "you are acting right; you will find peace and happiness in the path you seek. Be assured of my friendship and also my gratitude." Grace was mute, but she gave Lucy a look that might have melted a heart of stone.

"Grace," said Roland, "come back to us soon." He kept his promise to his sister, but his voice trembled, his hand lingered as it pressed hers in parting, and his eyes spoke a language she must have understood, had not her own been blinded with tears. She met a warm reception from the friends of her early days. The kind Susan, who had taken the first charge of her, and acted toward her a mother's part, opened her arms to receive her, and when she saw her faded colour and drooping eyes, she felt as the patriarch did when he took in his weary dove to the ark, for she knew the wanderer brought back no green olive branch of hope and joy. Susan had once known the gayeties of the world, and tasted its pleasures, but her heart had been blighted and her hopes betrayed, and finding all was vanity, to use her own expressive language she had "taken up her cross and followed her Saviour." Th seal of silence was placed on the history of her heart, and Grace dreamed not that one of that tranquil tribe had ever known the tumult of human passions. By some mysterious communion, however, between soul and soul, Grace felt an assurance of Susan's sympathy, and clung to her with increased affection. It was long before Mr. Worthington would consent to leave her behind. "Only a few months," pleaded she, "and

then I shall be well and strong again; all I need is quiet."
"The child is right," added Susan; "she is weary of the
world, and wants rest. She shall dwell in my tabernacle, and
share my pillow, and I will nourish and cherish her as my own
flesh and blood. She will not be compelled to join our worship, or follow our rites, for we now look upon her as our guest,
our daughter in love, but not our sister in the spirit of the
Lord." Satisfied with this promise, Mr. Worthington blessed
Grace, embraced her, and left her, bidding her be ready to return when the first leaf of autumn fell. She did not sit down
and brood over the blighted hopes of her youth. She interested
herself in all their neat and regular occupations, assisted them
in gathering the leaves of the medicinal plants, in spreading them
on pieces of pure white linen to dry; in collecting the garden
seeds and shelling them out of their shrunken capsules, with
as much readiness and grace as if she had never learned to
touch the keys of the piano, or to school her steps by the dancing master's rule. Dressed in the plainest robes the fashions of
the world allow, so as not to offend the austerity of their taste,
with no other ornament than her shining hair, simply parted
on her brow, she looked the incarnation of sweetness and humility; and Susan, seeing her dawning colour, believed she
had found peace. "Thus will I live," thought Grace, "till
Roland marries, and then if my adopted father claims me, I
will try to find happiness in administering to his."
    One evening, just as the sun had set, she returned from the
garden, her white apron gathered up before her, full of damask
rose leaves, while exercise and a bending position had given
her cheeks a hue, warm as the twilight's glow, and calling
eagerly to Susan, to present her offering for distillation, she
crossed the threshold and stood before—Roland Gray. Elec-
trified at the sight, she let go her apron, and the leaves fell in
a rosy shower around her. "Grace, dear Grace!" exclaimed
Roland, and both hands were clasped in his own. Now she
had been called dear Grace, and sweet Grace, and pretty Grace,
thousand times in her life, but never in such a tone, and
with such eyes looking down into her heart. It is easy to
imagine why Roland came, and how eloquently he proved to
Grace that he loved her better than all the world beside, and
that he could not, and would not live without her. For a moment a flood of rapture, deep and overwhelming, flowed in upon
her heart from the conviction that she was thus beloved; the
next, a cold and freezing thought shot through it and turned

the current to ice. Lucy—her threatened curse, her withering enmity, her own promise of never thinking of Roland, and of never revealing what had passed between Lucy and herself— all was remembered, and suddenly withdrawing her hand from his, she turned away and wept, without the power of self-control.

Roland was amazed. She had met his avowal with such a radiant blush and smile—such love and joy had just lighted up her modest eye, and now he witnessed every demonstration of the most passionate grief. " Oh, no !" she cried, " it never can be—I had forgotten it all; but I must not listen to you— oh, no !" and she repeated the interjection in such a plaintive accent, Roland was convinced there was no deception in her woe. In vain he entreated her for an explanation. She could not give any consistent with her promise to Lucy; she could only declare her unworthiness, her poor and perhaps disgraceful origin; and this only called forth a more impassioned assurance of his disinterested love, and his disdain of such scruples. He endeavoured to soothe and caress, till Grace felt her resolution and her truth fast yielding before his influence. If she could see Lucy, and be released from her rash promise, all might yet be well. Perhaps Lucy herself, finding her brother's pride had yielded to his love, would sanction the union. This idea once admitted, changed despair into hope. " Wait," said she, " till I return, and then, if the obstacle I fear no longer exists,"—she paused a moment, and her truth-telling lips constrained her to utter—" I shall be the happiest of human beings." Roland, now believing the obstacle to be Lucy, resolved she should not stand any longer in the way of their happiness, pressed for no further explanation. He had departed unknown to her, for he dreaded her violence. When Mr Worthington returned alone, he dreaded Grace might sacrifice herself, as Lucy insinuated, and determined to bear her away ere it was too late. Grace poured into Susan's calm but sympathizing ear the story of her love and the obstacles that opposed it. Her single heart was too narrow to contain the fulness of her emotions. Susan applauded her integrity, but trembled at her idolatry. She reminded her of the mutability and uncertainty of all earthly things, and strengthened her in the resolution never to accept the vows of Roland, with the threatened vengeance of Lucy hanging over her love. " Oh, she will relent !" cried Grace ; " Roland's sister cannot be such a monster " Had the chastened Susan witnessed her parting

with Roland, she would have read a still more solemn lesson
on the sinfulness of earthly affections; but she only saw the
consequent sorrow, which she was too gentle to reprove.

The leaves of autumn soon fell, and then everything was
changed in the destiny of Grace. Mr. Worthington claimed
his child, and when Susan resigned her, her last words bid her
pray for strength to keep her virtuous resolution.

It would be difficult to describe the passions that struggled
for mastery in Lucy's breast, when she learned from her brother
the part he had acted. Incapable of concealing them at first,
and believing she had lost the affection of Roland, she no
longer disguised the bitterness of her heart. She hated Grace
still more, since she was conscious she had injured her, and
when she, appealing in behalf of Roland's happiness as well
as her own, entreated her to free her from her promise, she
turned a deaf ear to the prayer, and claimed the fulfilment of
her word, renewing the same fearful penalty—"Unless," she
added, with a scornful smile, "you can prove your family
equal to ours, and that your alliance will bring no disgrace."

Strange paradox of the human heart! Had Lucy taken
scorpions into her bosom, she could not have suffered keener
pangs than the consciousness of Roland's alienated affection
caused her; yet she refused to bend her stubborn pride, and
wrapped herself up in the sulliness of self-will, feeling a kind
of stern joy that she had made others as wretched as herself.

*   *   *   *   *   *   *   *   *

Grace was standing in a lighted saloon, leaning on the arm
of Mr. Worthington, and an unwilling partaker of the gay
scene. A tall and majestic-looking man passed the spot where
she stood, whose appearance excited her interest and curiosity,
for he was evidently a stranger in the throng of fashion and
wealth, then gathered together. The suns of warmer climes
had darkened his face, and added gloom to features of a fine
and noble expression. As Grace lifted her mild gray eyes
his somewhat stern countenance relaxed, and turning round h
gazed earnestly in her face. Abashed by his scrutiny, she
moved into another part of the room; still the tall stranger
followed, with his melancholy eyes, pursuing her figure. Roland, never far from the object of his apparently hopeless
devotion, now jealous and irritated, drew to her side. "Oh,
Roland," said she, suddenly agitated by a new emotion, "there
is something in that stranger's face, resembling this!"—and

she drew from her bosom the miniature suspended from the golden chain. There was indeed a resemblance, only the face of the picture was younger, and the sable locks unbleached. The stranger observed the motions of Grace, and pressed forward, while the miniature was still open in her hand. "Pardon me, madam," said he, earnestly, "I must be pardoned —but allow me to look at that picture." Grace with trembling fingers unloosed the chain, and gave it into the stranger's hand. "It was once my mother's," said she, in a faltering voice, "and her name was Grace Goldman." "*Was*"—said the stranger—"and yet how could it be otherwise?—she was my sister—my only sister—and you"—he became too much agitated to finish the sentence, and entirely forgetting the throng that surrounded them, he clasped Grace to his bosom, as the living representative of his lost and lamented sister. Yes! in Mr. Maitland, the rich merchant, just returned from the East Indies, Grace had found an uncle, which proved her lineage to be such, that even the proud Lucy must acknowledge to be equal to her own. His sister, the mother of Grace, had eloped, when very young, with a handsome but profligate man, and being cast off by her parents, she was soon doomed to eat the bread of poverty, in consequence of her husband's excesses. Her brother, as soon as he learned her situation, offered to support her through life, declaring his intention never to marry, if she would leave her unprincipled husband. But she, in the strength of that passion which hopes all, believes all, and endures all, refused to leave the man she still loved, and whom she still trusted she might reclaim. Her brother, finding her wedded to her fate, left her with a purse of gold and his own miniature as a parting pledge of love, and departed for a foreign land. Forced to fly from the clamours of his creditors, Goldman removed his wife from place to place, till she was far out of the reach of former friends, when, plunging deeper and deeper in the gulf of inebriation, he left her to die, as we have described, of a broken heart. For himself, he died a drunkard's death by the wayside, and was buried by the same humane society that protected his orphan child. This circumstance had been concealed from Grace, nor did she learn it, till her subsequent visit to the Shaker village. Mr. Maitland, who had dwelt long in other lands, accumulating wealth, which his generous heart longed to share with the friends of his early youth, returned to mourn over the graves of his parents, and to seek in vain intelligence of his lost sister, till he saw

109

in the crowd the lovely form of Grace, such as her ill-fated mother was in the days of her beauty and youth.   Lucy could with sincerity offer her congratulations and welcome as a sister the niece of Mr. Maitland, though she had scorned the alliance of the humble Shaker girl.   But she felt she was degraded in her eyes, and this was a punishment to her proud spirit, keener than the task-master's lash.   Mr. Maitland's gratitude to Mr. Worthington was boundless as it was warm ; but he longed to see the kind Samaritans, who had soothed his sister's dying hours and guarded her orphan child.

It was a happy day for Grace, when, as the bride of Roland, she accompanied her husband and her uncle to the home of her early youth.   She introduced with pride the noble-looking stranger to all her true and single-hearted friends.   "But here," said she, throwing her arms round Susan, "here is my mother and my mother's friend."   Mr. Maitland would gladly have lavished wealth upon them, in remuneration for their cares, but they steadfastly refused his gifts, asserting they had only done their duty, and merited no reward.   "Do unto others, as we have done towards yours," replied these followers of our Saviour's golden rule.   "When you hear us reviled by the world, and our worship scorned, and our rites ridiculed, defend us if you can ; and if one of the disciples of our creed should be in need of succour, be unto him as a brother, and we ask no more."   "Dear Susan," said Grace, when the parting hour arrived, as she lingered behind to bid her farewell, "am I not the happiest of human beings?"   "I bless God that you *are* happy, my child," answered Susan, laying her hand solemnly on her head—"and long, long may you remain so ; but forget not, days of darkness may come, that the bridal garments may be changed for sackcloth, and ashes be scattered over the garlands of love.   Remember then, O Grace, there is a refuge from the woes and vanities of the world, where the spirit may wait in peace for its everlasting home."   Grace wept, but she smiled through her tears, and, seated once more at Roland's side, she felt as if darkness and sorrow could never be *her* portion.

A RAINY EVENING.

A SKETCH.

A PLEASANT little group was gathered round Uncle Ned's domestic hearth. He sat on one side of the fire-place, opposite Aunt Mary, who, with her book in her hand, watched the children seated at the table, some reading, others sewing, all occupied, but one, a child "of larger growth," a young lady, who, being a guest of the family, was suffered to indulge in the pleasure of idleness without reproof.

"Oh! I *love* a rainy evening," said little Ann, looking up from her book, and meeting her mother's smiling glance, "it is so nice to sit by a good fire and hear the rain pattering against the windows. Only I pity the poor people who have no house to cover them, to keep off the rain and the cold."

"And I love a rainy evening, too," cried George, a boy of about twelve. "I can study so much better. My thoughts stay at home, and don't keep rambling out after the bright moon and stars. My heart feels warmer, and I really believe I love everybody better than I do when the weather is fair."

Uncle Ned smiled, and gave the boy an approving pat on the shoulder. Every one smiled but the young lady, who with a languid, discontented air, now played with a pair of scissors, now turned over the leaves of a book, then, with an ill-suppressed yawn, leaned idly on her elbow, and looked into the fire.

"And what do you think of a rainy evening, Elizabeth?" asked Uncle Ned. "I should like to hear your opinion also."

"I think it over dull and uninteresting, indeed," answered

(127)

she. "I always feel so stupid, I can hardly keep myself awake —one cannot go abroad, or hope to see company at home; and one gets so tired of seeing the same faces all the time. I cannot imagine what George and Ann see to admire so much in a disagreeable rainy evening like this."

"Supposing I tell you a story, to enliven you?" said Uncle Ned.

"Oh! yes, father, please tell us a story," exclaimed the children, simultaneously.

Little Ann was perched upon his knee as if by magic, and even Elizabeth moved her chair, as if excited to some degree of interest. George still held his book in his hand, but his bright eyes, sparkling with unusual animation, were riveted upon his uncle's face.

"I am going to tell you a story about a *rainy evening*," said Uncle Ned.

"Oh! that will be *so* pretty!" cried Ann, clapping her hands; but Elizabeth's countenance fell below zero. It was an ominous annunciation.

"Yes," continued Uncle Ned, "a rainy evening. But though clouds darker than those which now mantle the sky were lowering abroad, and the rain fell heavier and faster, the rainbow of my life was drawn most beautifully on those dark clouds, and its fair colours still shine most lovely on the sight. It is no longer, however, the bow of promise, but the realization of my fondest dreams."

George saw his uncle cast an expressive glance towards the handsome matron in the opposite corner, whose colour perceptibly heightened, and he could not forbear exclaiming—

"Ah! Aunt Mary is blushing. I understand uncle's metaphor. *She* is his rainbow, and he thinks life one long rainy day."

"Not exactly so. I mean your last conclusion. But don't interrupt me, my boy, and you shall hear a lesson, which, young as you are, I trust you will never forget. When I was a young man I was thought quite handsome—"

"Pa is as pretty as he can be, now," interrupted little Ann, passing her hand fondly over his manly cheek.

Uncle Ned was not displeased with the compliment, for he pressed her closer to him, while he continued—

"Well, when I was young I was of a gay spirit, and a great favourite in society. The young ladies liked me for a partner in the dance, at the chess-board, or the evening walk, and I had reason to think several of them would have made no objection to take me as a partner for life. Among all my young acquaintances, there was no one whose companionship was so pleasing as that of a maiden whose name was Mary. Now, there are a great many Marys in the world, so you must not take it for granted I mean your mother or aunt. At any rate, you must not look so significant till I have finished my story. Mary was a sweet and lovely girl—with a current of cheerfulness running through her disposition that made music as it flowed. It was an under current, however, always gentle, and kept within its legitimate channel; never overflowing into boisterous mirth or unmeaning levity. She was the only daughter of her mother, *and she a widow.* Mrs. Carlton, such was her mother's name, was in lowly circumstances, and Mary had none of the appliances of wealth and fashion to decorate her person, or gild her home. A very modest competency was all her portion, and she wished for nothing more. I have seen her, in a simple white dress, without a single ornament, unless it was a natural rose, transcend all the gaudy belles, who sought by the attractions of dress to win the admiration of the multitude. But, alas! for poor human nature. One of these dashing belles so fascinated my attention, that the gentle Mary was for a while forgotten. Theresa Vane was, indeed, a rare piece of mortal mechanism. Her figure was the perfection of beauty, and she moved as if strung upon wires, so elastic and springing were her gestures. I never saw such lustrous hair—it was perfectly black, and shone like burnished steel; and then such ringlets! How they waved and rippled down her beautiful neck! She dressed with the most exquisite taste, delicacy, and neatness, and whatever she wore assumed a peculiar grace and fitness, as if art loved to adorn what nature made so fair. But what charmed me most was, the sunshiny smile that was always waiting to light up her countenance. To be sure, she sometimes laughed a little too loud, but then her laugh was so musical, and her teeth so white, it was impossible to believe her guilty of rudeness, or want of grace. Often, when I saw her in the social circle, so brilliant and smiling, the life and charm of everything around her, I thought how happy the constant companionship of such a being would make me—what brightness she would impart to the fireside of home—what light, what joy, to the darkest scenes of existence!"

"Oh! uncle," interrupted George, laughing, "if I were

Aunt Mary, I would not let you praise any other lady so warmly. You are so taken up with her beauty, you have forgotten all about the rainy evening."

Aunt Mary smiled, but it is more than probable that George really touched one of the hidden springs of her woman's heart, for she looked down, and said nothing.

"Don't be impatient," said Uncle Ned, "and you shall not be cheated out of your story. I began it for Elizabeth's sake, rather than yours, and I see she is wide awake.' She thinks I was by this time more than half in love with Theresa Vane, and she thinks more than half right. There had been a great many parties of pleasure, riding parties, sailing parties, and talking parties; and summer slipped by, almost unconsciously. At length the autumnal equinox approached, and gathering clouds, north-eastern gales, and drizzling rains, succeeded to the soft breezes, mellow skies, and glowing sunsets, peculiar to that beautiful season. For two or three days I was confined within doors by the continuous rains, and I am sorry to confess it, but the blue devils actually got complete possession of me—one strided upon my nose, another danced on the top of my head, one pinched my ear, and another turned somersets on my chin. You laugh, little Nanny; but they are terrible creatures, these blue gentlemen, and I could not endure them any longer. So the third rainy evening, I put on my overcoat, buttoned it up to my chin, and taking my umbrella in my hand, set out in the direction of Mrs. Vane's. ' Here,' thought I, as my fingers pressed the latch, 'I shall find the moonlight smile, that will illumine the darkness of my night —the dull vapours will disperse before her radiant glance, and this interminable equinoctial storm be transformed into a mere vernal shower, melting away in sunbeams in her presence.' My gentle knock not being apparently heard, I stepped into the ante-room, set down my umbrella, took off my drenched overcoat, arranged my hair in the most graceful manner, and, claiming a privilege to which, perhaps, I had no legitimate right, opened the door of the family sitting-room, and found myself in the presence of the beautiful Theresa—"

Here Uncle Ned made a provoking pause.

"Pray, go on." "How was she dressed?" "And was she glad to see you?" assailed him on every side.

"How was she dressed?" repeated he. "I am not very well skilled in the technicalities of a lady's wardrobe, but I can give you the general impression of her personal appearance. In the first place, there was a jumping up and an off-hand sliding step towards an opposite door, as I entered; but a disobliging chair was in the way, and I was making my lowest bow, before she found an opportunity of disappearing. Confused and mortified, she scarcely returned my salutation, while Mrs. Vane offered me a chair, and expressed, in somewhat dubious terms, their gratification at such an unexpected pleasure. I have no doubt Theresa wished me at the bottom of the Frozen Ocean, if I might judge by the freezing glances she shot at me through her long lashes. She sat uneasily in her chair, trying to conceal her slipshod shoes, and furtively arranging her dress about the shoulders and waist. It was a most rebellious subject, for the body and skirt were at open warfare, refusing to have any communion with each other. Where was the graceful shape I had so much admired? In vain I sought its exquisite outlines in the folds of that loose, slovenly robe. Where were those glistening ringlets and burnished locks that had so lately rivalled the tresses of Medusa? Her hair was put in tangled bunches behind her ears, and tucked up behind in a kind of Gordian knot, which would have required the sword of an Alexander to untie. Her frock was a soiled and dingy silk, with trimmings of sallow blonde, and a faded fancy handkerchief was thrown over one shoulder.

" ' You have caught me completely *en déshabille*,' said she, recovering partially from her embarrassment; ' but the evening was so rainy, and no one but mother and myself, I never dreamed of such an exhibition of gallantry as this.'

" She could not disguise her vexation, with all her efforts to conceal it, and Mrs. Vane evidently shared her daughter's chagrin. I was wicked enough to enjoy their confusion, and never appeared more at my ease, or played the agreeable with more signal success. I was disenchanted at once, and my mind revelled in its recovered freedom. My goddess had fallen from the pedestal on which my imagination had enthroned her, despoiled of the beautiful drapery which had imparted to her such ideal loveliness. I knew that I was a favourite in the family, for I was wealthy and independent, and perhaps of all Theresa's admirers what the world would call the best match. I maliciously asked her to play on the piano, but she made a thousand excuses, studiously keeping back the true reason, her disordered attire. I asked her to play a game of chess, but ' she had a headache; she was too stupid; she never *could* do anything on a *rainy evening*.'

"At length I took my leave, inwardly blessing the moving spirit which had led me abroad that night, that the spell which had so long enthralled my senses might be broken. Theresa called up one of her lambent smiles as I bade her adieu.

"'Never call again on a rainy evening,' said she, sportively; 'I am always so wretchedly dull. I believe I was born ·to live among the sunbeams, the moonlight, and the stars. Clouds will never do for me.'

"'Amen,' I silently responded, as I closed the door. While I was putting on my coat, I overheard, without the smallest intention of listening, a passionate exclamation from Theresa.

"'Good heavens, mother! was there ever anything so unlucky? I never thought of seeing my neighbour's *dog* to-night. If I have not been completely caught!'

"'I hope you will mind my advice next time,' replied her mother, in a grieved tone. 'I told you not to sit down in that slovenly dress. I have no doubt you have lost him for ever.'

"Here I made good my retreat, not wishing to enter the *penetralia* of family secrets.

"The rain still continued unabated, but my social feelings were very far from being damped. I had the curiosity to make another experiment. The evening was not very far advanced, and as I turned from Mrs. Vane's fashionable mansion, I saw a modest light glimmering in the distance, and I hailed it as the shipwrecked mariner hails the star that guides him o'er ocean's foam to the home he has left behind. Though I was gay and young, and a passionate admirer of beauty, I had very exalted ideas of domestic felicity. I knew that there was many a rainy day in life, and I thought the companion who was born alone for sunbeams and moonlight, would not aid me to dissipate their gloom. I had, moreover, a shrewd suspicion that the daughter who thought it a sufficient excuse for shameful personal neglect, that there was no one present but her *mother*, would, as a wife, be equally regardless of a *husband's* presence. While I pursued these reflections, my feet involuntarily drew nearer and more near to the light, which had been the loadstone of my opening manhood. I had continued to meet Mary in the gay circles I frequented, but I had lately become almost a stranger to her home. 'Shall I be a welcome guest?' said I to myself, as I crossed the threshold. 'Shall I find her *en déshabille*, likewise, and discover that feminine beauty and grace are incompatible with a rainy evening?' I heard a sweet voice reading aloud as I opened the door, and I knew it was the voice which was once music to my ears. Mary rose at my entrance, laying her book quietly on the table, and greeted me with a modest grace and self-possession peculiar to herself. She looked surprised, a little embarrassed, but very far from being displeased. She made no allusion to my estrangement or neglect; expressed no astonishment at my untimely visit, nor once hinted that, being alone with her mother, and not anticipating visiters, she thought it unnecessary to wear the habiliments of a *lady*. Never, in my life, had I seen her look so lovely. Her dress was perfectly plain, but every fold was arranged by the hand of the Graces. Her dark-brown hair, which had a natural wave in it, now uncurled by the dampness, was put back in smooth ringlets from her brow, revealing a face which did not consider its beauty wasted because a mother's eye alone rested on its bloom. A beautiful cluster of autumnal roses, placed in a glass vase on the table, perfumed the apartment, and a bright blaze on the hearth diffused a spirit of cheerfulness around, while it relieved the atmosphere of its excessive moisture. Mrs. Carlton was an invalid, and suffered also from an inflammation of the eyes. Mary had been reading aloud to her from her favourite book. What do you think it was? It was a very old-fashioned one, indeed. No other than the Bible. And Mary was not ashamed to have such a fashionable young gentleman as I then was to see what her occupation had been. What a contrast to the scene I had just quitted! How I loathed myself for the infatuation which had led me to prefer the artificial graces of a belle to this pure child of nature! I drew my chair to the table, and entreated that they would not look upon me as a stranger, but as a friend, anxious to be restored to the forfeited privileges of an old acquaintance. I was understood in a moment, and, without a single reproach, was admitted again to confidence and familiarity. The hours I had wasted with Theresa seemed a kind of mesmeric slumber, a blank in my existence, or, at least, a feverish dream. 'What do you think of a rainy evening, Mary?' asked I, before I left her.

" 'I love it of all things,' replied she, with animation. 'There is something so home-drawing, so heart-knitting, in its influence. The dependencies which bind us to the world seem withdrawn; and, retiring within ourselves, we learn more of the deep mysteries of our own being.'

" Mary's soul beamed from her eye as it turned, with a transient obliquity, towards heaven. She paused, as if fearful of unsealing the fountains of her heart. I said that Mrs. Carlton was an invalid, and consequently retired early to her chamber; but I lingered till a late hour, nor did I go till I had made a full confession of my folly, repentance, and awakened love; and, as Mary did not shut the door in my face, you may magine she was not sorely displeased."

"Ah! I know who Mary was. I knew all the time," exclaimed George, looking archly at Aunt Mary. A bright tear, which at that moment fell into her lap, showed that though a silent, she was no uninterested auditor.

"You haven't done, father?" said little Ann, in a disappointed tone; "I thought you were going to tell a story. You have been talking about yourself all the time."

"I have been something of an egotist, to be sure, my little girl, but I wanted to show my dear young friend here how much might depend upon a rainy evening. Life is not made all of sunshine. The happiest and most prosperous must have their seasons of gloom and darkness, and woe be to those from whose souls no rays of brightness emanate to gild those darkened hours. I bless the God of the rain as well as the sunshine. I can read His mercy and His love as well in the tempest, whose wings obscure the visible glories of His creation, as in the splendour of the rising sun, or the soft dews that descend after his setting radiance. I began with a metaphor. I said a rainbow was drawn on the clouds that lowered on that eventful day, and that it still continued to shine with undiminished beauty. Woman, my children, was sent by God to be the rainbow of man's darker destiny. From the glowing red, emblematic of that love which warms and gladdens his existence, to the violet melting into the blue of heaven, symbolical of the faith which links him to a purer world, her blending virtues, mingling with each other in beautiful harmony, are a token of God's mercy here, and an earnest of future blessings in those regions where no *rainy evenings* ever come to obscure the brightness of eternal day."

THREE SCENES IN THE LIFE OF A BELLE.

THERE was a rushing to and fro in the chamber of Ellen Loring, a tread of hurrying feet, a mingled hum of voices, an opening and shutting of doors, as if some event of overwhelming importance agitated the feelings, and moved the frames of every individual in the house. A stranger, in the apartment below, might have imagined an individual was dying, and that all were gathering round to offer the appliances of love and sympathy. But Ellen Loring, the object of all this commotion, was in all the bloom and beauty of health. She sat in a low chair and in front of a large mirror, half-arrayed in the habiliments of the ball-room, her head glowing with flowers, and streaming with ringlets, her feet encased in silk cobweb and white satin, her face flushed with excitement, her waist compressed into the smallest possible compass, while the strongest fingers the household could supply, were drawing together the last reluctant hook and eye, which fastened the rich and airy mixture of satin blonde, that fell in redundant folds round her slender person. "I am afraid, Ellen, your dress is *rather* too tight," said Mrs. Loring, who was superintending the process with a keen and experienced eye; "you had better not wear it, it may give you a consumption." "Ridiculous!" exclaimed Ellen, "it feels perfectly loose and comfortable; I am sure it fits delightfully. Look, Agnes," addressing a weary-looking girl who had been standing more than half an hour over her, arranging her hair in the most fashionable style. "Look, Agnes, is it not beautiful?"

"Very beautiful," answered Agnes; "but I think it would look much better if it were not so very low, and the night is so cold, I am sure you will suffer without something thrown over your shoulders.   These pearl beads are very ornamental, but they will not give warmth," lifting them up as she spoke, from a neck that "rivalled their whiteness."   Ellen burst into a scornful laugh, and declared she would rather catch her death-cold, than look so old-fashioned and old-womanish. Mrs. Loring here interposed, and insisted that Ellen should wear a shawl into the ball-room, and to be sure to put it around her when she was not dancing, "for you must remember," added she, "the dreadful cough you had last winter; when you caught cold, I was really apprehensive of a consumption."   .

"I do think, mother, you must be haunted by the ghost of consumption.   Everything you say begins and ends with *consumption*—*I* am not afraid of the ghost, or the reality, while such roses as these bloom on my cheeks, and such elastic limbs as these bear me through the dance."

Mrs. Loring looked with admiring fondness on her daughter, as she danced gayly before the looking-glass, called her a "wild, thoughtless thing," and thought it would be indeed a pity to muffle such a beautiful neck in a clumsy 'kerchief. The carriage was announced, and Agnes was despatched in a hundred directions for the embroidered handkerchief, the scented gloves, and all the *et ceteras*, which crowd on the memory at the last moment.   Agnes followed the retreating form of Ellen with a long and wistful gaze, then turned with a sigh to collect the scattered articles of finery that strewed the room.   "Happy Ellen!" said she to herself, "happy, beautiful Ellen! favoured by nature and fortune.   Every desire of her heart is gratified.   She moves but to be admired, flattered, and caressed.   While I, a poor, dependent relative, am compelled to administer to her vanity and wait upon her caprices—oh! if I were only rich and beautiful like Ellen! I would willingly walk over burning ploughshares to obtain the happiness that is in store for her to-night."

While the repining Agnes followed Ellen, in imagination, to scenes which appeared to her fancy like the dazzling pictures described in the Arabian Nights, let us enter the ball-room and follow the footsteps of her, whose favoured lot led her through the enchanted land.   The hall was brilliantly lighted, the music was of the most animating kind, airy forms floated on the gaze, most elaborately and elegantly adorned, and in the midst of these Ellen shone transcendent.   For a while, her enjoyment realized even the dreams of Agnes.   Conscious of being admired, she glided through the dance, gracefully holding her flowing drapery, smiling, blushing, coquetting and flirting. Compliments were breathed continually into her ears. She was compared to the sylphs, the graces, the muses, the houris, and even to the angels that inhabit the celestial city. Yes; this daughter of fashion, this devotee of pleasure, this vain and thoughtless being, who lived without God in the world, was told by flattering lips, that she resembled those pure and glorified spirits which surround the throne of the Most High, and sing the everlasting song of Moses and the Lamb—and she believed it. Perhaps some may assert that the daughters of fashion are not always forgetful of their God, for they are often heard to call upon his great and holy name, in a moment of sudden astonishment or passion, and were a saint to witness their uplifted eyes and clasped hands, he might deem them wrapt in an ecstasy of devotion.

Ellen, in the midst of almost universal homage, began to feel dissatisfied and weary. There was one who had been in the train of her admirers, himself the star of fashion, who was evidently offering incense at a new shrine. A fair young stranger, who seemed a novice in the splendid scene, drew him from her side, and from that moment the adulation of others ceased to charm. She danced more gayly, she laughed more loudly, to conceal the mortification and envy that was spreading through her heart; but the triumph, the joy was over. She began to feel a thousand inconveniences, of whose existence she seemed previously unconscious. Her feet ached from the lightness of her slippers, her respiration was difficult from the tightness of her dress; she was glad when the hour of her departure arrived. Warm from the exercise of the dance, and panting from fatigue, she stood a few moments on the pavement, waiting for some obstructions to be removed in the way of the carriage. The ground was covered with a sheet of snow, which had fallen during the evening, and made a chill bed for her feet, so ill defended from the inclement season. The night air blew damp and cold on her neck an shoulders, for her cloak was thrown loosely around her, tha, her beauty might not be entirely veiled, till the gaze of admiration was withdrawn.

Agnes sat by the lonely fireside, waiting for the return of Ellen. For a while she kept up a cheerful blaze, and as she heard the gust sweep by the windows, it reminded her that Ellen would probably come in shivering with cold and reproach her, if she did not find a glowing hearth to welcome her. She applied fresh fuel, till, lulled by the monotonous sound of the wind, she fell asleep in her chair, nor waked till the voice of Ellen roused her from her slumbers. A few dull embers were all that was left of the fire, the candle gleamed faintly beneath a long, gloomy wick—everything looked cold and comfortless. It was long before poor Agnes could recall the cheering warmth. In the mean time, Ellen poured upon her a torrent of reproaches, and tossing her cloak on a chair, declared she would never go to another ball as long as she lived—she had been tired *to death*, chilled *to death*, and now to be vexed *to death*, by such a stupid, selfish creature as Agnes. It was too much for human nature to endure. Agnes bore it all in silence, for she ate the bread of dependence, and dared not express the bitter feelings that rose to her lips. But she no longer said in her heart "happy, beautiful Ellen;" she wished her admirers could see her as she then did, and be disenchanted.

"Take off this horrid dress," cried Ellen, pulling the roses from her hair, now uncurled by the damp, and hanging in long straight tresses over her face. What a contrast did she now present to the brilliant figure which had left the chamber a few hours before! Her cheeks were pale, her eyes heavy, her limbs relaxed, her buoyant spirits gone. The terrible misfortune of not having reigned an unrivalled *belle*, completely overwhelmed her! He, whose admiration she most prized, had devoted himself to another, and she hated the fair, unconscious stranger, who had attracted him from his allegiance. The costly dress which the mantuamaker had sat up all night to complete, was thrown aside as a worthless rag; her flowers were scattered on the floor; every article of her dress bore witness to her ill-humour.

"I cannot get warm," said she; "I believe I *have* caught my death-cold;" and throwing her still shivering limbs on the bed, she told Agnes to bury her in blankets, and then let her leep. Can we suppose that guardian angels hovered over the couch, and watched the slumbers of this youthful beauty? There was no hallowed spot in her chamber, where she was accustomed to kneel in penitence, gratitude, and adoration, before the King of Kings and Lord of Lords. Perhaps, when a mere child, she had been taught to repeat the Lord's Prayer at her nurse's knee, but never had her heart ascended unto Him, who created her for his glory, and breathed into her frame a portion of his own immortal Spirit. She had been educated solely for the circles of fashion, to glitter and be admired—to dance, to sing, to dress, to talk, and that was all. She knew that she must one day die, and when the bell tolled, and the long funeral darkened the way, she was reluctantly reminded of her own mortality. But she banished the dreadful and mysterious thought, as one with which youth, beauty, and health had nothing to do, and as suited only to the infirmities of age, and the agonies of disease. As for the judgment beyond the grave, that scene of indescribable grandeur, when every created being must stand before the presence of un-created glory, "to give an account of the deeds done in the body," she deemed it shocking and sacrilegious to think of a subject so awful; and, to do her justice, she never heard it mentioned except from the pulpit (for there are fashionable churches, and Ellen was the belle of the church as well as of the ball-room). Thus living in practical atheism, labouring to bring every thought and feeling in subjection to the bondage of fashion, endeavouring to annihilate the great principle of immortality struggling within her, Ellen Loring was as much the slave of vice as the votary of pleasure. Like the king of Babylon, who took the golden vessels from the temple of the Lord, and desecrated them at his unhallowed banquet, she had robbed her *soul*, that temple of the living God, of its sacred treasures, and appropriated them to the revelries of life. But the hour was approaching, when the invisible angel of con-science was to write on the walls of memory those mystic characters which a greater than Daniel alone can interpret.

*　　*　　*　　*　　*　　*　　*

It was the afternoon of a mild summer's day, a lovely, smiling, joyous summer day, when two female figures were seen slowly walking along a shaded path, that led from a neat white cottage towards a neighbouring grove. One was beau-tiful, and both were young, but the beautiful one was so pale and languid, so fragile and fading, it was impossible to behold her without the deepest commiseration. She moved listlessly on, leaning on the arm of her less fair, but healthier companion, apparently insensible of the sweet and glowing scenery around her. The birds sung in melodious concert, from every green bough, but their music could not gladden her ear; the air played softly through her heavy locks, but awaked no elastic spring in her once bounding spirits. It was the late blooming

Ellen Loring, who, according to the advice of her physician, was inhaling the country air, to see if it could not impart an invigorating influence. She had never recovered from the deadly chill occasioned by her exposure, the night of the ball, when she stood with her thin slippers and uncovered neck in the snow and the blast, in all the "madness of superfluous health." It was said she had caught a "dreadful cold," which the warm season would undoubtedly relieve, and when the summer came, and her cough continued with unabated violence, and her flesh and her strength wasted, she was sent into the country, assured that a change of air and daily exercise would infallibly restore her. The fearful word *consumption*, which in the days of Ellen's health was so often on the mother's lips, was never mentioned now; and whenever friends inquired after Ellen, she always told them, "she had caught a bad cold, which hung on a long time, but that she was so young, and had so fine a constitution, she did not apprehend any danger." Ellen was very unwilling to follow the prescriptions of her medical friend. She left the city with great reluctance, dreading the loneliness of a country life. Agnes accompanied her, on whom was imposed the difficult task of amusing and cheering the invalid, and of beguiling her of every sense of her danger. "Be sure," said Mrs. Loring, when she gave her parting injunctions to Agnes, "that you do not suffer her to be alone: there is nothing so disadvantageous to a sick person as to brood over their own thoughts. It always occasions low spirits. I have put up a large supply of novels, and when she is tired of reading herself, you must read to her, or sing to her, or amuse her in every possible manner. If she should be very ill, you must send for me immediately, but I have no doubt that in a few weeks she will be as well as ever."

Poor Agnes sometimes was tempted to sink under the weary burden of her cares. She wondered she had ever thought it a task to array her for the ball-room, or to wait her return at the midnight-hour. But she no longer envied her, for Ellen pale and faded, and dejected, was a very different object from Ellen triumphant in beauty and bloom. The kind lady with whom they boarded, had had a rustic seat constructed under the trees, in the above-mentioned grove, for the accommodation of the invalid. As they now approached it, they found it already occupied by a gentleman, who was so intently reading he did not seem aware of their vicinity. They were about to retire, when lifting his eyes, he rose, and with a benignant countenance, requested them to be seated. Ellen was exhausted from the exercise of her walk; and, as the stranger was past the meridian of life, she did not hesitate to accept his offer, at the same time thanking him for his courtesy. His mild, yet serious eyes, rested on her face, with a look of extreme commiseration, as with a deep sigh of fatigue she leaned on the shoulder of Agnes, while the hectic flush flitting over her cheek, betrayed the feverish current that was flowing in her veins.

"You seem an invalid, my dear young lady," said he, so kindly and respectfully, it was impossible to be offended with the freedom of the address; "I trust you find there is a balm in Gilead, a heavenly Physician near."

Ellen gave him a glance of unspeakable astonishment, and coldly answered, "I have a severe cold, sir—nothing more."

The dry, continuous cough that succeeded, was a fearful commentary upon her words. The stranger seemed one not easily repulsed, and one, too, who had conceived a sudden and irrepressible interest in his young companions. Agnes, in arranging Ellen's scarf, dropped a book from her hand, which he stooped to raise, and as his eye glanced on the title, the gravity of his countenance deepened. It was one of ******'s last works, in which that master of glowing language and impassioned images, has thrown his most powerful spell around the senses of the reader, and dazzled and bewildered his perceptions of right and wrong.

"Suffer me to ask you, young lady," said he, laying down the book, with a sigh, "if you find in these pages instruction, consolation, or support? anything that as a rational being you ought to seek, as a moral one to approve, as an immortal one to desire?"

Ellen was roused to a portion of her former animation, by this attack upon her favourite author; and, in language warm as his from whom she drew her inspiration, she defended his sentiments and exalted his genius—she spoke of his godlike mind, when the stranger entreated her to forbear, in words of supplication, but in accents of command.

"Draw not a similitude," said he, "between a holy God, and a being who has perverted the noblest powers that God has given. Bear with me a little while, and I will show you what is truly godlike, a book as far transcending the produc

110

tions of him you so much admire, as the rays of the sun excel in glory the wan light of a taper."

Then, taking from his bosom the volume which had excited the curiosity of Ellen, on account of its apparent fascination, and seating himself by her side, he unfolded its sacred pages. She caught a glimpse of the golden letters on the binding, and drew back with a feeling of superstitious dread. It seemed to her, that he was about to read her death-warrant, and she involuntarily put out her hand, with a repulsive motion. Without appearing to regard it, he looked upon her with sweet and solemn countenance, while he repeated this passage, from a bard who had drank of the waters of a holier fountain than Grecian poets ever knew:

> "This book, this holy book, on every line
> Marked with the seal of high divinity,
> On every leaf bedewed with drops of love
> Divine, and with the eternal heraldry
> And signature of God Almighty stamped
> From first to last; this ray of sacred light,
> This lamp, from off the everlasting throne,
> Mercy took down, and in the night of time,
> Stood, casting on the dark her gracious bow;
> And evermore, beseeching men, with tears
> And earnest sighs, to read, believe, and live."

Ellen listened with indescribable awe. There was a power and sensibility in his accent, a depth of expression in his occasional upturned glance, that impressed and affected her as she had never been before.

"Forgive me," said he, "if, as a stranger, I seem intrusive; but I look upon every son and daughter of Adam, with the tenderness of a brother, and upon whom the Almighty has laid his chastening hand, with feelings of peculiar interest. If I were wandering through a barren wilderness, and found a fountain of living water, and suffered my fellow-pilgrim to slake his thirst at the noisome pool by the wayside, without calling him to drink of the pure stream, would he not have reason to upbraid me for my selfishness? Oh! doubly selfish then should I be, if, after tasting the waters of everlasting life, for ever flowing from this blessed Book, I should not seek to draw you from the polluted sources in which you vainly endeavour to quench the thirst of an immortal spirit. Dear young fellow-traveller to eternity, suffer me to lend you a guiding hand."

Ellen Loring, who had been famed in the circles of fashion for her ready wit and brilliant repartee, found no words in which to reply to this affectionate and solemn appeal. She turned aside her head, to hide the tears which she could no longer repress from flowing down her cheeks. As the polished, but darkened Athenians, when Paul, standing on Mars Hill, explained to them "that unknown God, whom they ignorantly worshipped," trembled before an eloquence they could not comprehend, she was oppressed by a power she could not define.   Agnes, who began to be alarmed at the consequences of this agitation, and who saw in perspective Mrs. Loring's displeasure and reproaches, here whispered Ellen it was time to return, and Ellen, glad to be released from an influence to · which she was constrained to bow, obeyed the signal.   Their new friend rose also; "I cannot but believe," said he, "that this meeting is providential.   It seems to me that heaven directed my steps hither, that I might lead you to those green pastures and still waters where the Shepherd of Israel gathers his flock.   You are both young, but there is one of you whose cheek is pale, and whose saddened glance tells a touching history of the vanity of all earthly things.   Take this blessed volume, and substitute it for the one you now hold, and believe me you will find in it an inexhaustible supply of entertainment and delight, a perennial spring of light, and love, and joy.   You will find it an unerring guide in life, and a torch to illumine the dark valley of the shadow of death.   Farewell—the blessing of Israel's God be yours!"

He placed the book in the hand of Agnes, and turned in a different path.   They walked home in silence.   Neither expressed to the other the thoughts that filled the bosom of each. Had an angel from heaven come down and met them in the grove, the interview could hardly have had a more solemnizing influence.   It was the first time they had ever been individually addressed as immortal beings, the first time they had been personally reminded that they were pilgrims of earth, and doomed to be dwellers of the tomb.   The voice of the stranger still rung in their ears, deep and mellow as the sound of the church-going bell.   Those warning accents, they could not forget them, for there was an echo in their own hearts, and an answer too, affirming the truth of what he uttered.   That night, when Ellen, unusually exhausted, reclined on her restless couch, she suddenly asked Agnes to read her something from *that book*, so mysteriously given.   It was the first time she

had addressed her, since their return, and there was something
startling in the sound of her voice, it was so altered.   There
was humility in the tone, that usually breathed pride or discon-
tent.   Agnes sat down, and turned the leaves with a trembling
hand.

"What shall I read? where shall I commence?" asked she,
fearful and irresolute, in utter ignorance of its hallowed contents.

"Alas! I know not," replied Ellen, then raising herself on
her elbow, with a wild and earnest look, "see if you can find
where it speaks of that dark valley, of which he told—the dark
valley of death."

By one of those unexpected coincidences which sometimes
occur, Agnes at that moment opened at the twenty-third Psalm, •
and the verse containing this sublime allusion met her eye.
She read aloud—"Though I walk through the valley of the
shadow of death, I will fear no evil, for thou art with me—
thy rod and thy staff, they comfort me."

"Strange," repeated Ellen, and making a motion for her to
continue, Agnes read the remainder of that beautiful Psalm,
and the two succeeding ones, before she paused.   Dark as was
their understanding with regard to spiritual things, and deep
as was their ignorance, they were yet capable of taking in
some faint glimpses of the glory of the Lord, pervading these
strains of inspiration.   Agnes was a pleasing reader, and her
voice, now modulated by new emotions, was peculiarly impressive.   Ellen repeated again and again to herself, after Agnes
had ceased, "Who is this King of glory? The Lord strong
and mighty?"   She had never thought of God, but as of a
Being dreadful in power, avenging in his judgments, and awful
in his mystery.   She had remembered him only in the whirlwind and the storm, the lightning and the thunder, never in
the still small voice.   She had thought of death, but it was of the
winding sheet and the dark coffin lid, and the lonely grave—
her fears had rested there, on the shuddering brink of decaying mortality.   Oh! as she lay awake during the long watches
of that night, and conscience, aroused from its deadly lethargy,
entered the silent chambers of memory and waked the slumbering shadows of the past—how cheerless, how dark was the
retrospect!   Far as the eye of memory could revert, she could
read nothing but *vanity, vanity!*   A wide, wide blank, on
which a spectral hand was writing *vanity*, and something told
her, too, that that same hand would ere long write this great

moral of life on her mouldering ashes. She cast her fearful gaze upon the future, but recoiled in shivering dread, from the vast illimitable abyss that darkened before her. No ray of hope illumined the dread immense. The Star of Bethlehem had never yet shed its holy beams on the horoscope of her destiny; not that its beams had ever ceased to shine, since that memorable night when, following its silvery pathway in the heavens, the wise men of the East were guided to the cradle of the infant Redeemer, to offer their adoration at his feet; but her eyes had never looked beyond the clouds of time, and in its high and pure resplendence it had shone in vain for her.

"I will seek him to-morrow, this holy man," said she, as hour after hour she lay gazing, through her curtains, on the starry depths of night, "and ask him to enlighten and direct me."

The morrow came, but Ellen was not able to take her accustomed work. For several days she was confined from debility to her own room, and had ample leisure to continue the great walk of self-examination. As soon as she was permitted to go into the open air, she sought her wonted retreat, and it was with feelings of mingled joy and dread, she recognised the stranger, apparently waiting their approach. This truly good man, though a stranger to them, was well known in the neighbourhood for his deeds of charity and labours of love. His name was M * * * *, and as there was no mystery in his character or life, he may be here introduced to the reader, that the appellation of stranger may no longer be necessary. He greeted them both with even more than his former kindness, and noticed with pain the increased debility of Ellen. He saw, too, from her restless glance, that her soul was disquieted within her.

"Oh, sir," said Ellen, mournfully, "you promised me joy, and you have given me wretchedness."

"My daughter," replied Mr. M * * * *, "before the sick found healing virtue in the waters at Bethesda, an angel came down and troubled the stillness of the pool."

Then, at her own request, he sat down by her side, and endeavoured to explain to her the grand yet simple truths of Christianity. And beginning with the law and the prophets, he carried her with him to the mount that burned with fire and thick smoke, where the Almighty, descending in shrouded majesty, proclaimed his will to a trembling world, in thunder and lightning and flame; he led her on with him, through the wilderness, pointing out the smitten rock, the descending manna, the brazen serpent, and all the miraculous manifestations of God's love to his chosen people; then, taking up the lofty strains of prophecy, from the melodious harp of David to the sublimer lyre of Isaiah, he shadowed forth the promised Messiah. In more persuasive accents he dwelt on the fulfilment of those wondrous prophecies. Gently, solemnly he guided her on, from the manger to the cross, unfolding as he went the glorious mysteries of redemption, the depth, the grandeur, the extent, and the exaltation of a Saviour's love. Ellen listened and wept. She felt as if she could have listened for ever. At one moment she was oppressed by the greatness of the theme, at another melted by its tenderness. Those who from infancy have been accustomed to hear these divine truths explained, who from their earliest years have surrounded the household altar, and daily read God's holy word, can have no conception of the overpowering emotions of Ellen and Agnes; neither can they, whose infant glances have taken in the visible glories of creation, comprehend the rapture and amazement of those who, being born blind, are made in after years to see.

From this hour Ellen and Agnes became the willing pupils of Mr. M * * * *, in the most interesting study in the universe; but it is with Ellen the reader is supposed most strongly to sympathize; the feelings of Agnes may be inferred from her going hand in hand with her invalid friend. Ellen lingered in the country till the golden leaves of autumn began to strew the ground, and its chill gales to sigh through the grove. What progress she made during this time in the lore of heaven, under the teachings and prayers of her beloved instructor, may be gathered from *another, and the last scene,* through which this once glittering belle was destined to pass.

    *   *   *   *   *   *   *   *   *

The chamber in which Ellen Loring was first presented to the reader, surrounded by the paraphernalia of the ball-room, was once more lighted—but what a change now met the eye! She, who then sat before the mirror to be arrayed in the adornments of fashion, whose vain eye gazed with unrepressed admiration on her own loveliness, and who laughed to scorn the apprehensions of her fatally indulgent mother, now lay pale and emaciated on her couch. No roses now bloomed in her damp, unbraided locks, no decorating pearl surrounded her wan neck, no sparkling ray of anticipated triumph flashed from her sunken eye. Pride, vanity, vainglory, strength, beauty—all were fled.

Come hither, ye daughters of pleasure, ye who live alone for the fleeting joys of sense, who give to the world the homage that God requires, and waste in the pursuits of time the energies given for eternity, and look upon a scene through which you must one day pass ! There is more eloquence in one dying bed, than Grecian or Roman orator ever uttered.

The dim eyes of Ellen turned towards the door, with a wistful glance. "I fear it will be too late," said she ; "mother, if he should not come before I die—"

"Die !" almost shrieked Mrs. Loring; "you are not going to die, Ellen. Do not talk so frightfully. You will be better soon—Agnes, bathe her temples. She is only faint."

"No, mother," answered Ellen, and her voice was surprisingly clear in its tones, "I feel the truth of what I utter, here," laying her wasted hand on her breast, as she spoke. "I did hope that I might live to hear once more the voice of him who taught me the way of salvation, and revealed to my benighted mind the God who created, the Saviour who redeemed me, that I might breathe out to him my parting blessing, and hear his hallowed prayer rise over my dying bed. But oh, my dear mother, it is for your sake, more than mine, I yearn for his presence—I.looked to him to comfort you, when I am gone." Mrs. Loring here burst into a violent paroxysm of tears, and wrung her hands in uncontrollable agony.

"Oh ! I cannot give thee up," she again and again repeated, "my beautiful Ellen, my good, my beautiful child !"

Mournfully, painfully did these exclamations fall on the chastened ears of the dying Ellen.

"Recall not the image of departed beauty, oh my mother ! I made it my idol, and my heavenly Father, in infinite mercy, consumed it with the breath of his mouth. Speak not of goodness—my life has been one long act of sin and ingratitude. I can look back upon nothing but wasted mercies, neglected opportunities, and perverted talents. But blessed be God, since I have been led in penitence and faith to the feet of a crucified Saviour, I dare to believe that my sins are forgiven, and that my trembling spirit will soon find rest in the bosom of Him, who lived to instruct and died to redeem me."

Ellen paused, for difficult breathing had often impeded her utterance ; but her prayerful eyes, raised to heaven, told the intercourse her soul was holding with One " whom not having seen she loved, but in whom believing, she rejoiced with joy inspeakable and full of glory." At this moment, the door oftly opened, and the gentle footsteps of him, whom on earth he most longed to behold, entered the chamber. As she caught a glimpse of that benign, that venerated countenance, she felt a glow of happiness pervading her being, of which she thought her waning life almost incapable. She clasped her feeble hands together, and exclaimed, " Oh ! Mr. M * * * *." It was all she could utter, for tears, whose fountains she had thought dried for ever, gushed into her eyes and rolled down her pallid cheeks. Mr. M * * * * took one of her cold hands in his, and looked upon her, for a time, without speaking.

. " My daughter," at length he said, and he did not speak without much emotion, " do you find the hand of God laid heavy upon your soul, or is it gentle, even as a father's hand ?"

" Gentle, most gentle," she answered. " Oh ! blessed, for ever blessed be the hour that sent you, heaven-directed, to guide the wanderer in the paths of peace ! Had it not been for you, I should now be trembling on the verge of a dark eternity, without one ray to illumine the unfathomable abyss. Pray for me once more, my beloved friend, and pray too for my dear mother, that she may be enabled to seek Him in faith, who can make a dying bed 'feel soft as downy pillows are.' "

Ellen clasped her feeble hands together, while Mr. M * * * *, kneeling by her bed-side, in that low, sweet solemn tone, for which he was so remarkable, breathed forth one of those deep and fervent prayers, which are, as it were, wings to the soul, and bear it up to heaven. Mrs. Loring knelt too, by the weeping Agnes, but her spirit, unused to devotion, lingered below, and her eyes wandered from the heavenly countenance of that man of God, to the death-like face of that child, whose beauty had once been her pride. She remembered how short a time since, she had seen that form float in airy grace before the mirror clothed in fair and flowing robes, and how soon she should see it extended in the awful immobility of death, wrapped in the still winding-sheet, that garment whose folds are never more waved by the breath of life. Then, conscience whispered in her shuddering ear, that, had she acted a mother's part, and disciplined her daughter to prudence and obedience, the blasts of death had not thus blighted her in her early bloom. And it whispered also, that *she* had no comfort to offer her dying child, in this last conflict of dissolving nature. It was for this world she had lived herself, it was for this world she had taught *her* to live, but for that untravelled world beyond, she had no guiding hand to extend. It was to a stranger's face the fading eyes of Ellen were directed. It was a stranger's prayers that hallowed her passage to the tomb. The realities of eternity for the first time pressed home, on that vain mother's heart. She felt, too, that *she* must one day die, and that earth with all its riches and pleasures could yield her no support in that awful moment. That there was something which earth could not impart, which had power to soothe and animate the departing spirit, she knew by the angelic expression of Ellen's upturned eyes, and by the look of unutterable serenity that was diffused over her whole countenance. The voice of Mr. M * * * * died away on her ear, and an unbroken silence reigned through the apartment. Her stormy grief had been stilled into calmness, during that holy prayer. The eyes of Ellen were now gently closed, and as they rose from their knees they sat down by her side, fearing, even by a deep-drawn breath, to disturb her slumbers. A faint hope began to dawn in the mother's heart, from the placidity and duration of her slumbers.

"I have never known her sleep so calm before," said she, in a low voice, to Mr. M * * * *. Mr. M * * * * bent forward and laid his hand softly on her marble brow.

"Calm indeed are her slumbers," said he, looking solemnly upward; "she sleeps now, I trust, in the bosom of her Saviour and her God."

Thus died Ellen Loring—just one year from that night when Agnes followed her retreating figure, with such a wistful gaze, as she left her for the ball-room, exclaiming to herself, "Happy, beautiful Ellen!" and Agnes now said within herself, even while she wept over her clay-cold form, "Happy Ellen!" but with far different emotions; for she now followed, with the eye of faith, her ascending spirit to the regions of the blest, and saw her, in imagination, enter those golden gates, which never will be closed against the humble and penitent believer.

A few evenings after, a brilliant party was assembled in one of those halls, where pleasure welcomes its votaries.—" Did you know that Ellen Loring was dead?" observed some one to a beautiful girl, the very counterpart of what Ellen once was. "Dead!" exclaimed the startled beauty, for one moment alarmed into reflection; "I did not think she would have died so soon. I am sorry you told me—it will throw a damp over my spirits the whole evening—poor Ellen!" It was but a moment, and the music breathed forth its joyous strains. She was led in haste to the dance, and Ellen Loring was forgotten.

THE FATAL COSMETIC.

CHARLES BROWN sat with Mr. Hall in a corner of the room, apart from the rest of the company. Mr. Hall was a stranger, Charles the familiar acquaintance of all present. The former evidently retained his seat out of politeness to the latter for his eyes wandered continually to the other side of the room, where a group of young ladies was gathered round a piano, so closely as to conceal the musician to whom they were apparently listening. The voice that accompanied instrument was weak and irregular, and the high tones excessively shrill and disagreeable, yet the performer continued her songs with unwearied patience, thinking the young gentlemen were turned into the very stones that Orpheus changed into breathing things, to remain insensible to her minstrelsy. There was one fair, blue-eyed girl, with a very sweet countenance, who stood behind her chair and cast many a mirthful glance towards Charles, while she urged the songstress to continue at every pause, as if she were spell-bound by the melody. Charles laughed, and kept time with his foot, but Mr. Hall bit his lips, and a frown passed over his handsome and serious countenance. "What a wretched state of society!" exclaimed he, "that admits, nay, even demands such insincerity. Look at the ingenuous countenance of that young girl—would you not expect from her sincerity and truth? Yet, with what practical falsehood she encourages her companion in her odious screeching!"

"Take care," answered Charles, "you must not be too severe. That young lady is a very particular friend of mine, and a very charming girl. She has remarkably popular manners, and if she *is* guilty of a few little innocent deceptions, such, for instance, as the present, I see no possible harm in them to herself, and they certainly give great pleasure to others. She makes Miss Lewis very happy, by her apparent admiration, and I do not see that she injures any one else."

Mr. Hall sighed.

"I fear," said he, "I am becoming a misanthropist. I find I have very peculiar views, such as set me apart and isolate me from my fellow beings. I cannot enjoy an artificial state of society. I consider *truth* as the corner stone of the great social fabric, and where this is wanting, I am constantly looking for ruin and desolation. The person deficient in this virtue, however fair and fascinating, is no more to me than the whited sepulchre and painted wall."

"You have, indeed, peculiar views," answered Charles, colouring with a vexation he was too polite to express in any other way; "and if you look upon the necessary dissimulations practised in society as falsehoods, and brand them as such, I can only say, that you have created a standard of morality more exalted and pure than human nature can ever reach."

"I cannot claim the merit of *creating* a standard, which the divine Moralist gave to man, when he marked out his duties from the sacred mount, in characters so clear and deep, that the very blind might see and the cold ear of deafness hear."

Mr. Hall spoke with warmth. The eyes of the company were directed towards him. He was disconcerted and remained silent. Miss Lewis rose from the piano, and drew towards the fire.

"I am getting terribly tired of the piano," said she, "I don't think it suits my voice at all. I am going to take lessons on the guitar and the harp—one has so much more scope with them; and then they are much more graceful instruments."

"You are perfectly right," replied Miss Ellis, the young lady with the ingenuous countenance, "I have no doubt you would excel on either, and your singing would be much better appreciated. Don't you think so, Margaret?" added she, turning to a young lady, who had hitherto been silent, and apparently unobserved.

"You know I do not," answered she, who was so abruptly addressed, in a perfectly quiet manner, and fixing her eyes serenely on her face; "I should be sorry to induce Miss Lewis to do anything disadvantageous to herself, and consequently painful to her friends."

"Really, Miss Howard," cried Miss Lewis, bridling, and tossing her head with a disdainful air, "you need not be so afraid of my giving you so much pain—I will not intrude my singing upon your delicate and refined ears."

Mr. Hall made a movement forward, attracted by the uncommon sincerity of Miss Howard's remark.

"There," whispered Charles, "is a girl after your own heart —Margaret Howard *will* speak the truth, however unpalatable it may be, and see what wry faces poor Miss Lewis makes in trying *not* to swallow it—I am sure Mary Ellis's flattery is a thousand times kinder and more amiable."

Mr. Hall did not answer. His eyes were perusing the face of her, whose lips had just given such honourable testimony to a virtue so rarely respected by the world of fashion. A decent boldness lighted up the clear hazel eyes that did not seem to be unconscious of the dark and penetrating glances at that moment resting upon them. She was dressed with remarkable simplicity. No decoration in colour relieved the spotless whiteness of her attire. Her hair of pale, yet shining brown, was plainly parted over a brow somewhat too lofty for mere feminine beauty, but white and smooth as Parian marble. Her features, altogether, bore more resemblance to a Pallas than a Venus. They were calm and pure, but somewhat cold and passionless—and under that pale, transparent skin, there seemed no under current, ebbing and flowing with the crimson tide of the heart. Her figure, veiled to the throat, was of fine, though not very slender proportions. There was evidently no artificial compression about the waist, no binding ligatures to prevent the elastic motions of the limbs, the pliable and graceful movements of nature.

"She has a fine face—a very handsome face," repeated Charles, responding to what Mr. Hall *looked*, for as yet he had uttered nothing; "but to me, it is an uninteresting one. She is not generally liked—respected, it is true, but feared— and fear is a feeling which few young ladies would wish to inspire. It is a dangerous thing to live above the world—at least, for a woman."

Charles availed himself of the earliest opportunity of introducing his friend to Miss Howard, glad to be liberated for a while from the close companionship of a man who made him feel strangely uncomfortable with regard to himself, and well pleased with the opportunity of conversing with his favourite, Mary Ellis.

"I feel quite vexed with Margaret," said this thoughtless girl, "for spoiling my compliment to Miss Lewis. I would give one of my little fingers to catch her for once in a white lie."

"Ask her if she does not think herself handsome," said Charles; "no woman ever acknowledged that truth, though none be more firmly believed."

He little expected she would act upon his suggestion, but Mary was too much delighted at the thought of seeing the uncompromising Margaret guilty of a prevarication, to suffer it to pass unheeded.

"Margaret," cried she, approaching her, unawed by the proximity of the majestic stranger—"Mr. Brown says you will deny that you think yourself handsome. Tell me the truth—don't you believe yourself *very* handsome?"

"I will tell you the truth, Mary," replied Margaret, blushing so brightly, as to give an actual radiance to her face, "that is, if I speak at all. But I would rather decline giving any opinion of myself."

"Ah! Margaret," persisted Miss Ellis, "I have heard you say that to *conceal* the truth, when it was required of us, unless some moral duty were involved, was equivalent to a falsehood. Bear witness, Charles, here is one subject on which even Margaret Howard dares not speak the truth."

"You are mistaken," replied Miss Howard; "since you force me to speak, by attacking my principles, I am very willing to say, I *do* think myself handsome; but not so conspicuously as to allow me to claim a superiority over my sex, or to justify so singular and unnecessary a question."

All laughed—even the grave Mr. Hall smiled at the frankness of the avowal—all but Miss Lewis, who, turning up her eyes and raising her hands, exclaimed, "Really, Miss Howard's modesty is equal to her politeness. I thought she despised beauty."

"The gifts of God are never to be despised," answered Miss Howard, mildly. "If he has graced the outer temple, we should only be more careful to keep the indwelling spirit pure."

She drew back, as if pained by the observation she had excited; and the deep and modest colour gradually faded from her cheek. Mr. Hall had not been an uninterested listener. He was a sad and disappointed man. He had been the victim of a woman's perfidy and falsehood—and was consequently distrustful of the whole sex; and his health had suffered from the corrosion of his feelings, and he had been compelled to seek, in a milder clime, a balm which time alone could yield. He had been absent several years, and was just returned to his native country, but not to the scene of his former residence. The wound was healed, but the hardness of the scar remained.

One greater and purer than the Genius of the Arabian Tale, had placed in his breast a mirror, whose lustre would be instantaneously dimmed by the breath of falsehood or dissimulation. It was in this mirror he saw reflected the actions of his fellow beings, and it pained him to see its bright surface so constantly sullied. Never, since the hour he was so fatally deceived, had he been in the presence of woman, without a melancholy conviction that she was incapable of standing the test of this bosom talisman. Here, however, was one, whose lips cast no cloud upon its lustre. He witnessed the marvellous spectacle of a young, beautiful, and accomplished woman, surrounded by the artifices and embellishments of fashionable life, speaking the truth, in all simplicity and godly sincerity, as commanded by the holy men of old. There was something in the sight that renovated and refreshed his blighted feelings. The dew falling on the parched herbage, prepares it for the influence of a kinder ray. Even so the voice of Margaret Howard, gentle in itself and persuasive, advocating the cause he most venerated, operated this night on the heart of Mr. Hall.

For many weeks the same party frequently met at the dwelling of Mrs. Astor. This lady was a professed patroness and admirer of genius and the fine arts. To be a fine painter, a fine singer, a fine writer, a traveller, or a foreigner, was a direct passport to her favour. To be distinguished in any manner in society was sufficient, provided it was not "bad eminence" which was attained by the individual. She admired Mr. Hall for the stately gloom of his mien, his dark and foreign air, his peculiar and high-wrought sentiments. She sought an intimacy with Margaret Howard, for it was a *distinction* to be her friend, and, moreover, she had an exquisite taste and skill in drawing and painting. Mary Ellis was a particular favourite of hers, because her own favourite cousin Charles Brown thought her the most fascinating young lady of his acquaintance. Mrs. Astor's house was elegantly furnished, and her rooms were adorned with rare and beautiful specimens of painting and statuary. She had one apartment which she called her Gallery of Fine Arts, and every new guest was duly ushered into this sanctuary, and called upon to look and admire the glowing canvas and the breathing marble. A magnificent pier-glass was placed on one side of the hall, so as to reflect and multiply these classic beauties. It had been purchased in Europe, and was remarkable for its thickness, brilliancy, and fidelity of re-flection. It was a favourite piece of furniture of Mrs. Astor's, and all her servants were warned to be particularly careful, whenever they dusted its surface. As this glass is of some importance in the story, it deserves a minute description. Mrs. Astor thought the only thing necessary to complete the fur-nishing of the gallery, were transparencies for the windows. Miss Howard, upon hearing the remark, immediately offered to supply the deficiency, an offer at once eagerly accepted, and Mrs. Astor insisted that her painting apparatus should be placed in the very room, that she might receive all the inspiration to be derived from the mute yet eloquent relics of genius, that there solicited the gaze. Nothing could be more delightful than the progress of the work. Margaret was an enthusiast in the art, and her kindling cheek always attested the triumph of her creating hand. Mrs. Astor was in a constant state of excitement, till the whole was completed, and it was no light task, as four were required, and the windows were of an extra size. Almost every day saw the fair artist seated at her easel, with the same group gathered round her. Mary Ellis admired everything so indiscriminately, it was impossible to attach much value to her praise; but Mr. Hall criticised as well as admired, and as he had the painter's eye, and the poet's tongue, Margaret felt the value of his suggestions, and the interest they added to her employment. Above all things, she felt their *truth*. She saw that he never flattered, that he dared to blame, and when he did commend, she was conscious the tribute was deserved. Margaret was not one of those beings, who cannot do but one thing at a time. She could talk and listen, while her hands were applying the brush or arranging the colours, and look up too from the canvas, with a glance that showed how entirely she participated in what was passing around her.

"I wonder you are not tired to death of that everlasting easel," said Mary Ellis to Margaret, who grew every day more interested in her task. "I could not endure such confine-ment."

"*Death* and *everlasting* are solemn words to be so lightly

used, my dear Mary," answered Margaret, whose religious ear
was always pained by levity on sacred themes.

"I would not be as serious as you are, for a thousand
worlds," replied Mary, laughing; "I really believe you think
it a sin to smile. Give me the roses of life, let who will take
the thorns. I am going now to gather some, if I can, and
leave you and Mr. Hall to enjoy all the briers you can find."

She left the room gayly singing, sure to be immediately followed by Charles, and Mr. Hall was left sole companion of the
artist. Mary had associated their names together, for the purpose of disturbing the self-possession of Margaret, and she
certainly succeeded in her object. Had Mr. Hall perceived
her heightened colour, his vanity might have drawn a flattering inference; but he was standing behind her easel, and his
eyes were fixed on the beautiful personification of Faith, Hope,
and Charity—those three immortal graces—she was delineat-
ing, as kneeling and embracing, with upturned eyes and celestial wings. It was a lovely group—the last of the transparencies, and Margaret lavished on it some of the finest touches
of her genius. Mary had repeated a hundred times that it
was finished, that another stroke of the pencil would ruin it,
and Mrs. Astor declared it perfect, and more than perfect, but
still Margaret lingered at the frame, believing every tint should
be the last. Every lover of the arts knows the fascination
attending the successful exercise and development of their
genius—of seeing bright and warm imaginings assume a colouring and form, and giving to others a transcript of the mind's
glorious creations; but every artist does not know what deeper
charm may be added by the conversation and companionship
of such a being as Mr. Hall. He was what might be called
a fascinating man, notwithstanding the occasional gloom and
general seriousness of his manners. For, when flashes of
sensibility lighted up that gloom, and intellect, excited and
brought fully into action, illumined that seriousness—it was
like moonlight shining on some ruined castle, beauty and
grandeur meeting together and exalting each other, from the
effect of contrast. Then there was a deep vein of piety pervading all his sentiments and expressions. The comparison of
the ruined castle is imperfect. The moonbeams falling on
some lofty cathedral, with its pillared dome and "long-drawn
aisles," is a better similitude, for devotion hallowed and elevated
every faculty of his soul. Margaret, who had lived in a world
of her own, surrounded by a purer atmosphere, lonely and

111

somewhat unapproachable, felt as if she were no longer solitary, for here was one who thought and sympathized with her; one, too, who seemed sanctified and set apart from others, by a kind of mysterious sorrow, which the instinct of woman told her had its source in the heart.

"I believe I am too serious, as Mary says," cried Margaret, first breaking the silence; "but it seems to me the thoughtless alone can be gay. I am young in years, but I began to reflect early, and from the moment I took in the mystery of life and all its awful dependencies, I ceased to be mirthful. I am doomed to pay a constant penalty for the singularity of my feelings: like the priestess of the ancient temples, I am accused of uttering dark sayings of old, and casting the shadows of the future over the joys of the present."

Margaret seldom alluded to herself, but Mary's accusation about the thorns and briers had touched her, where perhaps alone she was vulnerable; and in the frankness of her nature, she uttered what was paramount in her thoughts.

"Happy they who are taught by reflection, not experience, to look seriously, though not sadly on the world," said Mr. Hall, earnestly; "who mourn from philanthropy over its folly and falsehood, not because that falsehood and folly have blighted their dearest hopes, nay, cut them off, root and branch, for ever."

Margaret was agitated, and for a moment the pencil wavered in her hand. She knew Mr. Hall must have been unhappy—that he was still suffering from corroding remembrances—and often had she wished to pierce through the mystery that hung over his past life; but now, when he himself alluded to it, she shrunk from an explanation. He seemed himself to regret the warmth of his expressions, and to wish to efface the impression they had made, for his attention became riveted on the picture, which he declared wanted only one thing to make it perfect—"And what was that?"—"Truth encircling the trio with her golden band."

"It may yet be done," cried Margaret; and, with great animation and skill, she sketched the outline suggested.

It is delightful to have one's own favourite sentiments and feelings embodied by another, and that too with a graceful readiness and apparent pleasure, that shows a congeniality of thought and taste. Mr. Hall was not insensible to this charm in Margaret Howard. He esteemed, revered, admired, he wished that he dared to love her. But all charming and true as she seemed, she was still a woman, and he might be again deceived. It would be a terrible thing to embark his happiness once more on the waves which had once overwhelmed it; and find himself again a shipwrecked mariner, cast upon the cruel desert of existence. The feelings which Margaret inspired were so different from the stormy passions which had reigned over him, it is no wonder he was unconscious of their strength and believed himself still his own master.

"Bless me," said Mary, who, entering soon after, *banished,* as she said, Mr. Hall from her presence, for he retired; "if you have not added another figure to the group. I have a great mind to blot Faith, Hope, and Charity, as well as Truth from existence," and playfully catching hold of the frame, she pretended to sweep her arm over their faces.

"Oh! Mary, beware!" exclaimed Margaret; but the warning came too late. The easel tottered and fell instantaneously against the magnificent glass, upon which Mrs. Astor set such an immense value, and broke it into a thousand pieces. Mary looked aghast, and Margaret turned pale as she lifted her picture from amid the ruins.

"It is not spoiled," said she; "but the glass!"

"Oh! the glass!" cried Mary, looking the image of despair; "what shall I do? What will Mrs. Astor say? She will never forgive me!"

"She cannot be so vindictive!" replied Margaret; "but it is indeed an unfortunate accident, and one for which I feel particularly responsible."

"Do not tell her how it happened," cried Mary, shrinking with moral cowardice from the revealing of the truth. "I cannot brave her displeasure!—Charles, too, will be angry with me, and I cannot bear that. Oh! pray, dearest Margaret, pray do not tell her that it was I who did it—you know it would be so natural for the easel to fall without any rash hand to push it. Promise me, Margaret."

Margaret turned her clear, rebuking eye upon the speaker with a mingled feeling of indignation and pity.

"I will not expose you, Mary," said she, calmly; and, withdrawing herself from the rapturous embrace, in which Mary expressed her gratitude, she began to pick up the fragments of the mirror, while Mary, unwilling to look on the wreck she had made, flew out to regain her composure. It happened that Mr. Hall passed the window while Margaret was thus occupied; and he paused a moment to watch her, for in spite of himself, he felt a deep and increasing interest in every action of Margaret's. Margaret saw his shadow as it lingered, but she continued her employment. He did not doubt that she had caused the accident, for he had left her alone, a few moments before, and he was not conscious that any one had entered since his departure. Though he regretted any circumstance which might give pain to her, he anticipated a pleasure in seeing the openness and readiness with which she would avow herself the aggressor, and blame herself for her carelessness.

Margaret found herself in a very unpleasant situation. She had promised not to betray the cowardly Mary, and she knew that whatever blame would be attached to the act, would rest upon herself. But were Mrs. Astor to question her upon the subject, she could not deviate from the truth, by acknowledging a fault she had never committed. She felt an unspeakable contempt for Mary's weakness, for, had *she* been in *her* place, she would have acknowledged the part she had acted, unhesitatingly, secure of the indulgence of friendship and benevolence. " Better to leave the circumstance to speak for itself," said Margaret to herself, " and of course the burden will rest upon me." She sighed as she thought of the happy hours she had passed, by the side of that mirror, and how often she had seen it reflect the speaking countenance of Mr. Hall, that tablet of "unutterable thoughts," and then thinking how *his* hopes seemed shattered like that frail glass, and his memories of sorrow multiplied, she came to the conclusion that all earthly hopes were vain and all earthly memories fraught with sadness. Never had Margaret moralized so deeply as in the long solitary walk she stole that evening, to escape the evil of being drawn into the tacit sanction of a falsehood. Like many others, with equally pure intentions, in trying to avoid one misfortune she incurred a greater.

Mrs. Astor was very much grieved and astonished when she discovered her loss. With all her efforts to veil her feelings, Mary saw she was displeased with Margaret, and would probably never value as they deserved, the beautiful transparencies on which she had so faithfully laboured.

" I would not have cared if any other article had been broken," said Mrs. Astor, whose weak point Mary well knew; " but this can never be replaced. I do not so much value the cost, great as it was, but it was perfectly unique. I never saw another like it."

Mary's conscience smote her, for suffering another to bear

the imputation she herself deserved. A sudden plan occurred to her. She had concealed the truth, she was now determined to save her friend, even at the cost of a lie.

"I do not believe Margaret broke it," said she. "I saw Dinah, your little black girl in the room, just before Margaret left it, and you know how often you have punished her for putting her hands on forbidden articles. You know if Margaret had done it, she would have acknowledged it, at once."

"True," exclaimed Mrs. Astor; "how stupid I have been!" and glad to find a channel in which her anger could flow, unchecked by the restraints of politeness, she rung the bell and summoned the unconscious Dinah.

In vain she protested her innocence. She was black, and it was considered a matter of course that she would lie. Mrs. Astor took her arm in silence, and led her from the room, in spite of her prayers and protestations. We should be sorry to reveal the secrets of the prison-house, but from the cries that issued through the shut door, and from a certain whizzing sound in the air, one might judge of the nature of the punishment inflicted on the innocent victim of unmerited wrath. Mary closed her ears. Every sound pierced her heart. Something told her those shrieks would rise up in judgment against her at the last day. "Oh! how," thought she, "if I fear the rebuke of my fellow-creature for an unintentional offence, how can I ever appear before my Creator, with the blackness of falsehood and the hardness of cruelty on my soul?" She wished she had had the courage to have acted right in the first place, but now it was too late. Charles would despise her, and that very day he had told her that he loved her better than all the world beside. She tried, too, to soothe her conscience, by reflecting that Dinah would have been whipped for something else, and that as it was a common event to her, it was, after all, a matter of no great consequence. Mrs. Astor, having found a legitimate vent for her displeasure, chased the cloud from her brow, and greeted Margaret with a smile, on her return, slightly alluding to the accident, evidently trying to rise superior to the event. Margaret was surprised and pleased. She expressed her own regret, but as she imputed to herself no blame, Mrs. Astor was confirmed in the justice of her verdict. Margaret knew not what had passed in her absence, for Mrs. Astor was too refined to bring her domestic troubles before her guests. Mary, who was the only one necessarily initiated, was too deeply implicated to repeat it,

and the subject was dismissed.   But the impression remained
on one mind, painful and ineffaceable.

Mr. Hall marked Margaret's conscious blush on her entrance,
he had heard the cries and sobs of poor Dinah, and was not
ignorant of the cause.   He believed Margaret was aware of
the fact—she, the true offender.   A pang, keen as cold steel
can create, shot through his heart at this conviction.   He had
thought her so pure, so true, so holy, the very incarnation of
his worshipped virtue—and now, to sacrifice her principles for
such a bauble—a bit of frail glass.   He could not remain in
her presence, but, complaining of a headache, suddenly retired,
but not before he had cast a glance on Margaret, so cold and
freezing, it seemed to congeal her very soul.

" He believes me cowardly and false," thought she, for she
divined what was passing in his mind ; and if ever she was
tempted to be so, it was in the hope of reinstating herself in
his esteem.   She had given her promise to Mary, however,
and it was not to be broken.   Mary, whose feelings were as
evanescent as her principles were weak, soon forgot the whole
affair in the preparations of her approaching marriage with
Charles, an event which absorbed all her thoughts, as it involved
all her hopes of happiness.

Margaret finished her task, but the charm which had gilded
the occupation was fled.   Mr. Hall seldom called, and when
he did, he wore all his original reserve.   Margaret felt she
had not deserved this alienation, and tried to cheer herself
with the conviction of her own integrity ; but her spirits were
occasionally dejected, and the figure of Truth, which had such
a beaming outline, assumed the aspect of utter despondency.
Dissatisfied with her work, she at last swept her brush over
the design, and mingling Truth with the dark shades of the
back ground, gave up her office as an artist, declaring her
sketches completed.   Mrs. Astor was enraptured with the
whole, and said she intended to reserve them for the night of
Mary's wedding, when they would burst upon the sight, in one
grand *coup d'œil*, in the full blaze of chandeliers, bridal
lamps, and nuptial ornaments.   Margaret was to officiate as
one of the bridemaids, but she gave a reluctant consent.   She
could not esteem Mary, and she shrunk from her flattery and
caresses with an instinctive loathing.   She had once set her
foot on a flowery bank, that edged a beautiful stream.   The
turf trembled and gave way, for it was hollow below, and
Margaret narrowly escaped death.   She often shuddered at

the recollection. With similar emotions she turned from Mary Ellis's smiles and graces. There was beauty and bloom on the surface, but hollowness and perhaps ruin beneath.

A short time before the important day, a slight efflorescence appeared on the fair cheek and neck of Mary. She was in despair, lest her loveliness should be marred, when she most of all wished to shine. It increased instead of diminishing, and she resolved to have recourse to any remedy, that would remove the disfiguring eruption. She recollected having seen a violent erysipelas cured immediately by a solution of corrosive sublimate; and without consulting any one, she sent Dinah to the apothecary to purchase some, charging her to tell no one whose errand she was bearing, for she was not willing to confess her occasion for such a cosmetic. Dinah told the apothecary her mistress sent her, and it was given without questioning or hesitation. Her only confidant was Margaret, who shared her chamber and toilet, and who warned her to be exceedingly cautious in the use of an article so poisonous; and Mary promised with her usual heedlessness, without dreaming of any evil consequences. The eruption disappeared—Mary looked fairer than ever, and, clad in her bridal paraphernalia of white satin, white roses, and blonde lace, was pronounced the most beautiful bride of the season. Mr. Hall was present, though he had refused to take any part in the ceremony. He could not, without singularity, decline the invitation and, notwithstanding the blow his confidence in Margaret's character had received, he still found the spot where *she* was, enchanted ground, and he lingered near, unwilling to break at once the only charm that still bound him to society. After the short but solemn rite, that made the young and thoughtless, *one* by indissoluble ties, and the rush of congratulation took place, Margaret was forced by the pressure close to Mr. Hall's side. He involuntarily offered his arm as a protection, and a thrill of irrepressible happiness pervaded his heart, at this unexpected and unsought proximity. He forgot his coldness—the broken glass, everything but the feeling of the present moment. Margaret was determined to avail herself of the tide of returning confidence. Her just womanly modesty and pride prevented her *seeking* an explanation and reconciliation, but she knew without breaking her promise to Mary, she could not justify herself in Mr. Hall's opinion, if even the opportunity offered. She was to depart in the morning, with the new-married pair, who were going to take an excursion of pleasure, so fashionable after the wedding ceremony. She might never see him again. He had looked pale, his face was now flushed high with excited feeling.

"You have wronged me, Mr. Hall," said she, blushing, but without hesitation; "if you think I have been capable of wilful deception or concealment. The mirror was not broken by me, though I know you thought me guilty, and afraid or ashamed to avow the truth. I would not say so much to justify myself, if I did not think you would believe me, and if I did not value the esteem of one who sacrifices even friendship at the shrine of truth."

She smiled, for she saw she was believed, and there was such a glow of pleasure irradiating Mr. Hall's countenance, it was like the breaking and gushing forth of sunbeams. There are few faces, on which a smile has such a magic effect as on Margaret's. Her smile was never forced. It was the inspiration of truth, and all the light of her soul shone through it. Perhaps neither ever experienced an hour of deeper happiness than that which followed this simple explanation. Margaret felt a springtide of hope and joy swelling in her heart, for there was a deference, a tenderness in Mr. Hall's manner she had never seen before. He seemed entirely to have forgotten the presence of others, when a name uttered by one near, arrested his attention.

"That is Mrs. St. Henry," observed a lady, stretching eagerly forward. "She arrived in town this morning, and had letters of introduction to Mrs. Astor. She was the beauty of ——, before her marriage, and is still the leader of fashion and taste."

Margaret felt her companion start, as if a ball had penetrated him, and looking up, she saw his altered glance, fixed on the lady, who had just entered, with a dashing escort, and was advancing towards the centre of the room. She was dressed in the extremity of the reigning mode—her arms and neck entirely uncovered, and their dazzling whiteness, thus lavishly displayed, might have mocked the polish and purity of alabaster. Her brilliant black eyes flashed on either side, with the freedom of conscious beauty, and disdain of the homage it inspired. She moved with the air of a queen, attended by her vassals, directly forward, when suddenly her proud step faltered, her cheek and lips became wan, and uttering a sudden ejaculation, she stood for a moment perfectly still. She was opposite Mr. Hall, whose eye, fixed upon hers, seemed to have the effect of fascination. Though darkened by the burning sun of a tropical clime, and faded from the untimely blighting of the heart, that face could never be forgotten. It told her of perjury, remorse, sorrow—yes, of sorrow, for in spite of the splendour that surrounded her, this glittering beauty was wretched. She had sacrificed herself at the shrine of Mammon, and had learned too late the horror of such ties, unsanctified by affection. Appreciating but too well the value of the love she had forsaken, goaded by remorse for her conduct to him, whom she believed wasting away in a foreign land—she flew from one scene of dissipation to another, seeking in the admiration of the world an equivalent for her lost happiness. The unexpected apparition of her lover was as startling and appalling as if she had met an inhabitant of another world. She tried to rally herself and to pass on, but the effort was in vain—sight, strength, and recollection forsook her.

"Mrs. St. Henry has fainted! Mrs. St. Henry has fainted!" —was now echoed from mouth to mouth. A lady's fainting, whether in church, ball-room, or assembly, always creates a great sensation; but when that lady happens to be the centre of attraction and admiration, when every eye that has a loophole to peep through is gazing on her brilliant features, to behold her suddenly fall, as if smitten by the angel of death, pallid and moveless—the effect is inconceivably heightened. When, too, as in the present instance, a sad, romantic-looking stranger rushes forward to support her, the interest of the scene admits of no increase. At least Margaret felt so, as she saw the beautiful Mrs. St. Henry borne in the arms of Mr. Hall through the crowd, that fell back as he passed, into an adjoining apartment, speedily followed by Mrs. Astor, all wonder and excitement, and many others all curiosity and expectation, to witness the termination of the scene. Mr. Hall drew back, while the usual appliances were administered for her resuscitation. He heeded not the scrutinizing glances bent upon him. His thoughts were rolled within himself, and

"The soul of other days came rushing in."

The lava that had hardened over the ruin it created, melted anew, and the greenness and fragrance of new-born hopes were lost under the burning tide. When Mrs. St. Henry opened her eyes, she looked round her in wild alarm; then shading her brow with her hand, her glance rested where Mr. Hall stood, pale and abstracted, with folded arms, leaning against the wall—" I thought so," said she, in a low voice, " I thought so ;"—then covered her eyes and remained silent.   Mr. Hall, the moment he heard the sound of her voice and was assured of her recovery, precipitately retired, leaving behind him matter of deep speculation.   Margaret was sitting in a window of the drawing-room, through which he passed. She was alone, 'or even the bride was forgotten in the excitement of the pas cene.   He paused—he felt an explanation was due to her, but that it was impossible to make it.   He was softened by the sad and sympathizing expression of her countenance, and seated himself a moment by her side.

"I have been painfully awakened from a dream of bliss," said he, " which I was foolish enough to imagine might yet be realized. But the heart rudely shattered as mine has been, must never hope to be healed. I cannot command myself sufficiently to say more, only let me make one assurance, that whatever misery has been and may yet be my doom, guilt has no share in my wretchedness—I cannot refuse myself the consolation of your esteem."

Margaret made no reply—she could not. Had her existence depended on the utterance of one word, she could not have commanded it. She extended her hand, however, in token of that friendship she believed was hereafter to be the only bond that was to unite them.   Long after Mr. Hall was gone, she sat in the same attitude, pale and immovable as a statue ; but who can tell the changes and conflicts of her spirit, in that brief period ?

Mrs. St. Henry was too ill to be removed, and Mrs. Astor was unbounded in her attentions.   She could hardly regret a circumstance which forced so interesting and distinguished a personage upon the acceptance of her hospitality.   Margaret remained with her during the greater part of the night, apprehensive of a renewal of the fainting fits, to which she acknowledged she was constitutionally subject.   Margaret watched ner as she lay, her face scarcely to be distinguished from the sheet, it was so exquisitely fair, were it not for the shading of the dark locks, that fell unbound over the pillow, still heavy with the moisture with which they had been saturated ; and, as she contemplated her marvellous loveliness, she wondered not at the influence she exercised over the destiny of another. Mr. Hall had once spoken of himself as being the victim of falsehood.   Could she have been false—and loving him, how could she have married another? If she had voluntarily broken her troth, why such an agitation at his sight? and if she were worthy of his love, why such a glaring display of her person, such manifest courting of the free gaze of admiration? These, and a thousand similar interrogations, did Margaret make to herself during the vigils of the night, but they found no answer. Towards morning, the lady slept; but Margaret was incapable of sleep, and her wakeful eyes caught the first gray tint of the dawn, and marked it deepening and kindling, till the east was robed with flame, the morning livery of the skies. All was bustle till the bridal party was on their way. Mrs. St. Henry still slept, under the influence of an opiate, and Margaret saw her no more. Farewells were exchanged, kind wishes breathed, and the travellers commenced their journey. Margaret's thoughts wandered from Mrs. St. Henry to Mr. Hall, and back again, till they were weary of wandering and would gladly have found rest; but the waters had not subsided, there was no green spot where the dove of peace could fold her drooping wings. Charles and Mary were too much occupied by each other to notice her silence; and it was not till they paused in their journey, she was recalled to existing realities. Mary regretted something she had left behind—a sudden recollection came over Margaret.

"Oh! Mary," said she, "I hope you have been cautious, and not left any of that dangerous medicine, where mischief could result from it. I intended to remind you of it before our departure."

"Certainly—to be sure I took especial care of it, I have it with me in my trunk," replied Mary, but her conscience gave her a remorseful twinge as she uttered the *white lie,* for she had forgotten it, and where she had left it, she could not remember. As Margaret had given her several warnings, she was ashamed to acknowledge her negligence, and took refuge in the shelter she had too often successfully sought. Had she anticipated the fatal consequences of her oblivion, her bridal felicity would have been converted into agony and despair. She had left the paper containing the powder, yet undissolved, on the mantelpiece of her chamber. The chambermaid who arranged the room after her departure, seeing it and supposing it to be medicine, put it in the box which Mrs. Astor devoted to that department, in the midst of calomel, salts, antimony, &c. It was folded in brown paper, like the rest, and there was no label to indicate its deadly qualities. Mrs. St. Henry continued the guest of Mrs. Astor, for her indisposition assumed a more serious aspect, and it was impossible to remove her. She appeared feverish and restless, and a physician was called in to prescribe for her, greatly in opposition to her wishes. She could not bear to acknowledge herself ill. It was the heat of the room that had oppressed her—a transient cold, which would soon pass away—she would not long trespass on Mrs. Astor's hospitality. The doctor was not much skilled in diseases of the heart, though he ranked high in his profession. His grand panacea for almost all diseases was calomel, which he recommended to his patient, as the most efficient and speediest remedy. She received the prescription with a very ill grace, declaring she had never tasted of any in her life, and had a horror of all medicines. Mrs. Astor said she had an apothecary's shop at command in her closet, and that she kept doses constantly prepared for her own use. After the doctor's departure, Mrs. St. Henry seemed much dejected, and her eyes had an anxious, inquiring expression as they turned on Mrs. Astor.

"You say," said she to her, in a low tone, "that friends have been kind in their inquiries for me? Most of them are strangers, and yet I thank them."

"Mr. Hall has called more than once," replied Mrs. Astor, "he, I believe, is well known to you."

. "He is indeed," said Mrs. St. Henry—"I wish I could see him—but it cannot be; no, it would not answer."

Mrs. Astor longed to ask the nature of their former acquaintance, but a conviction that the question would be painful, restrained the expression of her curiosity.

"Would you not like to send for some of your friends?" inquired Mrs. Astor—"your husband? My servants shall be at your disposal."

"You are very kind," answered Mrs. St. Henry, quickly—"but it is not necessary—my husband is too infirm to travel, and believing me well, he will suffer no anxiety on my account—I think I shall be quite well, after taking your sovereign medicine. Give it me now, if you please, while I am in a vein of compliance."

She turned, with so lovely a smile, and extended her hand with so much grace, Mrs. Astor stood a moment, thinking what a beautiful picture she would make; then taking the lamp in her hand, she opened her closet, and took down the medicine casket. It happened that the first paper she touched was that which Mary had left, and which the servant had mingled with the others.

" Here is one already prepared," cried she—" I always keep them ready, the exact number of grains usually given, as we often want it suddenly and at night."

She mixed the fatal powder with some delicious jelly, and holding it to the lips of her patient, said with a cheerin smile—" Come, it has no disagreeable taste at all."

Mrs. St. Henry gave a nervous shudder, but took it, unconscious of its deadly properties ; and Mrs. Astor, praising her resolution, seated herself in an easy chair by the bedside, and began to read. She became deeply interested in her book, though she occasionally glanced towards her patient to see if she slept. She had placed the lamp so that its light would not shine on the bed, and the most perfect quietness reigned in the apartment. How long this tranquillity lasted it is impossible to tell, for she was so absorbed in her book, time passed unheeded. At length Mrs. St. Henry began to moan, and toss her arms over the covering, as if in sudden pain. Mrs. Astor leaned over her, and took her hand. It was hot and burning, her cheek had a scarlet flush on it, and when she opened her eyes they had a wild and alarming expression.

" Water," she exclaimed, leaning on her elbow, and shading back her hair hurriedly from her brow—" Give me water, for I die of thirst."

" I dare not," said Mrs. Astor, terrified by her manner— " anything but that to quench your thirst."

She continued still more frantically to call for water, till Mrs. Astor, excessively alarmed, sent for the doctor, and called in other attendants. As he was in the neighbourhood, he came immediately. He looked aghast at the situation of his patient, for she was in a paroxysm of agony at his entrance, and his experienced eye took in the danger of the case. " What have you given her, madam ?" said he, turning to Mrs Astor, with a countenance that made her tremble.

" What have you given me ?" exclaimed Mrs. St. Henry, grasping her wrist with frenzied strength—" You have killed me—it was poison—I feel it in my heart and in my brain !"

Mrs. Astor uttered a scream, and snatched up the paper which had fallen on the carpet.

" Look at it, doctor—it was calomel, just as you prescribed —what else could it be !"

The doctor examined the paper—there was a little powder still sticking to it.

"Good heavens, doctor," cried Mrs. Astor, "what makes you look so?—what is it?—what was it?"

"Where did you get this?" said he, sternly.

"At the apothecary's—I took it from that chest—examine 't, pray."

The doctor turned away with a groan, and approached his beautiful patient, now gasping and convulsed. He applied the most powerful antidotes, but without effect.

"I am dying," she cried, "I am dying—I am poisoned— but oh, doctor, save me—save me—let me see him, if I must die—let me see him again;" and she held out her hands imploringly to Mrs. Astor, who was in a state little short of distraction.

"Only tell me, if you mean Mr. Hall."

"Who should I mean but Augustus?" she cried. "Perhaps in death he may forgive me."

The doctor made a motion that her request should be complied with, and a messenger was despatched.

What an awful scene was presented, when he entered that chamber of death! Was that the idol of his young heart, the morning star of his manhood; she, who lay livid, writhing and raving there? Her long, dark hair hung in dishevelled masses over her neck and arms, her large black eyes were fearfully dilated, and full of that unutterable agony which makes the spirit quail before the might of human suffering. Cold sweat-drops gleamed on her marble brow, and her hands were damp with that dew which no morning sunbeam can ever exhale.

"Almighty Father!" exclaimed Mr. Hall, "what a sight is this!"

The sound of that voice had the power to check the ravings of delirium. She shrieked, and stretched out her arms towards him, who sunk kneeling by the bedside, covering his face with his hands, to shut out the appalling spectacle.

"Forgive me," she cried, in hollow and altered accents— 'Augustus, you are terribly avenged—I loved you, even when I left you for another. Oh! pray for me to that great and dreadful God, who is consuming me, to have mercy on me hereafter."

He did pray, but it was in spirit, his lips could not articulate; but his uplifted hands and streaming eyes called down pardon and peace on the dying penitent. The reason, that had flashed out for a moment, rekindled by memory and passion, was now gone for ever. All the rest was but the striving of mortal pain, the rending asunder of body and soul. In a short time all was over, and the living were left to read one of the most tremendous lessons on the vanity of beauty, and the frailty of life, mortality could offer in all its gloomy annals.

"This is no place for you, now," said the doctor, taking Mr. Hall's arm, and drawing him into another apartment, where, secure from intrusion, he could be alone with God and his own heart. There was another duty to perform—to investigate the mystery that involved this horrible tragedy. The apothecary was summoned, who, after recovering from his first consternation, recollected that a short time before, he had sold a quantity of corrosive sublimate to a little black girl, according to her mistress's orders. The servants were called for examination, and Dinah was pointed out as the culprit—Dinah, the imputed destroyer of the mirror, whose terror was now deemed the result of conscious guilt. Mrs. Astor vehemently protested she had never sent her, that it was the blackest falsehood; and Dinah, though she told the whole truth, how Mary had forbid her telling it was for her, and she merely used her mistress's name on that account, gained no belief. The chambermaid, who had found the paper and put it in the chest, withheld her testimony, fearing she might be implicated in the guilt. Everything tended to deepen the evidence against Dinah. The affair of the broken looking-glass was revived. She had been heard to say, after her memorable flagellation, that she wished her mistress was dead, that she would kill her if she could; and many other expressions, the result of a smarting back and a wounded spirit, were brought up against her. It was a piteous thing to see the fright, and hear the pleadings of the wretched girl: "Oh! don't send me to jail—don't hang me—send for Miss Mary," she repeated, wringing her hands, and rolling her eyes like a poor animal whom the hunters have at bay. But to jail she was sent—for who could doubt her crime, or pity her after witnessing its terrific consequences?—a damp, dreary prison-house, where, seated on a pallet of straw, she was left to brood day after day over her accumulated wrongs, hopeless of sympathy or redress. Let those who consider a *white lie* a venial offence, who look upon deception as necessary to the happiness and harmony of society, reflect on the consequences of Mary Ellis's moral delinquency, and tremble at the view.   She had not done more than a thousand others have done, and are daily doing; and yet what was the result?   The soul of the lovely, the erring, and the unprepared had been sent shuddering into eternity, a household made wretched, the innocent condemned, a neighbourhood thrown into consternation and gloom.   Had Mary confessed her negligence to Margaret, instead of telling an unnecessary and untempted falsehood, a warning message could have then been easily sent back, and the wide-spread ruin prevented.   There is no such thing as a *white lie;* they are all black as the blackest shades of midnight; and no fuller on earth can whiten them.

When Mrs. Astor had recovered from the shock of these events in a sufficient degree, she wrote to Mary a detailed account, begging her and Margaret to return immediately, and cheer the home which now seemed so desolate.   The letter was long in reaching her, for the travellers were taking a devious course, and could leave behind them no precise directions. Mary was in one of her gayest, brightest humours, when she received the epistle.   She was putting on some new ornaments, which Charles had presented to her, and he was looking over her shoulder at the fair image reflected in the glass, whose brow was lighted up with the triumph of conscious beauty.

"I look shockingly ugly to-day," said she, with a smile that belied her words.

"You tell stories with such a grace," replied her flattering husband, "I am afraid we shall be in love with falsehood."

"A letter from our dear Mrs. Astor; open it, Charles, while I clasp this bracelet; and read it aloud, then Margaret and I both can hear it."

Before Charles had read one page, Mary sunk down at his feet, rending the air with hysterical screams.   Her husband, who was totally unaware of the terrible agency she had had in the affair, raised her in indescribable alarm.   Her own wild expressions, however, revealed the truth, which Margaret's shivering lips confirmed.

"Oh! had you told me but the *truth,*" cried Margaret, raising her prayerful eyes and joined hands to heaven—"how simple, how easy it had been—Charles, Charles," added she, with startling energy, "praise not this rash, misguided girl, for the grace with which she *lies*—I will not recall the word. By the worth of your own soul and hers, teach her, that as there is a God above, he requires truth in the inward heart."

Charles trembled at the solemnity of the adjuration; and conscience told him, that all the agonies his wife suffered, and all the remorse which was yet to be her portion, were just. Margaret sought the solitude of her chamber, and there, on her knees, she endeavoured to find calmness. The image of Mr. Hall, mourning over the death-bed of her once so madly loved, the witness of her expiring throes, the receiver of her last repentant sigh rose, between her and her Creator. Then, ▲ that radiant face, that matchless form, which had so lately excited a pang of envy, even in *her* pure heart, now blasted by consuming poison, and mouldering in the cold grave; how awful was the thought, and how fearful the retribution! She, whose vain heart had by falsehood endangered the very existence of another, was the victim of the very vice that had blackened her own spirit. Yes! there is retribution even in this world.

Mary returned, but how changed from the gay and blooming bride! Her cheek was pale, and her eye heavy. She hastened to repair the only wrong now capable of anyremedy. The prison doors of poor Dinah were thrown open, and her innocence declared: but could the long and lonely days and nights spent in that weary, gloomy abode be blotted out? Could the pangs of cold, shuddering fear, the dream of the gallows, the rope, the hangman's grasp round the gurgling throat, the dark coffin seat, the scoffing multitude, be forgotten? No!—Dinah's spirit was broken, for though her skin was black, there was sensibility and delicacy too beneath her ebon colouring. Could Mary bring back the gladness that once pervaded the dwelling of Mrs. Astor? Everything there was changed. The room in which Mrs. St. Henry died was closed, for it was haunted by too terrible remembrances. Bitterly did Mary mourn over the grave of her victim; but she could not recall her by her tears. No remorse could open the gates of the tomb, or reclothe with beauty and bloom the ruins of life.

Margaret, the true, the pure-hearted and upright Margaret, was not destined, like Mary, to gather the thorns and briers of existence. Long did the fragrance of *her* roses last, for she had not plucked them with too rash a hand. She and Mr. Hall again met. The moral sympathy that had drawn them together, was not weakened by the tragic event that had intervened; it had rather strengthened through suffering and sorrow. Mr. Hall could never forget the death scene of Laura

112

St. Henry. The love expressed for him at a moment when
all earthly dissimulation was over had inexpressibly affected
him. Her unparalleled sufferings seemed an expiation for her
broken faith. It was at her grave that he and Margaret first
met after their sad separation, when the falling shades of
evening deepened the solemnity of the scene. Sorrow, sympathy, devotion, and truth, form a holy groundwork for love;
and when once the temple is raised on such a foundation, the
winds and waves may beat against it in vain. Mr. Hall found
by his own experience, that the bruised heart can be healed,
for Margaret's hand poured oil and balm on its wounds. He
could repose on her faith as firmly as on the rock which ages
have planted. He knew that she loved him, and felt it due
to her happiness as well as his own, to ask her to be the companion of his pilgrimage. If they looked back upon the clouds
that had darkened their morning, it was without self-reproach,
and remembrance gradually lost its sting. Who will say she
was not happier than Mary, who carried in her bosom, through
life, that which "biteth like a serpent, and stingeth like an
adder?"

ABYSSINIAN NEOPHYTE.

ADELLAN, an Abyssinian youth, approached one of those consecrated buildings, which crown almost every hill of his native country. Before entering, he drew off his shoes, and gave them in charge to a servant, that he might not soil the temple of the Lord, with the dust of the valley; then bending down, slowly and reverentially, he pressed his lips to the threshold, performed the same act of homage to each post of the door, then passed into the second division of the church, within view of the curtained square, answering to the mysterious *holy of holies* in the Jewish temple. He gazed upon the pictured saints that adorned the walls, long and earnestly, when, kneeling before them, he repeated, with deep solemnity, his customary prayers. He rose, looked towards the mystic veil, which no hand but that of the priest was permitted to raise, and anticipated with inexplicable emotions the time when, invested with the sacred dignity of that office, he might devote himself exclusively to Heaven. From early childhood, Adellan had been destined to the priesthood. His first years were passed mid the stormy scenes of war, for his father was soldier, fighting those bloody battles, with which the province of Tigre had been more than once laid waste. Then followed the dreadful discipline of famine, for the destroying locusts, the scourge of the country, had followed up the desolation of war, and year succeeding year, gleaned the last hope of man. The parents of Adellan fled from these scenes of devastation, crossed the once beautiful and fertile banks of the Tacazze, and sought refuge in the ample monastery of Walduba, where

(175)

a brother of his father then resided. Here, he was placed entirely under the protection of his uncle, for his father, sickened with the horrors he had witnessed, and loathing the ties which were once so dear to him, recrossed his native stream, became a gloomy monk in another convent, where, with several hundred of his brethren, he soon after perished a victim to those barbarities, which had robbed him of all that gave value to life. Adellan had never known the joys of childhood. The greenness and bloom of spring had been blotted from his existence. Famine had hollowed his boyish cheek, and fear and distrust chilled and depressed his young heart. After entering the convent of Walduba, where all his physical wants were supplied, the roundness and elasticity of health were restored to his limbs, but his cheek was kept pale by midnight vigils, and long and painful fastings. The teacher, whom his uncle placed over him, was severe and exacting. He gave him no relaxation by day, and the stars of night witnessed his laborious tasks. He was compelled to commit lessons to memory, in a language which he did not then understand, a drudgery from which every ardent mind must recoil. Yet, such was his thirst for knowledge, that he found a pleasure, even in this, that sweetened his toils. All the strains of the devout Psalmist were familiar to his lips, but they were in an *unknown tongue*, for in this manner are the youth of those benighted regions taught. Often, when gazing on the magnificent jewelry of a tropical sky, shining down on the darkness and solitude of night, had he unconsciously repeated the words of the royal penitent—"The heavens declare the glory of God. The firmament showeth his handy work." He understood not their meaning, but the principle of immortality was striving within him, and every star that gemmed the violet canopy, seemed to him eye-beams of that all-seeing Divinity he then darkly adored.

Adellan left the enclosure of the church, and lingered beneath the shade of the cedars, whose trunks supported the roof, and thus formed a pleasant colonnade sheltered from the sun and the rain. Beautiful was the prospect that here stretched itself around him. All the luxuriance of a mountainous country, constantly bathed with the dews of heaven, and warmed by the beams of a vertical sun, was richly unfolded. Odoriferous perfumes, wafted from the forest trees, and exhaled from the roses, jessamines, and wild blossoms, with which the fields were covered, scented the gale. Borne from afar, the fragrance of Judea's balm mingled with the incense of the flowers and the richer breath of the myrrh. A cool stream murmured near, where those who came up to worship, were accustomed to perform their ablutions and purifying rites, in conformance with the ancient Levitical law. Wherever Adellan turned his eyes, he beheld some object associated with the ceremonies of his austere religion. In that consecrated stream he had bathed, he had made an altar beneath every spreading tree, and every rock had witnessed his prostrations. He thought of the unwearied nature of his devotions, and pride began to swell his heart. He knew nothing of that meek and lowly spirit, that humiliation of soul, which marks the followers of a crucified Redeemer. He had been taught to believe that salvation was to be found in the observance of outward forms, but never had been led to purify the inner temple so as to make it a meet residence for a holy God.

Near the close of the day, he again walked forth, meditating on his contemplated journey to Jerusalem, the holy city, where he was not only to receive the remission of his own sins, but even for seven generations yet unborn, according to the superstitious belief of his ancestors. He was passing a low, thatched dwelling, so lost in his own meditations, as scarcely to be aware of its vicinity, when a strain of low, sweet music, rose like a stream of "rich distilled perfumes." Woman's softer accents mingled with a voice of manly melody and strength ; and as the blending strains stole by his ear, he paused, convinced that the music he heard was an act of adoration to God, though he understood not the language in which it was uttered. The door of the cabin was open, and he had a full view of the group near the entrance. A man, dressed in a foreign costume, whose prevailing colour was black, sat just within the shade of the cedars that sheltered the roof. Adellan immediately recognised the pale face of the European, and an instinctive feeling of dislike and suspicion urged him to turn away. There was something, however, in the countenance of the stranger that solicited and obtained more than a passing glance. There was beauty in the calm, thoughtful features, the high marble brow, the mild devotional dark eye, and the soft masses of sable heir that fell somewhat neglected over his lofty temples. There was a tranquillity, a peace, an elevation diffused over that pallid face, which was reflected back upon the heart of the beholder : a kind of moon-

light brightness, communicating its own peculiar sweetness
and quietude to every object it shone upon. Seated near him,
and leaning over the arm of his chair, was a female, whose
slight delicate figure, and dazzlingly fair complexion, gave her
a supernatural appearance to the unaccustomed eye of the
dark Abyssinian. Her drooping attitude and fragile frame
appealed at once to sympathy and protection, while her placid
eyes, alternately lifted to heaven and turned towards him on
whose arm she leaned, were expressive not only of meekness
and submission, but even of holy rapture. A third figure
belonged to this interesting group : that of an infant girl,
about eighteen months old, who, seated on a straw matting, at
the feet of her parents, raised her cherub head as if in the act
of listening, and tossed back her flaxen ringlets with the playful grace of infancy.

Adellan had heard that a Christian missionary was in the
neighbourhood of Adorva, and he doubted not that he now
beheld one whom he had been taught to believe his most
dangerous enemy. Unwilling to remain longer in his vicinity,
he was about to pass on, when the stranger arose and addressed
him in the language of his country. Surprised at the salutation, and charmed, in spite of himself, with the mild courtesy
of his accents, Adellan was constrained to linger. The fair-
haired lady greeted him with a benign smile, and the little
child clapped its hands as if pleased with the novelty and
grace of his appearance ; for though the hue of the olive dyed
his cheek, his features presented the classic lineaments of
manly beauty, and though the long folds of his white robe
veiled the outlines of his figure, he was formed in the finest
model of European symmetry. The missionary spoke to him
of his country, of the blandness of the climate, the magnifi-
cence of the trees, the fragrance of the air, till Adellan forgot
his distrust, and answered him with frankness and interest.
Following the dictates of his own ardent curiosity, he questioned the missionary with regard to his name, his native
country, and his object in coming to his own far land. He
learned that his name was M——, that he came from the
banks of the Rhine to the borders of the Nile, and, following
its branches, had found a resting-place near the waters of the
beautiful Tacazze.

" And why do you come to this land of strangers ?" asked
the abrupt Abyssinian.

" I came as an humble servant of my divine Master," replied

the missionary, meekly; "as a messenger of 'glad tidings of great joy,' to all who will receive me, and as a friend and brother, even to those who may persecute and revile me."

"What tidings can you bring us," said Adellan, haughtily, "that our priests and teachers can not impart to us?"

"I bring my credentials with me," answered Mr. M——, and taking a Testament, translated into the Amharic language, he offered it to Adellan; but he shrunk back with horror, and refused to open it.

"I do not wish for your books," said he; "keep them. We are satisfied with our own. Look at our churches. They stand on every hill, far as your eye can reach. See that stream that winds near your dwelling. There we wash away the pollution of our souls. I fast by day, I watch by night. The saints hear my prayers, and the stars bear witness to my penances. I am going to the holy city, where I shall obtain remission for all my sins, and those of generations yet unborn. I shall return holy and happy."

Mr. M—— sighed, while the youth rapidly repeated his claims to holiness and heaven.

"You believe that God is a spirit," said he; "and the worship that is acceptable in his eyes, must be spiritual also. In vain is the nightly vigil and the daily fast, unless the soul is humbled in his eyes. We may kneel till the rock is worn by our prostrations, and torture the flesh till every nerve is wakened to agony, but we can no more work out our own salvation by such means, than our feeble hands can create a new heaven and a new earth, or our mortal breath animate the dust beneath our feet, with the spirit of the living God."

The missionary spoke with warmth. His wife laid her gentle hand on his arm. There was something in the glance of the young Abyssinian that alarmed her. But the spirit of the martyr was kindled within him, and would not be quenched.

"See," said he, directing the eye of the youth towards the neighbouring hills, now clothed in the purple drapery of sunset; "as sure as those hills now stand, the banner of the cross shall float from their summits, and tell to the winds of heaven the triumphs of the Redeemer's kingdom. Ethiopia shall stretch out her sable hands unto God, and the farthest isles of the ocean behold the glory of his salvation."

Adellan looked into the glowing face of the missionary, remembered the cold and gloomy countenance of his religious teacher, and wondered at the contrast. But his prejudices were unshaken, and his pride rose up in rebellion against the man who esteemed him an idolater.

"Come to us again," said the missionary, in a subdued tone, as Adellan turned to depart; "let us compare our different creeds, by the light of reason and revelation, and see what will be the result."

"Come to us again," said the lady, in Adellan's native ongue; and her soft, low voice sounded sweet in his ears, as the fancied accents of the virgin mother. That night, as he sat in his lonely chamber, at the convent, conning his task in the stillness of the midnight hour, the solemn words of the missionary, his inspired countenance, the ethereal form of his wife, and the cherub face of that fair child, kept floating in his memory. He was angry with himself at the influence they exercised. He resolved to avoid his path, and to hasten his departure to Jerusalem, where he could be not only secure from his arts, but from the legions of the powers of darkness.

*   *   *   *   *   *   *   *   *   *

Months passed away. The humble cabin of the missionary was gradually thronged with those who came from curiosity, or better motives, to hear the words of one who came from such a far country. His pious heart rejoiced in the hope, that the shadows of idolatry which darkened their religion would melt away before the healing beams of the Sun of Righteousness. But he looked in vain for the stately figure of the young Adellan. His spirit yearned after the youth, and whenever he bent his knees at the altar of his God, he prayed for his conversion, with a kind of holy confidence that his prayer would be answered. At length he once more presented himself before them, but so changed they could scarcely recognise his former lineaments. His face was haggard and emaciated, his hair had lost its raven brightness, and his garments were worn and soiled with dust. He scarcely answered the anxious inquiries of Mr. M——, but sinking into a seat, and covering his face with his hands, large tears, gathering faster and faster, glided through his fingers, and rained upon his knees. Mary, the sympathizing wife of the missionary, wept in unison; but she did not limit her sympathy to tears, she gave him water to wash, and food to eat, and it was not until he rested his weary limbs, that they sought to learn the history of his sufferings. It would be tedious to detail them at length, though he had indeed experienced "a sad variety of woe." He had commenced his journey under the guidance and protection of a man in whose honour he placed unlimited confidence, had been deceived and betrayed, sold as a slave, and, though he had escaped this degradation, he had been exposed to famine and nakedness, and the sword.

"I have been deserted by man," said Adellan; "the saints have turned a deaf ear to my prayers; I have come to you to learn if there is a power in *your* Christianity to heal a wounded spirit, and to bind up a broken heart."

The missionary raised his eyes in gratitude to Heaven.

"The Spirit of the Lord God is upon me," cried he, repeating the language of the sublimest of the prophets: "because the Lord hath anointed me to preach good tidings unto the meek; he hath sent me to bind up the broken-hearted, to proclaim liberty to the captive, and the opening of the prison to them that are bound."

"Blessed are they that mourn, for they shall be comforted," repeated Mary, softly; and never were promises of mercy pronounced in a sweeter voice. Afflictions had humbled the proud spirit of Adellan. But his was not the humility of the Christian. It was rather a gloomy misanthropy, that made him turn in loathing from all he had once valued, and to doubt the efficacy of those forms and penances, in which he had wasted the bloom of his youth, and the morning strength of his manhood. But he no longer rejected the proffered kindness of his new friends. He made his home beneath their roof. The Testament he had formerly refused, he now gratefully received, and studied it with all the characteristic ardour of his mind. Persevering as he was zealous, as patient in investigation as he was quick of apprehension, he compared text with text, and evidence with evidence, till the prejudices of education yielded to the irresistible force of conviction. When once his understanding had received a doctrine, he cherished it as a sacred and eternal truth, immutable as the word of God, and immortal as his own soul.

He now went down into the hitherto untravelled chambers of his own heart, and, throwing into their darkest recesses the full blaze of revelation, he shuddered to find them infested by inmates more deadly than the serpent of the Nile. Passions, of whose existence he had been unconscious, rose up from their hiding places, and endeavoured to wrap him in their giant folds. Long and fearful was the struggle, but

Adellan opposed to their power the shield of Faith and the sword of the Spirit, and at last came off conqueror, and laid down his spoils at the foot of the cross. The missionary wept over him, "tears such as angels shed." "Now," exclaimed he, "I am rewarded for all my privations, and my hitherto unavailing toils. Oh! Adellan, now the friend and brother of my soul, I feel something like the power of prophecy come over me, when I look forward to your future destiny. The time will shortly come, when you will stand in the high places of the land, and shake down the strong holds of ancient idolatry and sin. The temples, so long desecrated by adoration of senseless images, shall be dedicated to the worship of the living God. Sinners, who so long have sought salvation in the purifying waters of the stream, shall turn to the precious fountain of the Redeemer's blood. Oh! glorious, life-giving prospect! They who refuse to listen to the pale-faced stranger, will hearken to the accents of their native hills. Rejoice, my beloved Mary! though I may be forced to bear back that fading frame of yours to a more congenial clime, our Saviour will not be left without a witness, to attest his glory, and confirm his power."

To fulfil this prophecy became the ruling desire of Adellan's life. He longed to liberate his deluded countrymen from the thraldom of that superstition to which he himself had served such a long and gloomy apprenticeship. He longed, too, for some opportunity of showing his gratitude to his new friends. But there is no need of signal occasions to show what is passing in the heart. His was of a transparent texture, and its emotions were visible as the pebbles that gleam through the clear waters of the Tacazze. The beautiful child of the missionary was the object of his tenderest love. He would carry it in his arms for hours, through the wild groves that surrounded their dwelling, and, gathering for it the choicest productions of nature, delight in its smiles and infantine caresses. Sometimes, as he gazed on the soft azure of its eyes, and felt its golden ringlets playing on his cheek, he would clasp it to his bosom and exclaim, "Of such is the kingdom of heaven."

Mary idolized her child, and Adellan's great tenderness for it, inexpressibly endeared him to her heart. She loved to see the fair face of her infant leaning against the dark cheek of Adellan, and its flaxen locks mingling with his jetty hair. One evening, as it fell asleep in his arms, he was alarmed at the scarlet brightness of its complexion, and the burning heat of its skin. He carried it to its mother. It was the last time the cherub ever slumbered on his bosom. It never again lifted up its head, but faded away like a flower scorched by a noonday sun.

Day and night Adellan knelt by the couch of the dying infant, and prayed in agony for its life; yet even in the intensity of his anguish, he felt how sublime was the resignation of its parents. They wept, but no murmur escaped their lips. They prayed, but every prayer ended with the submissive ejaculation of their Saviour, "Not our will, O Father! but thine be done." And when the sweet, wistful eyes were at last closed in death, and the waxen limbs grew stiff and cold, when Adellan could not restrain the bitterness of his grief, still the mourners bowed ther heads and cried, "The Lord gave, the Lord taketh away—blessed be the name of the Lord."

Adellan had witnessed the stormy sorrow of his country-women, whose custom it is to rend their hair, and lacerate their faces with their nails, and grovel, shrieking, in the dust; but never had his heart been so touched as by the resignation of this Christian mother. But, though she murmured not, she was stricken by the blow, and her fragile frame trembled beneath the shock. Her husband felt that she leaned more heavily on his arm, and though she smiled upon him as wont, the smile was so sad, it often brought tears into his eyes. At length she fell sick, and the missionary saw her laid upon the same bed on which his infant had died. Now, indeed, it might be said that the hand of God was on him. She, the bride of his youth, the wife of his fondest affections, who had given up all the luxuries of wealth, and the tender indulgences of her father's home, for the love of him and her God; who had followed him not only with meekness, but joy, to those benighted regions, that she might share and sweeten his labours, and join to his, her prayers and her efforts for the extension of the Redeemer's kingdom; she, whose presence had been able to transform their present lowly and lonely dwelling into a place lovely as the Garden of Eden—could he see *her* taken from him, and repeat, from his heart, as he had done over the grave of his only child, " Father, thy will be done ?"

Bitter was the conflict, but the watchful ear of Adellan again heard the same low, submissive accents, which were so lately breathed over his lost darling. Here, too, Adellan acted a brother's part; but female care was requisite, and this

his watchful tenderness supplied. He left them for a while,
and returned with a young maiden, whose olive complexion,
graceful figure, and long braided locks, declared her of Abyssinian birth. Her voice was gentle, and her step light, when
she approached the bed of the sufferer. Ozora, for such was
the name of the maiden, was a treasure in the house of sickness. Mary's languid eye followed her movements, and often
brightened with pleasure, while receiving her sympathizing
attentions. In her hours of delirious agony, she would hold
her hand, and call her sister in the most endearing tone, and
ask her how she had found her in that land of strangers.
Sometimes she would talk of the home of her childhood, and
imagine she heard the green leaves of her native bowers rus-
tling in the gale. Then she thought she was wandering through
the groves of Paradise, and heard the angel voice of her child
singing amid the flowers.

Ozora was familiar with all the medicinal arts and cooling
drinks of her country. She possessed not only native gentleness, but skill and experience as a nurse. She was an orphan,
and the death-bed of her mother had witnessed her filial tenderness and care. She was an idolater, but she loved Adellan,
and for his sake would gladly embrace the faith of the European. Adellan was actuated by a twofold motive in bringing
her to the sick-bed of Mary; one was, that she might exercise a healing influence on the invalid, and another, that she
might witness the triumphs of Christian faith over disease,
sorrow, and death. But Mary was not doomed to make her
grave in the stranger's land. The fever left her burning veins,
and her mind recovered its wonted clearness. She was able
to rise from her couch, and sit in the door of the cabin, and
feel the balmy air flowing over her pallid brow.

She sat thus one evening, supported by the arm of her husband, in the soft light of the sinking sunbeams. Adellan and
her gentle nurse were seated near. The eyes of all were simultaneously turned to a small green mound, beneath the shade
of a spreading cedar, and they thought of the fairy form that
had so often sported around them in the twilight hour.

"Oh! not there," cried Mary, raising her glistening eyes
from that lonely grave to heaven—"Not there must we seek
our child. Even now doth her glorified spirit behold the face
of our Father in heaven She is folded in the arms of Him,
who, when on earth, took little children to his bosom and
blessed them And I, my beloved husband—a little while

and ye shall see my face no more. Though the Almighty has raised me from that couch of pain, there is something tells me," continued she, laying her hand on her heart, "that my days are numbered; and when my ashes sleep beside that grassy bed, mourn not for me, but think that I have gone to my Father and your Father, to my God and your God." Then, leaning her head on her husband's shoulder, she added, in a low trembling voice—"to my child and your child."

It was long before Mr. M—— spoke; at length he turned to Adellan, and addressed him in the Amharic language: "My brother! it must be that I leave you. The air of her native climes may revive this drooping flower. I will bear her back to her own home, and, if God wills it, I will return and finish the work he has destined me to do."

Mary clasped her hands with irrepressible rapture as he uttered these words; then, as if reproaching herself for the momentary selfishness, she exclaimed, "And leave the poor Abyssinians!"

"I will leave them with Adellan," he answered, "whom I firmly believe God has chosen, to declare his unsearchable riches to this portion of the Gentile world. The seed that has been sown has taken root, and the sacred plant will spring up and increase, till the birds of the air nestle in its branches, and the beasts of the forest lie down beneath its shade. Adellan, does your faith waver?"

"Never," answered the youth, with energy, "but the arm of my brother is weak. Let me go with him on his homeward journey, and help him to support the being he loves. I shall gather wisdom from his lips, and knowledge from the glimpse of a Christian land. Then shall I be more worthy to minister to my brethren the word of life."

A sudden thought flashed into the mind of the missionary. "And would you, Adellan," asked he, "would you indeed wish to visit our land, and gain instruction in our institutions of learning, that you might return to enrich your countr with the best treasures of our own? You are very young, and might be spared awhile now, that you may be fitted for more extensive usefulness hereafter."

Adellan's ardent eye told more expressively than words could utter, the joy which filled his soul at this proposition. "Too happy to follow you," cried he; "how can I be sufficiently grateful for an added blessing?"

Ozora, who had listened to the conversation, held in her

own language, with intense interest, here turned her eyes upon
Adellan, with a look of piercing reproach, and suddenly rising,
left the cabin.

"Poor girl!" exclaimed Mary, as Adellan, with a saddened
countenance, followed the steps of Ozora; "how tenderly has
she nursed me, and what is the recompense she meets? We
are about to deprive her of the light that gladdens her exist-
nce. She has not yet anchored her hopes on the Rock of
Ages, and where else can the human heart find refuge, when
the wild surges of passion sweep over it!"

"Adellan is in the hands of an all-wise and all-controlling
power," answered the missionary, thoughtfully; "the tears
of Ozora may be necessary to prove the strength of his resolution; if so, they will not fall in vain."

A few weeks after, everything being in readiness for the
departure of the missionary and his family, he bade farewell
to the Abyssinians, who crowded round his door to hear his
parting words. He took them with him to the hillside, and,
under the shadow of the odoriferous trees, and the covering of
the heavens, he addressed them with a solemnity and fervour
adapted to the august temple that surrounded him. His deep
and sweet-toned voice rolled through the leafy colonnades and
verdant aisles, like the rich notes of an organ in some ancient
cathedral. The Amharic language, soft and musical in itself,
derived new melody from the lips of Mr. M——.

"And now," added he, in conclusion, "I consign you
to the guardianship of a gracious and long-suffering God.
Forget not the words I have just delivered unto you, for
remember they will rise up in judgment against you in that
day when we shall meet face to face before the bar of eternal
justice. This day has the Gospel been preached in your ears.
Every tree that waves its boughs over your heads, every flower
that embalms the atmosphere, and every stream that flows
down into the valley, will bear witness that the hallowed name
of the Redeemer has been breathed in these shades, and promises of mercy so sweet that angels stoop down from heaven
to listen to the strains that have been offered, free, free as the
very air you inhale. I go, my friends, but should I never
return, this place will be for ever precious to my remembrance.
It contains the ashes of my child. That child was yielded up
in faith to its Maker, and the spot where it sleeps is, therefore, holy ground. Will ye not guard it from the foot of the
stranger, and the wild beast of the mountain? Let the flower

of the hills bloom ungathered upon it, and the dew of heaven
rest untrodden on its turf, till he, who is the resurrection and
the life, shall appear, and the grave give back its trust."

He paused, overpowered by the strength of his emotions,
and the sobs of many of his auditors attested the sympathy of
these untutored children of nature. He came down from the
elevated position on which he had been standing, and taking
the hand of Adellan, led him to the place he had just occupied. The people welcomed him with shouts, for it was the
first time he had presented himself in public, to declare the
change in his religious creed, and such was the character he
had previously obtained for sanctity and devotion, they looked
upon him with reverence, notwithstanding his youth. He
spoke at first with diffidence and agitation, but gathering confidence as he proceeded, he boldly and eloquently set forth
and defended the faith he had embraced. That young, enthusiastic preacher would have been a novel spectacle to an European audience, as well as that wild, promiscuous assembly.
His long, white robes, girded about his waist, according to the
custom of his country, his black, floating hair, large, lustrous
eyes, and dark but now glowing complexion, formed a striking
contrast with the sable garments, pallid hue, and subdued
expression of the European minister. They interrupted him
with tumultuous shouts, and when he spoke of his intended
departure and attempted to bid them farewell, their excitement became so great, he was compelled to pause, for his voice
strove in vain to lift itself above the mingled sounds of grief
and indignation.

"I leave you, my brethren," cried he, at length, "only to
return more worthy to minister unto you. My brother will
open my path to the temples of religion and knowledge. He
needs my helping arm in bearing his sick through the lonely
desert and over the deep sea—what do I not owe him? I
was a stranger and he took me in; I was naked and he clothed
me; hungry and he fed me, thirsty and he gave me drink;
and more than all, he has given me to eat the bread of heaven,
and water to drink from the wells of salvation. Oh! next to
God, he is my best friend and yours."

The shades of night began to fall, before the excited crowd
were all dispersed, and Mr. M——, and Adellan were left in
tranquillity. Mary had listened to the multitudinous sounds,
with extreme agitation. She reproached herself for allowing
her husband to withdraw from the scene of his missionary

labours out of tenderness for her. She thought it would be better for her to die and be laid by her infant's grave, than the awakened minds of these half Pagan, half Jewish people, be allowed to relapse into their ancient idolatries. When the clods of the valley were once laid upon her breast, her slumbers would not be less sweet because they were of the dust of a foreign land.

Thus she reasoned with her husband, who, feeling that her life was a sacred trust committed to his care, and that it was his first duty to guard it from danger, was not moved from his purpose by her tearful entreaties. They were to depart on the following morning.

That night Adellan sat with Ozora by the side of a fountain, that shone like a bed of liquid silver in the rising moonbeams. Nature always looks lovely in the moonlight, but it seemed to the imagination of Adellan he had never seen her clothed with such resplendent lustre as at this moment, when every star shone with a farewell ray, and every bough, as it sparkled in the radiance, whispered a melancholy adieu.

Ozora sat with her face bent over the fountain, which lately had often been fed by her tears. Her hair, which she had been accustomed to braid with oriental care, hung dishevelled over her shoulders. Her whole appearance presented the abandonment of despair. Almost every night since his contemplated departure, had Adellan followed her to that spot, and mingled the holiest teachings of religion with the purest vows of love. He had long loved Ozora, but he had struggled with the passion, as opposed to that dedication of himself to heaven, he had contemplated in the gloom of his conventual life. Now enlightened by the example of the missionary, and the evangelical principles he had embraced, he believed Christianity sanctioned and hallowed the natural affections of the heart. He no longer tried to conquer his love, but to make it subservient to higher duties.

Mary, grieved at the sorrow of Ozora, would have gladly taken her with her, but Adellan feared her influence. He knew he would be unable to devote himself so entirely to the eternal truths he was one day to teach to others, if those soft and loving eyes were always looking into the depths of his heart, to discover their own image there. He resisted the proposition, and Mr. M—— applauded the heroic resolution. But now Adellan was no hero; he was a young, impassioned lover, and the bitterness of parting pressed heavily on his soul.

"Promise me, Ozora," repeated he, "that when I am gone, you will never return to the idolatrous worship you have abjured. Promise me, that you will never kneel to any but the one, invisible God, and that this blessed book, which I give you, as a parting pledge, shall be as a lamp to your feet and a light to your path. Oh! should you forget the faith you have vowed to embrace, and should I, when I come back to my country, find you an alien from God, I should mourn, I should weep tears of blood over your fall; but you could never be the wife of Adellan. The friend of his bosom must be a Christian."

"I cannot be a Christian," sobbed the disconsolate girl, "for I love you better than God himself, and I am still an idolater. Oh! Adellan, you are dearer to me than ten thousand worlds, and yet you are going to leave me."

The grief she had struggled to restrain, here burst its bounds. Like the unchastened daughters of those ardent climes, she gave way to the wildest paroxysms of agony. She threw herself on the ground, tore out her long raven locks, and startled the silence of night by her wild, hysterical screams. Adellan in vain endeavoured to soothe and restore her to reason; when, finding his caresses and sympathy worse than unavailing, he knelt down by her side, and lifting his hands above her head, prayed to the Almighty to forgive her for her sacrilegious love. As the stormy waves are said to subside, when the wing of the halcyon passes over them, so were the tempestuous emotions that raged in the bosom of this unhappy maiden, lulled into calmness by the holy breath of prayer. As Adellan continued his deep and fervent aspirations, a sense of the omnipresence, the omnipotence and holiness of God stole over her. She raised her weeping eyes, and as the moonbeams glittered on her tears, they seemed but the glances of his all-seeing eye. As the wind sighed through the branches, she felt as if *His* breath were passing by her, in mercy and in love. Filled with melting and penitential feelings, she lifted herself on her knees, by the side of Adellan, and softly whispered a response to every supplication for pardon.

"Oh! Father, I thank thee for this hour!" exclaimed Adellan, overpowered by so unlooked-for a change, and throwing his arms around her, he wept from alternate ecstasy and

113

sorrow. Let not the feelings of Adellan be deemed too refined
and exalted for the region in which he dwelt. From early
boyhood he had been kept apart from the companionship of
the ruder throng; his adolescence had been passed in the
shades of a convent, in study, and deep observation, and more
than all he was a Christian; and wherever Christianity sheds
its pure and purifying light, it imparts an elevation, a sub-
limity to the character and the language, which princes, un-
taught of God, may vainly emulate.

The morning sunbeam lighted the pilgrims on their way.
The slight and feeble frame of Mary was borne on a litter by
four sturdy Ethiopians. Seven or eight more accompanied to
rest them, when weary, and to bear Mr. M—— in the same
manner, when overcome by fatigue, for it was a long distance
to Massowak. Their journey led them through a desert wilderness, where they might vainly sigh for the shadow of the rock,
or the murmur of the stream. Adellan walked in silence by
the side of his friend. His thoughts were with the weeping
Ozora, and of the parting hour by the banks of the moon-
lighted fountain. Mary remembered the grave of her infant,
and wept, as she caught a last glimpse of the hill where she
had dwelt. The spirit of the missionary was lingering with
the beings for whose salvation he had laboured, and he made
a solemn covenant with his own soul, that he would return
with Adellan, if God spared his life, and leave his Mary under
the shelter of the paternal roof, if she indeed lived to behold
it. On the third day, Mr. M—— was overcome with such
excessive languor, he was compelled to be borne constantly by
the side of his wife, unable to direct, or to exercise any con-
trolling influence on his followers. Adellan alone, unwearied
and energetic, presided over all, encouraged, sustained, and
soothed. He assisted the bearers in upholding their burdens,
and whenever he put his shoulder to the litter, the invalids
immediately felt with what gentleness and steadiness they
were supported. When they reached the desert, and camels
were provided for the travellers, they were still often obliged
to exchange their backs for the litter, unable long to endure
the fatigue. Adellan was still unwilling to intrust his friends
to any guidance but his own. He travelled day after day
through the burning sands, animating by his example the exhausted slaves, and personally administering to the wants of
the sufferers. When they paused for rest or refreshment,
before he carried the cup to his own parched lips, he brought

it to theirs. It was his hand that bathed with water their feverish brows, and drew the curtain around them at night, when slumber shed its dews upon their eyelids. And often, in the stillness of the midnight, when the tired bearers and weary camels rested and slept after their toils, the voice of Adellan rose sweet and solemn in the loneliness of the desert, holding communion with the high and holy One who inhabiteth eternity.

There was a boy among the negro attendants, who was the object of Adellan's peculiar kindness. He seemed feeble and incapable of bearing long fatigue, and at the commencement of the journey Adellan urged him to stay behind, but he expressed so strong a desire to follow the good missionary, he could not refuse his request. He wore his face muffled in a handkerchief, on account of some natural deformity, a circumstance which exposed him to the derision of his fellow slaves, but which only excited the sympathy of the compassionate Adellan. Often, when the boy, panting and exhausted, would throw himself for breath on the hot sand, Adellan placed him on his own camel and compelled him to ride. And when they rested at night, and Adellan thought every one but himself wrapped in slumber, he would steal towards him, and ask him to tell him something out of God's book, that he, Adellan, had been reading. It was a delightful task to Adellan to pour the light of divine truth into the dark mind of this poor negro boy, and every moment he could spare from his friends was devoted to his instruction.

One evening, after a day of unusual toil and exertion, they reached one of those verdant spots, called the Oases of the desert; and sweet to the weary travellers was the fragrance and coolness of this green resting-place. They made their tent under the boughs of the flowering acacia, whose pure white blossoms diffused their odours even over the sandy waste they had passed. The date tree, too, was blooming luxuriantly there, and, more delicious than all, the waters of a fountain, gushing out of the rock, reminded them how God had provided for the wants of his ancient people in the wilderness. The missionary and his wife were able to lift their languid heads, and drink in the freshness of the balmy atmosphere All seemed invigorated and revived but the negro boy, who lay drooping on the ground, and refused the nourishment which the others eagerly shared.

"What is the matter, my boy?" asked Adellan, kindly,

and taking his hand in his, was struck by its burning heat. "You are ill," continued he, "and have not complained." He made a pallet for him under the trees, and they brought him a medicinal draught. Seeing him sink after a while in a deep sleep, Adellan's anxiety abated. But about midnight he was awakened by the moanings of the boy, and bending over him, laid his hand on his forehead. The sufferer opened his eyes, and gasped, "Water, or I die!" Adellan ran to the fountain, and brought the water immediately to his lips. Then kneeling down, he removed the muffling folds of the handkerchief from his face, and unbound the same from his head, that he might bathe his temples in the cooling stream. The moon shone as clearly and resplendently as when it beamed on Ozora's parting tears, and lighted up with an intense radiance the features of the apparently expiring negro. Adellan was astonished that no disfiguring traces appeared on the regular outline of his youthful face; his hair, too, instead of the woolly locks of the Ethiopian, was of shining length and profusion, and as Adellan's hand bathed his brow with water, he discovered beneath the jetty dye of his complexion the olive skin of the Abyssinian.

"Ozora!" exclaimed Adellan, throwing himself in agony by her side; "Ozora, you have followed me, but to die!"

"Forgive me, Adellan," cried she, faintly; "it was death to live without you; but oh! I have found everlasting life, in dying at your feet. Your prayers have been heard in the desert, and I die in the faith and the hope of a Christian."

Adellan's fearful cry had roused the slumberers of the tent. Mr. M——, and Mary, herself, gathering strength from terror, drew near the spot. What was her astonishment to behold her beloved nurse, supported in the arms of Adellan, and seemingly breathing out her last sighs! Every restorative was applied, but in vain. The blood was literally burning up in her veins.

This last fatal proof of her love and constancy wrung the heart of Adellan. He remembered how often he had seen her slender arms bearing the litter, her feet blistering in the sands; and when he knew, too, that it was for the love of him she had done this, he felt as if he would willingly lay down his life for hers. But when he saw her mind, clear and undimmed by the mists of disease, bearing its spontaneous testimony to the truth of that religion which reserves its most glorious triumphs for the dying hour, he was filled with rejoicing emotions.

"My Saviour found me in the wilderness," cried she, "while listening to the prayers of Adellan. His head was filled with dew, and his locks were heavy with the drops of night. Oh, Adellan, there is a love stronger than that which has bound my soul to yours. In the strength of that love I am willing ɔ resign you. I feel there is forgiveness even for me."

She paused, and lifting her eyes to heaven, with a serene expression, folded her hands on her bosom. The missionary saw that her soul was about to take its flight, and kneeling over her, his feeble voice rose in prayer and adoration. While the holy incense was ascending up to heaven, her spirit winged its upward way, so peacefully and silently, that Adellan still clasped her cold hand, unconscious that he was clinging to dust and ashes.

They made her grave beneath the acacia, whose blossoms were strewed over her dying couch. They placed a rude stone at the head, and the hand of Adellan carved upon it this simple, but sublime inscription, "I know that my Redeemer liveth." The name of *Ozora*, on the opposite side, was all the memorial left in the desert, of her whose memory was immortal in the bosom of her friends. But there was a grandeur in that lonely grave which no marble monument could exalt. It was the grave of a Christian:

"And angels with their silver wings o'ershade
The ground now sacred by her relics made."

It would be a weary task to follow the travellers through every step of their journey. Adellan still continued his unwearied offices to his grateful and now convalescent friends, but his spirit mourned for his lost Ozora. When, however, he set foot on Christian land, he felt something of the rapture that swelled the breast of Columbus on the discovery of a new world. It was, indeed, a new world to him, and almost realized his dreams of Paradise.

The friends of Mary and her husband welcomed him, as the guardian angel who had watched over their lives in the desert, at the hazard of his own; and Christians pressed forward to open their hearts and their homes to their Abyssinian brother. Mary, once more surrounded by the loved scenes of her youth, and all the appliances of kindred love, and all

the medicinal balms the healing art can furnish, slowly recovered her former strength.   All that female gratitude and
tenderness could do, she exerted to interest and enliven the
feelings of Adellan, when, after each day of intense study, he
returned to their domestic circle.   The rapidity with which
he acquired the German language was extraordinary.   He
found it, however, only a key, opening to him treasures of
unknown value.   Mr. M—— feared the effects of his excessive application, and endeavoured to draw him from his books
and studies.   He led him abroad amongst the works of nature,
and the wonders of art, and tried to engage him in the athletic
exercises the youth of the country delighted in.

Whatever Adellan undertook he performed with an ardour
which no obstacles could damp, no difficulties subdue.   Knowledge, purified by religion, was now the object of his existence; and, while it was flowing in upon his mind, from such
various sources, finding, instead of its capacities being filled,
that they were constantly enlarging and multiplying, and the
fountains, though overflowing, still undrained : and knowing
too, that it was only for a short time that his spirit could
drink in these immortal influences, and that through them he
was to fertilize and refresh, hereafter, the waste places of his
country, he considered every moment devoted to relaxation
alone, as something robbed from eternity.

One day, Adellan accompanied a number of young men
belonging to the institution in which he was placed, in an excursion for the collection of minerals.   Their path led them
through the wildest and most luxuriant country, through
scenes where nature rioted in all its virgin bloom ; yet, where
the eye glancing around, could discern the gilding traces of
art, the triumphs of man's creating hand.   Adellan, who beheld in every object, whether of nature or of art, the mani-
festation of God's glory, became lost in a trance of ecstasy.
He wandered from his companions.   He knelt down amid the
rocks, upon the green turf, and on the banks of the streams.
In every place he found an altar, and consecrated it with the
incense of prayer and of praise.   The shades of night fell
around him, before he was conscious that the sun had declined.
The dews fell heavy on his temples, that still throbbed with
the heat and the exertions of the day.   He returned chilled
and exhausted.   The smile of rapture yet lingered on his lips,
but the damps of death had descended with the dews of night,
and from that hour consumption commenced its slow but

certain progress. When his friends became aware of his danger, they sought by every possible means to ward off the fatal blow. Mr. M—— induced him to travel, that he might wean him from his too sedentary habits. He carried him with him, through the magnificent valleys of Switzerland, those valleys, embosomed in hills, on whose white and glittering summits Adellan imagined he could see the visible footprints of the Deity. "Up to the hills," he exclaimed, with the sweet singer of Israel, in a kind of holy rapture, "up to the hills do I lift mine eyes, from whence cometh my help." When returning, they lingered on the lovely banks of the Rhine, his devout mind, imbued with sacred lore, recalled "the green fields and still waters," where the Shepherd of Israel gathered his flock.

The languid frame of Adellan seemed to have gathered strength, and his friends rejoiced in their reviving hopes; but "He who seeth not as man seeth," had sent forth his messenger to call him to his heavenly home. Gentle was the summons, but Adellan knew the voice of his divine Master, and prepared to obey. One night, as he reclined in his easy chair, and Mr. M—— was seated near, he stretched out his hand towards him, with a bright and earnest glance: "My brother," said he, "I can now say from my heart, the will of God be done. It was hard to give up my beloved Abyssinians, but I leave them in the hands of One who is strong to deliver, and mighty to save. You, too, will return, when you have laid this wasted frame in its clay-cold bed."

"I made a vow unto my God," answered Mr. M——, "that I would see them again, and that vow shall not be broken. When they ask me the parting words of Adellan, tell me what I shall utter."

"Tell them," exclaimed Adellan, raising himself up, with an energy that was startling, and in a voice surprisingly clear, while the glow of sensibility mingled with the hectic fires that burned upon his cheek; "tell them that the only reflection that planted a thorn in my dying pillow, was the sorrow I felt that I was not permitted to declare to them once more, the eternal truths of the Gospel. Tell them, with the solemnities of death gathering around me, in the near prospect of judgment and eternity, I declare my triumphant faith in that religion your lips revealed unto me, that religion which was sealed by the blood of Jesus, and attested by the Spirit of Almighty God; and say, too, that had I ten thousand lives, and for every life ten thousand years to live, I should deem them all too short to devote to the glory of God, and the service of my Redeemer."

He sunk back exhausted in his chair, and continued, in a lower voice, "You will travel once more through the desert, but the hand of Adellan will no longer minister to the friend he loves. Remember him when you pass the grave of Ozora, and hallow it once more with the breath of prayer. She died for love of me, but she is gone to him who loved her *as man never loved.* Her spirit awaits my coming."

The last tear that ever dimmed the eye of Adellan here fell to the memory of Ozora. It seemed a parting tribute to the world he was about to leave. His future hours were gilded by anticipations of the happiness of heaven, and by visions of glory too bright, too holy for description. He died in the arms of the missionary, while the hand of Mary wiped from his brow the dews of dissolution. Their united tears embalmed the body of one, who, had he lived, would have been a burning and a shining light, in the midst of the dark places of the earth; one, who combined in his character, notwithstanding his youth and his country, the humility of the Publican, the ardour of Peter, the love of John, and the faith and zeal of the great Apostle of the Gentiles. Perhaps it should rather be said, with the reverence due to these holy evangelists and saints, that a large portion of their divine attributes animated the spirit of the Abyssinian Neophyte.

VILLAGE ANTHEM.

"WHAT is that bell ringing for?" asked Villeneuve of the waiter, who was leaving the room.

"For church," was the reply.

"For church! Oh! is it Sunday? I had forgotten it. I did not think there was a church in this little village."

"Yes, indeed," answered the boy, his village pride taking the alarm, "and a very handsome one, too. Just look out at that window, sir. Do you see that tall, white steeple, behind those big trees there? That is the church, and I know there is not a better preacher in the whole world than Parson Blandford. He was never pestered for a word yet, and his voice makes one feel so warm and tender about the heart, it does one good to hear him."

Villeneuve cast a languid glance through the window, from the sofa on which he was reclining, thinking that Parson Blandford was very probably some old hum-drum, puritanical preacher, whose nasal twang was considered melodious by the vulgar ears which were accustomed to listen to him. Dull as his present position was, he was resolved to keep it, rather than inflict upon himself such an intolerable bore. The boy, who had mounted his hobby, continued, regardless of the unpropitious countenance of his auditor.

"Then there is Miss Grace Blandford, his daughter, plays so beautifully on the organ! You never heard such music in your life. When she sits behind the red curtains, and you can't see anything but the edge of her white skirt below, I

can't help thinking there's an angel hid there; and when she
comes down and takes her father's arm, to walk out of church,
she looks like an angel, sure enough."

Villeneuve's countenance brightened.   Allowing for all the
hyperbole of ignorance, there were two positive things which
were agreeable in themselves—music and a young maiden.   He
ose from the sofa, threw aside his dressing-gown, called for
is coat and hat, and commanded the delighted boy to direct
nim to the church, the nearest way.   His guide, proud of
ushering in such a handsome and aristocratic-looking stranger,
conducted him to one of the most conspicuous seats in the
broad aisle, in full view of the pulpit and the orchestra, and
Villeneuve's first glance was towards the red curtains, which
were drawn so close, not even a glimpse of white was granted
to the beholder.   He smiled at his own curiosity.   Very likely
this angel of the village boy was a great red-faced, hard-handed
country girl, who had been taught imperfectly to thrum the
keys of an instrument, and consequently transformed by rustic
simplicity into a being of superior order.   No matter, any
kind of excitement was better than the ennui from which he
had been aroused.   A low, sweet, trembling prelude stole on
his ear.   "Surely," thought he, "no vulgar fingers press
those keys—that is the key-note of true harmony."   He listened, the sound swelled, deepened, rolled through the arch
of the building, and sank again with such a melting cadence,
the tears involuntarily sprang into his eyes.   Ashamed of his
emotions, he leaned his head on his hand, and yielded unseen
to an influence, which, coming over him so unexpectedly, had
all the force of enchantment.   The notes died away, then
swelled again in solemn accompaniment with the opening
hymn.   The hymn closed with the melodious vibrations of
the instrument, and for a few moments there was a most profound silence.

"The Lord is in his holy temple; let all the earth keep
silence before him:" uttered a deep, solemn voice.

Villeneuve raised his head and gazed upon the speaker.   He
was a man rather past the meridian of life, but wearing un-
marred the noblest attributes of manhood.   His brow was
unwrinkled, his piercing eye undimmed, and his tall figure
majestic and unbowed.   The sun inclined from the zenith, but
the light, the warmth, the splendour remained in all their
power, and the hearts of the hearers radiated that light and
warmth, till an intense glow pervaded the assembly, and the

opening words of the preacher seemed realized. Villeneuve was an Infidel; he looked upon the rites of Christianity as theatrical machinery, necessary, perhaps, towards carrying on the great drama of life, and when the springs were well adjusted and oiled, and the pulleys worked without confusion, and every appearance of art was kept successfully in the background, he was willing to sit and listen as he would to a fine actor when reciting the impassioned language of the stage. "This man is a very fine actor," was his first thought, "he knows his part well. It is astonishing, however, that he is willing to remain in such a limited sphere—with such an eye and voice—such flowing language and graceful elocution, he might make his fortune in any city. It is incomprehensible that he is content to linger in obscurity." Thus Villeneuve speculated, till his whole attention became absorbed in the sermon, which as a literary production was exactly suited to his fastidiously refined taste. The language was simple, the sentiments sublime. The preacher did not bring himself down to the capacities of his auditors, he lifted them to his, he elevated them, he spiritualized them. He was deeply read in the mysteries of the human heart, and he knew that however ignorant it might be of the truths of science and the laws of metaphysics, it contained many a divine spark which only required an eliciting touch to kindle. He looked down into the eyes upturned to him in breathless interest, and he read in them the same yearnings after immortality, the same reverence for the Infinite Majesty of the Universe, which moved and solemnized his own soul. His manner was in general calm and affectionate, yet there were moments when he swept the chords of human passion with a master's hand, and the hectic flush of his cheek told of the fire burning within.

"He is a scholar, a metaphysician, a philosopher, and a gentleman," said Villeneuve to himself, at the close of his discourse. "If he is an actor, he is the best one I ever saw. He is probably an enthusiast, who, if he had lived in ancient days, would have worn the blazing crown of martyrdom. I should like to see his daughter." The low notes of the organ again rose, as if in response to his heart's desire. This time there was the accompaniment of a new female voice. The congregation rose as the words of the anthem began. It was a kind of doxology, the chorus terminating with the solemn expression—"for ever and ever." The hand of the organist no longer trembled. It swept over the keys, as if the enthu-

siasm of an exalted spirit were communicated to every pulse
and sinew. The undulating strains rolled and reverberated
till the whole house was filled with the waves of harmony.
But high, and clear, and sweet above those waves of harmony
and the mingling voices of the choir, rose that single female
voice, uttering the burden of the anthem, "for ever and ever."
Villeneuve closed his eyes. He was oppressed by the novelty
of his sensations. Where was he? In a simple village church,
listening to the minstrelsy of a simple village maiden, and he
had frequented the magnificent cathedral of Notre Dame, been
familiar there with the splendid ritual of the national religion,
and heard its sublime chantings from the finest choirs in the
Universe. Why did those few monotonous words so thrill
through every nerve of his being? That eternity which he
believed was the dream of fanaticism, seemed for a moment
an awful reality, as the last notes of the pæan echoed on his
ear.

When the benediction was given, and the congregation was
leaving the church, he watched impatiently for the foldings
of the red curtains to part, and his heart palpitated when he
saw a white-robed figure glide through the opening and immediately disappear. The next minute she was seen at the
entrance of the church, evidently waiting the approach of her
father, who, surrounded by his people, pressing on each other
to catch a kindly greeting, always found it difficult to make
his egress. As she thus stood against a column which supported the entrance, Villeneuve had a most favourable opportunity of scanning her figure, which he did with a practised
and scrutinizing glance. He was accustomed to Parisian and
English beauty, and comparing Grace Blandford to the high-
born and high-bred beauties of the old world, she certainly
lost in the comparison. She was very simply dressed, her
eyes were downcast, and her features were in complete repose.
Still there was a quiet grace about her that pleased him—a
blending of perfect simplicity and perfect refinement that was
extraordinary. Mr. Blandford paused as he came down the
aisle. He had noticed the young and interesting looking
stranger, who listened with such devout attention to all the
exercises. He had heard, for in a country village such things
are rapidly communicated, that there was a traveller at the
inn, a foreigner and an invalid—two strong claims to sympathy
and kindness. The pallid complexion of the young man was a
sufficient indication of the latter, and the air of high breeding

which distinguished him was equal to a letter of recommendation in his behalf. The minister accosted him with great benignity, and invited him to accompany him home.

" You are a stranger," said he, "and I understand an invalid. Perhaps you will find the quiet of our household more congenial this day than the bustle of a public dwelling."

Villeneuve bowed his delighted acceptance of this most unexpected invitation. He grasped the proffered hand of the minister with more warmth than he was aware of, and followed him to the door where Grace yet stood, with downcast eyes.

" My daughter," said Mr. Blandford, drawing her hand through his arm. This simple introduction well befitted the place where it was made, and was acknowledged by her with a gentle bending of the head and a lifting of the eyes, and they walked in silence from the portals of the church. What a change had the mere uplifting of those veiled lids made in her countenance! Two lines of a noble bard flashed across his memory—

> "The light of love, the purity of grace,
> The mind, the music breathing from her face."

Then another line instantaneously succeeded—

> "And oh! that eye is in itself a soul."

There was one thing which disappointed him. He did not notice a single blush flitting over her fair cheek. He feared she was deficient in sensibility. It was so natural to blush at a stranger's greeting. He did not understand the nature of her feelings. He could not know that one so recently engaged in sublime worship of the Creator, must be lifted above fear or confusion in the presence of the creature. Villeneuve had seen much of the world, and understood the art of adaptedness, in the best sense of the word. He could conform to the circumstances in which he might be placed with grace and ease, and though he was too sincere to express sentiments he did not feel, he felt justified in concealing those he did feel, when he knew their avowal would give pain or displeasure It was a very singular way for him to pass the Sabbath. The guest of a village pastor, breathing an atmosphere redolent of the sweets of piety, spirituality, and holy love. The language of levity and flattery, so current in society, would be considered profanation here; and a conviction deeply mortifying to his

vanity forced itself upon him, that all those accomplishments
for which he had been so much admired, would gain him no
favour with the minister and his daughter. He could not
forbear expressing his surprise at the location Mr. Blandford
had chosen.

" I would not insult you by flattery," said Villeneuve,
ngenuously, " but I am astonished you do not seek a wider
phere of usefulness. It is impossible that the people here
should appreciate your talents, or estimate the sacrifices you
make to enlighten and exalt them."

Mr. Blandford smiled as he answered—" You think my
sphere too small, while I tremble at the weight of responsibility
I have assumed. If I have the talents which you kindly
ascribe to me, I find here an ample field for their exercise.
There are hundreds of minds around me that mingle their
aspirations with mine, and even assist me in the heavenward
journey. In a larger, more brilliant circle, I might perhaps
gain a more sounding name and exercise a wider influence, but
that influence would not be half as deep and heartfelt. I was
born and bred in a city, and know the advantages such a life
can offer; but I would not exchange the tranquillity of this
rural residence, the serenity of my pastoral life, the paternal
influence I wield over this secluded village, and the love
and reverence of its upright and pure-minded inhabitants,
for the splendid sinecure of the Archbishops of our mother-
land."

Villeneuve was astonished to see a man so nobly endowed,
entirely destitute of the principle of ambition. He wanted to
ask him how he had thus trampled under his feet the honours
and distinctions of the world. " You consider ambition a
vice, then ?" said he.

" You are mistaken," replied Mr. Blandford, " if you believe
me destitute of ambition. I am one of the most ambitious
men in the world. But I aspire after honours that can resist
the mutations of time, and partake of the imperishability of
their Great Bestower."

There was a silence of some moments, during which Mr
Blandford looked upward, and the eyes of Grace followed her
father's with kindling ray.

" But, your daughter," continued Villeneuve, " can she find
contentment in a situation for which nature and education have
so evidently unfitted her ?"

" Let Grace answer for herself," said Mr. Blandford, mildly ;

" I have consulted her happiness as well as my own, in the choice I have made."

Villeneuve was delighted to see a bright blush suffuse the modest cheek of Grace—but it was the blush of feeling, not of shame.

" I love the country rather than the town," said she, " for I prefer nature to art, meditation to action, and the works of God to the works of man; and in the constant companionship of my father I find more than contentment—I find happiness, joy."

Villeneuve sighed—he felt the isolation of his own destiny. The last of his family, a traveller in a strange land, in pursuit of health; which had been sacrificed in the too eager pursuit of the pleasures of this world, without one hope to link him to another. Affluent and uncontrolled, yet sated and desponding, he envied the uncorrupted taste of the minister's daughter. He would have bartered all his wealth for the enthusiasm that warmed the character of her father. That night he was awakened by a singular dream. He thought he was alone in the horror of thick darkness. It seemed that he was in the midst of infinity, and yet chained to one dark spot, an immovable speck in the boundless ocean of space. " Must I remain here for ever?" he cried in agony, such as is only known in dreams, when the spirit's nerves are all unsheathed. " For ever and ever," answered a sweet, seraphic voice, high above his head, and looking up he beheld Grace, reclining on silver-bosomed clouds, so distant she appeared like a star in the heavens, yet every lineament perfectly defined. " Am I then parted from thee for ever?" exclaimed he, endeavouring to stretch out his arms towards the luminous point. " For ever and ever," responded the same heavenly accents, mournfully echoing till they died away, and the vision fled. He was not superstitious, but he did not like the impression of his dream. He rose feverish and unrefreshed, and felt himself unable to continue his journey. Mr. Blandford came to see him. He was deeply interested in the young stranger, and experienced the pleasure which every sensitive and intellectual being feels in meeting with kindred sensibility and intellect The intimacy, thus commenced, continued to increase, and week after week passed away, and Villeneuve still lingered near the minister and his daughter. His health was invigorated, his spirits excited by the novel yet powerful influences that surrounded him. It was impossible, in the course of this deepening intimacy, that the real sentiments of Villeneuve should remain concealed, for hypocrisy formed no part of his character. Mr. Blandford, relying on the reverence and affection Villeneuve evidently felt for him, believed it would be an easy task to interest him in the great truths of religion. And it was an easy task to interest him, particularly when the father's arguments were backed by the daughter's persuasive eloquence; but it was a most difficult one to convince. The prejudices of education, the power of habit, the hardening influence of a worldly life, presented an apparently impenetrable shield against the arrows of divine truth.

"I respect, I revere the principles of your religion," Villeneuve was accustomed to say at the close of their long and interesting conversations. "I would willingly endure the pangs of death; yea, the agonies of martyrdom, for the possession of a faith like yours. But it is a gift denied to me. I cannot force my belief, nor give a cold assent with my lips to what my reason and my conscience belie."

Mr. Blandford ceased not his efforts, notwithstanding the unexpected resistance he encountered, but Grace gradually retired from the conflict, and Villeneuve found to his sorrow and mortification that she no longer appeared to rejoice in his society. There was a reserve in her manners which would have excited his resentment, had not the sadness of her countenance touched his heart. Sometimes when he met her eye it had an earnest, reproachful, pitying expression, that thrilled to his soul. One evening he came to the Parsonage at a later hour than usual. He was agitated and pale. "I have received letters of importance," said he; "I must leave you immediately. I did not know that all my happiness was centered in the intercourse I have been holding with your family, till this summons came." Grace, unable to conceal her emotions, rose and left the apartment. Villeneuve's eyes followed her with an expression which made her father tremble. He anticipated the scene which followed. "Mr. Blandford," continued Villeneuve, "I love your daughter. I cannot live without her—I cannot depart without an assurance of her love and your approbation."

Mr. Blandford was too much agitated to reply—the blood rushed to his temples, then retreating as suddenly, left his brow and cheek as colourless as marble. "I should have foreseen this," at length he said. "It would have spared us all much misery."

" Misery !" replied Villeneuve, in a startling tone.

" Yes," replied Mr. Blandford, "I have been greatly to blame—I have suffered my feelings to triumph over my judgment. Villeneuve, I have never met a young man who won upon my affections as you have done. The ingenuousness, ardour, and generosity of your character impelled me to love you. I still love you; but I pity you still more. I can never trust my daughter's happiness in your hands. There is a gulf between you—a wall of separation—high as the heavens and deeper than the foundations of the earth." He paused, and bowed his face upon his hands. The possibility that his daughter's happiness might be no longer in her own keeping, completely overpowered him. Villeneuve listened in astonishment and dismay. He, in all the pride of affluence and rank (for noble blood ran in lineal streams through his veins), to be rejected by an obscure village pastor, from mere religious scruples. It was incredible—one moment his eye flashed haughtily on the bending figure before him; the next it wavered, in the apprehension that Grace might yield to her father's decision, and seal their final separation. "Mr. Blandford," cried he, passionately, "I can take my rejection only from your daughter—I have never sought her love unsanctioned by your approbation—I have scorned the guise of a hypocrite, and I have a right to claim this from you. You may destroy *my* happiness—it is in your power—but tremble lest you sacrifice a daughter's peace."

Mr. Blandford recovered his self-command, as the passions of the young man burst their bounds. He summoned Grace into his presence. "I yield to your impetuous desire," said he, "but I would to Heaven you had spared me a scene like this. Painful as it is, I must remain to be a witness to it." He took his daughter's hand as she entered, and drew her towards him. He watched her countenance while the first vows of love to which she had ever listened were breathed into her ear with an eloquence and a fervour which seemed irresistible, and these were aided by the powerful auxiliary of a most handsome and engaging person, and he trembled as he gazed. Her cheek kindled, her eye lighted up with rapture, her heart panted with excessive emotion. She leaned on her father's arm, unable to speak, but looked up in his face with an expression that spoke volumes.

"You love him, then, Grace," said he mournfully. "Oh, my God! forgive me the folly, the blindness, the madness of which I have been guilty!"

114

Grace started, as if wakening from a dream. Her father's words recalled her to herself—one brief moment of ecstasy had been hers—to be followed, she knew, by hours of darkness and sorrow. The warm glow faded from her cheek, and throwing her arms round her father's neck, she wept unrestrainedly.

"She loves me," exclaimed Villeneuve; "you yourself witness her emotions—you will not separate us—you will not suffer a cruel fanaticism to destroy us both."

"Grace," said Mr. Blandford, in a firm voice, "look up. Let not the feelings of a moment, but the principles of a life decide. Will you hazard, for the enjoyment of a few fleeting years, the unutterable interests of eternity? Will you forsake the Master *he* abjures for the bosom of a stranger? In one word, my daughter, will you wed an Infidel?"

Grace lifted her head, and clasping her hands together, looked fervently upward.

"Thou art answered," cried Mr. Blandford, with a repelling motion towards Villeneuve. "The God she invokes will give her strength to resist temptation. Go, then, most unhappy yet beloved young man—you have chosen your destiny, and we have chosen ours. *You* live for time. *We*, for eternity. As I said before, there is a deep gulf between us. Seek not to drag her down into the abyss into which you would madly plunge. My soul hath wrestled with yours, and you have resisted, though I fought with weapons drawn from Heaven's own armory. Farewell—our prayers and our tears will follow you."

He extended his hand to grasp Villeneuve's for the last time, but Villeneuve, with every passion excited beyond the power of control, rejected the motion; and, snatching the hand of Grace, which hung powerless over her father's shoulder, drew her impetuously towards him. "She loves me," exclaimed he, "and I will never resign her; I swear it by the inexorable Power you so blindly worship. Perish the religion that would crush the dearest and holiest feelings of the human heart! Perish the faith that exults in the sacrifice of nature and of love!"

With one powerful arm Mr. Blandford separated his daughter from the embrace of her lover, and holding him back with the other, commanded him to depart. He was dreadfully agitated, the veins of his temples started out like cords, and his eyes flashed with imprisoned fires. Villeneuve writhed for a moment in his unrelaxing grasp, then, reeling backward, sunk upon a sofa. He turned deadly pale, and held his handkerchief to his face.

"Oh! father! you have killed him!" shrieked Grace, springing to his side; "he faints! he bleeds, he dies!"

Even while Grace was speaking, the white handkerchief was crimsoned with blood, the eyes of the young man closed, and he fell back insensible.

"Just Heaven! spare me this curse!" cried Mr. Blandford. "Great God! I have killed them both!"

They did indeed look like two murdered victims, for the blood which oozed from the young man's lips not only dyed his own handkerchief and neckcloth, but reddened the white dress of Grace and stiffened on her fair locks, as her head drooped unconsciously on his breast. All was horror and confusion in the household. The physician was immediately summoned, who declared that a blood-vessel was ruptured, and that the life of the young man was in the most imminent danger. Grace was borne to her own apartment and consigned to the care of some kind neighbours, but Mr. Blandford remained the whole night by Villeneuve's side, holding his hand in his, with his eyes fixed on his pallid countenance, trembling lest every fluttering breath should be his last. About daybreak he opened his eyes, and seeing who was watching so tenderly over him, pressed his hand and attempted to speak, but the doctor commanded perfect silence, assuring him that the slightest exertion would be at the hazard of his life. For two or three days he hovered on the brink of the grave, during which time Mr. Blandford scarcely left his side, and Grace lingered near the threshold of the door, pale and sleepless, the image of despair. One night, when he seemed to be in a deep sleep, Mr. Blandford knelt by his couch, and in a low voice breathed out his soul in prayer. His vigil had been one long prayer, but he felt that he must find vent in language for the depth and strength of his emotions. He prayed in agony for the life of the young man; for his soul' life. He pleaded, he supplicated; till, language failing, sigh and tears alone bore witness to the strivings of his spirit "Yet, not my will, oh! God!" ejaculated he again, "but thine be done."

"Amen!" uttered a faint voice. The minister started as if he had heard a voice from the dead. It was Villeneuve who spoke, and whose eyes fixed upon him had a most intense and thrilling expression. "Your prayer is heard," continued he. "I feel that God is mercifnl. A ray of divine light illumines my parting hour. Let me see Grace before I die, that our souls may mingle once on earth, in earnest of their union hereafter."

The minister led his daughter to the couch of Villeneuve. He joined her hand in his. "My daughter," cried he, "rejoice. I asked for him life. God giveth unto him long life; yea, life for evermore."

Grace bowed her head on the pale hand that clasped her own, and even in that awful moment, a torrent of joy gushed into her soul. It was the foretaste of an eternal wedlock, and death seemed indeed swallowed up in victory. Mr. Blandford knelt by his kneeling daughter, and many a time during that night they thought they saw the spirit of Villeneuve about to take its upward flight; but he sunk at length into a gentle slumber, and when the doctor again saw him, he perceived a favourable change in his pulse, and told Mr. Blandford there was a faint hope of his recovery. "With perfect quiet and tender nursing," said he, looking meaningly at Grace, "he may yet possibly be saved."

The predictions of the excellent physician were indeed fulfilled, for in less than three weeks Villeneuve, though still weak and languid, was able to take his seat in the family circle. Mr. Blandford saw with joy that the faith which he had embraced in what he believed his dying hour, was not abandoned with returning health. He had always relied on the rectitude of his principles, and now, when religion strengthened and sanctified them, he felt it his duty to sanction his union with his daughter. The business which had summoned him so unexpectedly to his native country still remained unsettled, and as the physician prescribed a milder climate, he resolved to try the genial air of France. It was no light sacrifice for Mr. Blandford to give up his daughter, the sole treasury of his affections, and doom himself to a solitary home; but he did it without murmuring, since he hoped the blessing f heaven would hallow their nuptials. Villeneuve promised to return the ensuing year, and restore Grace again to her beloved parsonage.

The Sunday before their departure, Grace accompanied her father and husband to the village church. Villeneuve saw the boy who had guided him there the first time, standing at the portal. He returned his respectful salutation with a warm grasp of the hand. "He led me to the gate of heaven," thought he; "he shall not go unrewarded."

"She will be too proud to play on the organ any more," said the boy to himself, "now that she has married a great man and a foreigner;" but Grace ascended the steps as usual, and drew the red curtains closely round her. What the feelings of the musician were, within that sacred sanctuary, as she pressed the keys, probably for the last time, could only be judged from a trembling touch; but at the close of the services, when the same sublime anthem, with the burden "for ever and ever," was sung by the choir, Villeneuve recognised the same clear, adoring accents which first fell so thrillingly on his ear. He remembered his dream. It no longer filled him with superstitious horror. It was caused by the workings of his dark and troubled mind. Now every thought flowed in a new channel; he seemed a new being to himself.

"Are we indeed united?" said he, while his soul hung on the echoes of that sweet strain, "and shall we be united for ever?"

"For ever and ever," returned the voice of the worshipper; and the whole choir, joining in, in a full burst of harmony, repeated again and again, "for ever and ever."

THE BOSOM SERPENT.

"I HAVE something to tell you, Rosamond," said Cecil Dormer, taking Rosamond Clifford on his knee and seating himself in a corner of her mother's sofa—"Don't you want to hear a story to-night?"

"Is it a sure enough story?" asked Rosamond, "or a fairy tale, like the Arabian Nights Entertainment?"

"Every word of it truth," answered Cecil—"though some portions of it may 'freeze your young blood.' It is of a little girl, about your own age, and a woman who I verily believe is Lucifer himself, dressed in woman's clothes."

"You have excited my curiosity," said Mrs. Clifford closing her book, and taking a seat on the sofa—"for as every story must have a hero, I suspect you are the hero of your own."

"Please tell it," cried Rosamond, with the impatience of a petted child—"I want to hear about the little girl."

"Well," said Cecil, "you recollect how bright and beautiful the moon shone last night, and how peaceful and lovely everything looked. As I was returning to my lodgings, rather later than usual, I passed through a lane, which shortened the distance, though the walk itself was rough and unpleasant. As I was indulging in my old habit of building castles by the moonlight, I heard the most piercing shrieks issuing from a low building to which I was directly opposite. There must be murder going on, thought I, and like the giant, I imagined I could 'smell the blood of an Englishman.' I rushed to the door, almost shook it from its hinges in opening it, and found myself in the narrow, dark passage—but, guided by the cries, I soon reached another door, which I opened with as little ceremony, and what do you think I saw?"

"Were they killing the poor little girl?" cried Rosamond, drawing a long breath, her eyes growing larger and darker.

"You shall hear. In the centre of the room, there was a large, iron-framed woman, with her right hand extended, brandishing a leathern thong over the head of a pale, shrinking girl, whom she grasped with her left hand, and from whose bare shoulders the blood was oozing through grooves that thong had cut. You may well start and shudder, for a more hideous spectacle never met the eye. She was just in the act of inflicting another lash, when I arrested her arm with a force which must have made it ache to the marrow of the bones, and caused her involuntarily to loosen her hold of her victim, who fell exhausted to the floor. The woman turned on me, with the fury of a wolf interrupted in its bloody banquet."

"Did she look like the picture of the wolf in little *Red Riding Hood?*" asked Rosamond.

"Yes, a most striking resemblance. Her cap was blown back to the crown of her head by the barbarous exercise in which she had been engaged, her tongue actually protruded from her mouth, in the impotence of her rage, and her hard, dull-coloured eyes glowed like red-hot stones in their deep sockets."

"'What do you want?' cried she, in a voice between a growl and a scream—'and who are you, and what is your business? You had better take care, or I'll make your back smart, in spite of your fine coat.'

"I could not help smiling at the idea of being whipped by a woman, but I answered as sternly as possible—'I want humanity, for I am a man. My business is to snatch this child from your clutches, and to give you up to the city authorities for disturbing the public peace.'

"'It is her fault, not mine,' replied she, a little intimidated by my threat—'she always screams and hollows when I whip her, as if I were murdering her, if I but scratch her skin. I gave her a task to do, and told her if she did not do it I would whip her—a good-for-nothing, lazy thing!—mope, mope from morning to night, nothing but mope and fret, while I'm drudging like a slave. I'm not going to support her any longer, if I have to turn her out of doors. She thinks because her mother happened to die here, I must give her a home, forsooth, and she do nothing to pay for it, the ungrateful hussy!'"

"Oh! don't tell any more about that horrid old woman,"

interrupted Rosamond—"I want to hear about the little girl. What did she do?"

"Why, she wept and sobbed, and said she did all she could, but that she was sick and weak, and she wished she was in the grave, by her poor mother's side, for there was nobody in the world to take care of her, and she knew not what would become of her. I told her impulsively that *I* would see she was taken care of, and if that vile woman but lifted her finger against her once more, she should rue it to her heart's core."

"There, Cecil, you have made a rhyme, so you must wish before you speak again," said Rosamond, laughing.

"Well, I wish that poor, desolate child had a home like this, and a mother like Mrs. Clifford, and a companion like Rosamond—or I wish that I had a kind mother and sister, to whose care I could intrust her, or a sweet gentle wife—and it is the first time in my life I ever breathed that wish—who would be willing to protect and cherish her for my sake."

"Is she a pretty child?" interrogated Mrs. Clifford, feelings best known to herself prompting the question.

"Yes!" repeated Rosamond, eagerly, stealing a look in the glass at her own bright eyes, fair complexion, and curling locks —"is she pretty, and was she dressed nice?"

"No!" answered Cecil, "the only emotion she could excite is that of the deepest pity. She is thin to emaciation, sallow to cadaverousness, and her eyes occupy the greatest portion of her face, they look so large and hollow and wild. She might sit for a miniature representation of famine, disease, or woe. There is something about her, however, that speaks of gentle blood and early gentle breeding. Her name at least is aristocratic, and bespeaks a French extraction—Eugenia St. Clair."

Rosamond was delighted with the name, and wondered how she could help being pretty with such a beautiful name.

"Poor child!" said Mrs. Clifford, "it is a pity she is not handsome, it would add so much to the romance of the adventure."

"She is helpless and oppressed," cried Cecil warmly, "and if she had the beauty of a cherub her claims would not plead more eloquently than they do in my heart. I should think I were guilty of murder, if I left her in the hands of that virago. It is true I put a *douceur* in her hand, terrifying her at the same time with the threatenings of the law, but this will only

purchase the child's security for a short time. I made a vow
to myself, when she clung to me convulsively, as I attempted
to leave her, that I would place her in some situation where
she could find kindness and protection, till fitting arrangements
can be made for her education."

"You are indeed romantic," said Mrs. Clifford, seriously,
"and know not what you may entail upon yourself."

"I am sorry if you think me so," said Cecil, with a look
of mortification and disappointment—"I see I have as usual
drawn too hasty conclusions. You have been so very kind to
me, so kind as to make me forget in your household the
absence of domestic ties. I dared to hope you would assist me
in my design, and perhaps receive for a little while, under your
own roof, this neglected child of orphanage and want. I have
no other friend of whom I could ask a similar favour, and if I
find I am presuming too much on you, I believe I must try to
fall in love and get married, so that I can take my protegée to
a home of my own."

Mrs. Clifford had not the most distant idea of permitting
him to do so preposterous a thing, for she had long since appropriated him to Rosamond, whom as a child he now petted
and caressed, and whom, if he continued as he now was, fancy
free, as a woman he must inevitably love. When he first
mentioned the girl, and expressed such a strong interest in
her behalf, she began to tremble in anticipation, fearing a
future rival in her views; but the lean, sallow face, half eyes
and half bone, just delineated, tranquillized her fears, and as
her fears subsided, her pity strengthened. And Rosamond,
though too young to enter into her mother's speculations, felt
her sympathy increased tenfold since she had learned that
nature had gone hand in hand with fortune, and been equally
niggard of her boons. She was unfortunately an only child,
and accustomed to be an object of exclusive attention in the
household, from her idolizing mother down to the lowest
menial. The guests too easily understood the way to Mrs.
Clifford's heart, and as Rosamond was pretty and sprightly,
they derived amusement from her little airs and graces. But
what flattered her vanity and elated her pride more than anything else, Cecil Dormer, so distinguished for wealth and
accomplishments, so courted and admired, seemed to prefer her
company to the society of grown ladies, who had often declared
themselves jealous of her, and threatened, when she was a few
years older, to shut her up in some convent or cell. Thus imper-

ceptibly acquiring an exaggerated idea of her own consequence, and believing the love and admiration of all her inalienable right, had Cecil represented the orphan Eugenia as beautiful and charming, it is more than probable she would have regarded her as a dreaded encroacher on boundaries which nature had prescribed and fortune guarded—but for the ugly Eugenia all her sympathies were enlisted, and she pleaded her mother so varmly to bring her there directly, and take her away from that roadful woman *for good and all,* that Cecil was delighted with her sensibility and benevolence, and rejoiced in such a juvenile coadjutor.

The next morning Mrs. Clifford accompanied Dormer to Mrs. Grundy's, the woman of the leathern thong, of whom she requested the history of Eugenia. Mrs. Grundy was sullen, and but little disposed to be communicative. She declared she knew nothing about her mother, only that she came there as a boarder, with barely sufficient to pay the expenses of her lodgings; that she fell sick soon after, and died, leaving the little girl on her hands, with nothing in the world but a grand name for her support. She expressed no gratitude or pleasure at the prospect of being released from the burthen under which she groaned, but grumbled about her own hard lot, insinuating that idleness and ingratitude were always sure to be rewarded. Eugenia's appearance was a living commentary on the truth of Dormer's story. Her neck and shoulders were streaked with swollen and livid lines, and her large, blood-shot eyes spoke of repressed and unutterable anguish. When told of the new home to which she was to be transferred, that she was to be placed by Dormer under the protection of Mrs. Clifford, and that if she were a good girl, and merited such advantages, she should be sent to school, and be fitted for a respectable station in society—she stood like one bewildered, as if awaking from a dream. Then, after taking in the truth of her position, she turned towards Dormer with wonderful quickness and even grace of motion, and clasping her hands together, attempted to speak, but burst into a passionate fit of weeping.

"There!" cried Mrs. Grundy, "you see what an ungrateful cretur she is. Do what you will for her, she does nothing but cry. Well, all I hope, you'll not be sick of your bargain, and be imposing her on me, before the week comes round again. But I give you warning, when once she gets out of my doors, she never darkens them a second time."

Dormer cast upon her a withering look, but, disdaining to reply to mere vulgarity and insolence, he took the hand of the sobbing child, and motioning to Mrs. Clifford, they left the room, while Mrs. Grundy's voice, keeping up a deep thorough bass, followed them till the door of the carriage was closed and the rumbling of the wheels drowned accents which certainly "by distance were made more sweet."

Eugenia had not been an hour under the roof of Mrs. Clifford, before a complete transformation was effected, by the supervising care of the proud and busy Rosamond. Her waiting-maid was put in active employment, in combing, brushing, and perfuming Eugenia's neglected hair, her wardrobe was ransacked to supply her fitting apparel, her mother's medicine chest was opened to furnish a healing liniment for her lacerated neck, which was afterwards covered by a neat muslin apron.

"Now look at yourself in the glass," said Rosamond, leading her to a large mirror, which reflected the figure at full length; "don't you look nice?"

Eugenia cast one glance, then turned away with a deep sigh. The contrast of her own tawny visage and meagre limbs with the fair, bright, round, joyous face and glowing lineaments of Rosamond, was too painful; but Rosamond loved to linger where a comparison so favourable to herself could be drawn, and her kind feelings to Eugenia rose in proportion to the self-complacency of which she was the cause.

It was a happy little circle which met that evening around Mrs. Clifford's table. Mrs. Clifford was happy in the new claim she had acquired over Cecil Dormer, and the probable influence it might exert on her future plans. Rosamond was happy in enacting the character of Lady Bountiful, and being praised by Cecil Dormer; and Cecil himself was happy in the consciousness of having performed a benevolent action. Eugenia's spirits had been so crushed by sorrow and unkindness, it seemed as if their elastic principle were destroyed. She was gentle, but passive, and appeared oppressed by the strangeness of her situation. Yet, as she expressed no vulgar amazement at the elegancies that surrounded her, and had evidently been taught the courtesies of society, Mrs. Clifford became convinced that Dormer was right in his belief that she was of gentle blood, and the fear that Rosamond's manners might be injured by contact with an unpolished plebeian subsided. When Eugenia was somewhat accustomed to her new situation, Mrs. Clifford questioned her minutely with regard to her parentage and the peculiar circumstances of her mother's death. She gathered from her broken and timid answers, that her father was wealthy, and that the first years of her life were passed in affluence; that as she grew older her mother seemed unhappy and her father stern and gloomy, why she could not tell; that one night, during her father's absence, her mother had left her home, accompanied by herself and one servant girl, and taken passage in a steamboat for that city. They boarded in obscure lodgings, never went abroad, or received visitors at home. Her mother grew paler and sadder. At length the servant girl, who seemed greatly attached to them, died. Then she described her mother as being much distressed for money to pay her board, being obliged to part with her watch and jewels, and when these resources failed, thankful to obtain sewing from her landlady, or, through her, from others. As they became more wretched and helpless, they were compelled to go from house to house, where her mother could find employment, till she was taken sick at Mrs. Grundy's, and never lifted her head again from the pillow so grudgingly supplied. A diamond ring, the most valued and carefully preserved of all her jewels, procured for her the sad privilege of dying there. Over her consequent sufferings Eugenia only wept, and on this subject Mrs. Clifford had no curiosity.

It was about six years after these events, that Cecil Dormer again was seated on the sofa in Mrs. Clifford's drawing-room, but Rosamond no longer sat upon his knee. The rosy-cheeked child, with short curling hair, short frock, and ruffled pantalettes, had disappeared, and, in her stead, a maiden with longer and more closely fitting robes, smoother and darker hair, and cheeks of paler and more mutable roses. Cecil was unchanged in face, but there was that in his air and manner which spoke a higher degree of elegance and fashion, and a deeper acquaintance with the world. He had passed several years at Paris. Rosamond had been in the mean time at a distant boarding-school, where Eugenia still remained.

"What are you going to do with Eugenia," asked Mrs. Clifford, "when she returns? Will you not find a young female protegée rather an embarrassing appendage to a bachelor's establishment?"

"I have just been thinking of the same thing," replied Cecil. "I believe I must still encroach on your kindness as I was wont to do in former days, and request you to receive her under your protection, till some permanent arrangement can be made for her home."

"That permanent arrangement must be your own marriage, I should presume," said Mrs. Clifford; "and indeed, Cecil, I wonder that with your fortune and rare endowments, you do not think seriously of assuming the responsibility of a household."

"What! the sensible Benedict a married man?" cried Cecil, with a theatrical start. "I shall lose all my consequence in society—I shall dwindle down into complete insignificance. No—I am not quite old enough to be married yet. I must act, too, as protector and elder brother to Rosamond, on her entrance into the world, an office which I promised to perform, when I dandled her a child in my arms."

"I am sure Rosamond would not wish to interfere with your personal arrangements," replied Mrs. Clifford, in a tone of pique—she was vexed and astonished at Cecil's coldness and indifference. She could not imagine the stoicism which could resist the influence of Rosamond's blooming beauty. She had looked forward to their meeting, after an absence of years, as the moment which should realize her long-cherished hopes, and nothing could be more provoking than the nonchalance of Cecil, unless it was the warm interest he manifested in everything respecting Eugenia.

"No, indeed," said Rosamond, laughing, "I willingly relinquish every claim on your protection, for Eugenia's sake. Perhaps some one else will take pity on my forlorn condition, and volunteer as my champion." Rosamond laughed, but her voice was unsteady, and a bright blush suffused her cheek.

Cecil noticed the vibration of her voice, and the sudden crimson rushing even to her temples. Her emotion surprised—interested him—was it possible, his marriage was an event capable of awakening such visible agitation? He looked at her more intently. Sensibility had added wonderful charms to her features. His vanity was flattered. He had been much admired in the world, and the language of adulation was familiar to his ear. But here was a young girl, in all the freshness and purity of life's vernal season, incapable of artifice, unpractised in the blandishments of society, one too whom he had known and loved as a beautiful child, and caressed with the familiarity of a brother, who was paying him an involuntary homage, as unexpected as it was fascinating. It was

surprising what a long train of images swept over his mind,
rapid and dazzling as lightning, called up by that deep maiden
blush.   How delightful it would be to secure the possession
of a heart which had never yet known the pulsations of passion,
whose master chords were waiting the magic of his touch to
respond the deep music of feeling and love!   How happy
Eugenia would be in the constant companionship of her
juvenile benefactress, her schoolmate and friend!   Mrs. Clifford, too, had always shown him the tenderness of a mother,
and was so interested in his future establishment.   Strange,
what slight circumstances sometimes decide the most solemn,
the most important events of life!   The opportune blush of
Rosamond sealed her own destiny, and that of Cecil Dormer.
In less than one month the "sensible Benedict" was indeed a
married man, the husband of the young and happy Rosamond.
Seldom indeed was there a prouder and happier bride—ambition, pride, vanity, love—all were gratified, and could she
have purchased the lease of immortality on earth, she would
have asked no other heaven.   But, even in the fulness of
love's silver honeymoon, a dark cloud rose.   The mother, who
had lived but for her, and who was basking in the blaze of her
daughter's prosperity, without one thought beyond it, was
stricken by a sudden and fatal disease, and Rosamond's bridal
paraphernalia was changed to the garments of mourning.   It
was her first felt misfortune, for her father died in her infancy;
and the blow was terrible.   At any other time it would have
been so, but now this sudden and startling proof of mortality,
in the morn of her wedded felicity, was chill and awful.
Still there was a consolation in the sympathy of Cecil, that
disarmed sorrow of its keenest pang, and there were moments,
when she felt it even a joy to weep, since her tears were shed
on the bosom of a husband so passionately loved.   The arrival
of Eugenia, a few weeks after this melancholy event, turned
her feelings into a new channel.   Cecil had often asked of her
a description of Eugenia, whose letters, breathing so eloquently
of gratitude and affection, and so indicative of enthusiasm and
refinement of character, had been a source of pleasure and
pride to him.   "If her person has improved only half as much
as her mind," he would say, "she cannot be ugly."   Rosamond,
who had been her daily associate, was hardly sensible of the
gradual transformation that was going on in her external appearance.   The strength of her first impression remained, and
whenever she thought of Eugenia, she remembered her as she

stood, pale and hollow-eyed, by her side, before the mirror, which gave back the blooming image of her own juvenile beauty. Still, though she felt her immeasurable superiority to this poor, dependent girl, she was agitated at her coming, and regretted the commanding claims she had on her husband's kindness and protection.

"Can this indeed be Eugenia?" exclaimed Cecil, in a tone of delighted surprise, when, unbonneted and unshawled, she stood before him, tearful, smiling, and agitated. "Rosamond, are we not deceived? Tell me, can this indeed be our Eugenia?"

"It is indeed that Eugenia whom your bounty has cherished, the child whom you"—Eugenia paused in unconquerable emotion, and clasped her hands together with characteristic fervour and grace. Cecil was deeply affected. He recollected the little girl whose emaciated features told a tale of such unutterable woe, whose shoulders were furrowed with bleeding streaks, whose cries of agony had pierced the silence of his evening walk. He contrasted the image drawn on his remembrance, with the figure of exquisite symmetry, the face moulded into the softness of feminine loveliness, the eyes of such rare beauty and lustre, that they actually illuminated her whole countenance. His heart swelled with the consciousness of rewarded benevolence, it softened into tenderness towards every human being, and overflowed with a love for Rosamond, such as he had never felt before. So true it is that the exercise of every kind and generous affection increases the soul's capacities for loving, instead of draining and impoverishing them. "You must henceforth be sisters," said he, taking a hand of each, and seating himself between them. "I need not tell you to love each other as such. I am sure that injunction is unnecessary. But there is one task I must impose upon you, Rosamond. You must teach Eugenia to look upon me as a brother, a friend, not as a benefactor, for I feel repaid a thousand times over, for all I have done for her, in the happiness of this moment. Let the idea of obligation be banished for ever, and we can be the happiest trio in the universe, bound together by a threefold and indissoluble cord."

"My mother!" ejaculated Rosamond, and drawing away her hand from her husband, she covered her face and wept. He reproached himself for his transient oblivion of her sorrow, and in endeavouring to soothe it, Eugenia was for a while forgotten. But he little dreamed of the fountain of Rosamond's

tears. It would have been difficult for herself to have ana-
lyzed the strange feelings struggling within her. The *bosom
serpent*, of whose existence she had been previously unconscious,
then wound its first cold coil in her heart, and instead of
shuddering at its entrance, and closing its portals on the deadly
guest, she allowed it to wind itself in its deepest foldings,
where its hissings and writhings were no less terrible, because
unheard and unseen. Rosamond from earliest childhood had
been the object of exclusive devotion from those she loved.
She had never known a sharer in her mother's love, for un-
happily she was an only child. The undivided fondness of her
husband had hitherto been all that her exacting heart required.
Now, she must admit an acknowledged sharer of his thoughts
and affections, not as an occasional visiter, but as an constant
inmate, an inseparable companion. The hallowed privacy of
the domestic altar was destroyed, for the foot of the stranger
had desecrated it. She could no longer appropriate to herself
every look and smile of him, whose glances and smiles she believed her own inalienable right. If she walked abroad,
another beside herself, must henceforth lean upon his arm.
If she remained at home, another must also be seated at his
side. And this invasion of her most precious immunities, was
not to be endured for a short season, for weeks or months,
but years, perhaps for life. These new and evil anticipations
swept darkly across the troubled surface of Rosamond's mind,
as she gazed on the varying countenance of Eugenia, and
wondered she had never thought her handsome before. The
gratitude and sensibility that beamed from her eyes whenever
they turned on her benefactor, seemed to her diseased imagination the harbingers of a warmer emotion, and the constitutional ardour and frankness of her expressions were indicative
of the most dangerous of characters. It was well for Rosamond
that the recent death of her mother was a legitimate excuse
for her pensiveness and gloom, as the incipient stage of the
malady that was beginning to steal into her soul must otherwise have been perceived. Cecil, frank, confident, and un-
suspecting, never dreamed that every attention bestowed on
Eugenia was considered as a robbery to herself. Eugenia,
warm-hearted, impulsive, and grateful, as little imagined that
the overflowings of her gratitude were construed into feelings
she would have blushed to have cherished. Cecil was passionately fond of music. Since her mother's death, Rosamond
could not be prevailed upon to touch the keys of the instru-

ment, and he was too kind to urge upon her a task repugnant to her feelings. But when Eugenia discovered that she possessed an accomplishment capable of imparting pleasure to him who had given her the means of acquiring it, she was never weary of exercising it. She sang too with rare sweetness and power, and never refused to sing the songs that Cecil loved to hear. Rosamond could not sing. She had never mourned over this deficiency before, but now she could not bear to think that another should impart a pleasure to her husband, she had not the means of bestowing. She forgot that she had selfishly denied to gratify his taste, in the way she had the power of doing, because it would have interrupted the indulgence of her filial grief. Another thing deeply wounded Rosamond's feelings: always accustomed to being waited upon by others, to have all her wishes anticipated, she never thought of showing her love by those active manifestations which most men love to receive. She would have laid down her life for her husband, if the sacrifice were required, but she never thought of offering him a glass of water with her own hand, because it was the office of the servants to supply his recurring wants. Never till she saw these attentions bestowed by another who was not a menial, did she imagine that affection could give an added relish, even to a cup of cold water, when offered to the thirsty lip. One warm, sultry day, Cecil entered after a long walk, and throwing himself on a sofa exclaimed, "Give me some drink, Titania—for I faint—even as a sick girl." Rosamond smiled at his theatrical assumption of Cæsar's dignity, and reaching out her hand, rang the bell. Eugenia flew out of the room, and returned long before a servant could answer the summons, with a glass of water, and bending one knee to the ground, with sportive grace she offered it to his acceptance.

"Eugenia!" cried Rosamond, colouring very high, "we have no lack of servants. I am sure there is no necessity of your assuming such a trouble."

"Oh! but it is such a pleasure!" exclaimed Eugenia, springing up, and placing the empty glass on the sideboard. "It is all I can do. You would not deprive me of the privilege if you knew how dearly I prize it."

Had Cecil observed the heightened colour of Rosamond, he might have conjectured that all was not right in her bosom, but she sat in the shadow of a curtain, and her emotion was unperceived. A few evenings afterwards, they were walking

115

together, when they met a woman bustling through the streets, with her arm a-kimbo, and an air of boldness and defiance, that spoke the determined Amazon. Eugenia clung closely to Cecil's arm as she approached, and turned deadly pale; she recognised in those stony eyes and iron features the dreaded Mrs. Grundy, the tyrant of her desolate childhood, and she felt as if the thong were again descending on her quivering flesh, and the iron again entering into her soul. Such a rush of painful recollections came over her, she was obliged to lean against a railing for support, while Cecil, who saw what was the cause of her agitation, gave a stern glance at the woman, who had stopped, and was gazing in her face with an undaunted stare.

"Heyday!" cried she, "who's this? 'Tisn't Giny, sure enough? I never should have thought of such a thing, if it hadn't been for the gentleman. Well! can't you speak to a body, now you have got to be such a fine lady? This is all the gratitude one gets in the world."

"Gratitude!" repeated Cecil, "how dare you talk of gratitude to her, before me? Pass on and leave her, and be thankful that your sex shields you a second time from my indignation."

"Well you needn't bristle up so, sir," cried she, with a sneer. "I'm not going to kill her. I suppose you've got married to her by this time. But you'd better look sharp, lest she gets into a rambling way, as her mother did before her." With a malignant laugh the virago passed on, delighted to find that she had drawn quite a crowd to the spot where Eugenia still leaned, incapable of motion, and Rosamond stood, pale as a statue, brooding over the words of the woman, as if, like a Delphian priestess, she had uttered the oracles of fate.

"Why should she imagine *her* to be his wife," whispered the bosom serpent, subtle as its arch prototype in the bowers of Eden, "if she had not witnessed in him evidences of tenderness, such as a husband only should bestow? That random sentence spoke volumes, and justifies thy fearful suspicions. Alas for thee, Rosamond! The young blossoms of thy happiness are blighted in the sweet springtime of their bloom. There is no more greenness or fragrance for thee—better that thou hadst died, and been laid by thy mother's side, than live to experience the bitter pangs of deceived confidence and unrequited love."

Cecil, unconscious of the secret enemy that was operating

so powerfully against him in the breast of Rosamond, wondered at her coldness to Eugenia; a coldness which became every day more apparent, and was even assuming the character of dislike. It seemed so natural in one so young and affectionate as Rosamond, to wind her affections round a being of corresponding youth and sensibility, so foreign to her gentle nature to treat one entirely dependent on her kindness, with such reserve and distrust—he wondered, regretted, and at length remonstrated. Eugenia had just anticipated a servant's movements in bringing him a book from the library, which he expressed a desire to see, and he had taken it from her hand with a smile of acknowledgment, when the instantaneous change in the countenance of Rosamond arrested his attention. It was so chilling, so inexplicable, he dropped the book to the ground in his confusion, which Eugenia, with her usual graceful readiness, again lifted and laid upon his knee. In raising her face from her bending position, she encountered the glance of Rosamond, which seemed to have upon her the momentary effect of fascination. She stood as if rooted to the spot, gazing steadfastly on her, then with a cheek as hueless as ashes, turned and precipitately left the apartment. Cecil and Rosamond looked at each other without speaking. Never had they exchanged such a look before. "Good heavens!" he exclaimed, rising and walking two or three times across the apartment, with a resounding tread. "Good heavens! what a transformation! I must know the cause of it. Tell me, Rosamond, and tell me truly and unreservedly, what means your mysterious and unkind behaviour to one who never can have offended you? What has Eugenia done to forfeit your affection as a friend, your consideration as a guest, your respect to the claims of your husband's adopted sister?"

"It were far better to subject your own heart and conscience to this stern inquisition, than mine, Cecil," replied Rosamond bitterly. "Had you informed me sooner of the length and breadth of my duties, I might have fulfilled them better I did not know, when Eugenia was received into our household, how overwhelming were her claims. I did not know that I was expected to exalt *her* happiness on the ruins of my own."

"Rosamond! Rosamond!" interrupted Cecil, vehemently —"Beware what you say—beware lest you strike a death-blow to our wedded love. I can bear anything in the world but suspicion. Every feeling of my heart has been laid bare

before you.   There is not a thought that is not as open to your
scrutiny as the heavens in the blaze of noonday.   How unworthy
of yourself, how disgraceful to me, how wounding to Eugenia,
this unjustifiable conduct !"

Every chord of Rosamond's heart quivered with agony at
this burst of indignant feeling from lips which had never
before addressed her but in mild and persuasive tones.   Had
he wealth of worlds been laid at her feet, she would have
given it to recall the last words she had uttered.   Still, in the
midst of her remorse and horror, she felt the overmastering
influence of her imagined wrongs, and that influence triumphed
over the suggestions of reason and the admonitions of prudence.

" It is ungenerous—it is unmanly," she cried, " to force
me into the confession of sentiments which you blame me for
declaring—I had said nothing, done nothing—yet you arraign
me before the bar of inexorable justice, as the champion of the
injured Eugenia.   If the sincerity of my countenance offends
you, it is my misfortune, not my fault.   I cannot smile on the
boldness I condemn, or the arts I despise."

" Boldness ! arts !" repeated Cecil.   " If there was ever an
unaffected, impulsive child of nature, it is she whom you so
deeply wrong; but you wrong yourself far more.   You let
yourself down from the high station where I had enthroned
you, and paid you a homage scarcely inferior to an angel of
light.   You make me an alien from your bosom, and nourish
there a serpent which will wind you deeper and deeper in its
envenomed folds, till your heart-strings are crushed beneath its
coils."

" I am indeed most wretched," exclaimed Rosamond ; " and
if I have made myself so, I deserve pity rather than upbraiding.   Cecil, you never could have loved me, or you would not
so lightly cast me from you."

Cecil, who had snatched up his hat, and laid his hand on
the latch of the door, turned at the altered tone of her voice.
Tears, which she vainly endeavoured to hide, gushed from her
eyes, and stole down her colourless cheeks.

" Rosamond," said he, in a softened tone, approaching her
as he spoke, " if you believe what you last uttered, turn away
from me, and let us henceforth be strangers to each other ;—
but if your heart belies their meaning, if you can restore me
the confidence you have withdrawn, and which is my just due,
if you are willing to rely unwaveringly on my integrity, my

honour, and my love, come to my arms once more, and they shall shelter you through life with unabated tenderness and undivided devotion."

Poor, foolish Rosamond! she had wrought herself up to a state bordering on despair, and the revulsion of her feelings was so great that she almost fainted in the arms that opened to enfold her. Her folly, her madness, her injustice and selfishness stared her so fearfully in the face, she was appalled nd self-condemned. Like the base Judean, she had been about to throw away from her "a gem richer than all its tribe," a gem of whose priceless worth she had never till this moment been fully conscious. She made the most solemn resolutions for the future, invoking upon herself the most awful penalties if she ever again yielded to a passion so degrading. But passion once admitted is not so easily dispossessed of its hold. Every self-relying effort is but a flaxen withe bound round the slumbering giant, broken in the first grasp of temptation. Jealousy is that demon, whose name is Legion, which flies from the rebuking voice of Omnipotence alone. Rosamond did not say, "If God give me strength, I will triumph over my indwelling enemy." She said, "The tempter shall seek me in vain—I am strong, and I defy its power." Rosamond was once more happy, but she had planted a thorn in the bosom of another, sharp, deep, and rankling. No after kindness could obliterate the remembrance of that involuntary, piercing glance. It was but the sheathing of a weapon. Eugenia felt that the cold steel was still lurking in the scabbard, ready to flash forth at the bidding of passion. A few evenings after the scene just described, when she had been playing and singing some of Cecil's favourite songs, at the magnanimous request of Rosamond, she turned suddenly to Cecil and said—

"I think I overheard a friend of yours say to you the other day, that I might make my fortune on the stage. Now," added she, blushing, "I do not wish to go upon the stage, but if my musical talents could give me distinction there, they migh be made useful in the domestic circle. I have been told of a lady who wishes an instructress for her daughters. Suffer me to offer myself for the situation. If through your bounty I am possessed of accomplishments which may be subservient to myself or others, is it not my duty to exercise them? I should have done this sooner—I have been too long an idler."

"No, no, Eugenia," said Rosamond, warmly, every good

and generous feeling of her heart in full and energetic operation—"we can never sanction such a proposition. Is not this your home as well as mine? Are you not our sister? Remember the threefold cord that never was to be broken." She pressed Eugenia's hand in both her own, and continued, in a trembling voice—"If I have ever seemed cold or unkind, forgive me, Eugenia, for I believe I am a strange, fitful being. You found me a sad mourner over the grave of my mother, with weakened nerves and morbid sensibilities. My mind is getting a healthier tone. Remain with us—we shall be happier by and by."

Completely overcome by this unexpected and candid avowal, Eugenia threw her arms round Rosamond's neck, and exclaimed —"I shall be the happiest being in the world, if you indeed love me. I have no one else in the world to love but you and my benefactor."

Cecil felt as if he could have prostrated himself at Rosamond's feet, and thanked her for her noble and generous conduct. He had waited in trembling eagerness for her reply. It was more than he expected. It was all he wished or required.

"Be but true to yourself, my beloved Rosamond," said he, when he was alone with her, "and you can never be unjust to me. Continue in the path you have now marked out, and you shall be repaid not only with my warmest love, but with my respect, my admiration, and my gratitude."

Thus encouraged, Rosamond felt new life flowing in her veins. Though she could not sing according to scientific rules, her buoyant spirit burst forth in warbling notes, as she moved about her household duties, with light, bounding steps, rejoicing in the consciousness of recovered reason. Week after week glided away, without any circumstance arising to remind them of the past. Indeed all seemed to have forgotten that anything had ever disturbed their domestic peace.

"Oh! what beautiful flowers!" exclaimed Rosamond, as, riding with her husband, on a lovely autumnal evening, they passed a public garden, ornamented with the last flowers of the season. "I wish I had some of them. There are the emblems of love, constancy, and devotion. If I had them now, I would bind them on my heart, in remembrance of this enchanting ride."

"You shall have them speedily, dear Rosamond," replied he,

"even if, like the gallant knight who named the sweet flower *Forget-me-not*, I sacrifice my life to purchase them."

Rosamond little thought those flowers, sought with such childish earnestness, and promised with such sportive gallantry, were destined to be so fatal to her newly acquired serenity. As soon as they reached home, Cecil returned to seek the flowers which Rosamond desired, and selecting the most beautiful the garden afforded, brought them with as much enthusiasm of feeling as if it were the bridegroom's first gift. When he entered the room Eugenia was alone, Rosamond being still engaged in changing her riding apparel.

"Oh! what an exquisitely beautiful nosegay," cried Eugenia, involuntarily stretching out her hand—"how rich, how fragrant!"

"Yes! I knew you would admire them," he replied—"I brought them expressly for——" Rosamond, he was just going to add, when he was suddenly called out, leaving the flowers in the hand of Eugenia, and the unfinished sentence in her ear. Not knowing anything of their appropriation, Eugenia believed the bouquet a gift to herself, and she stood turning them to the light in every direction, gazing on their rainbow hues with sparkling eyes, when Rosamond entered the apartment, with a cheek glowing like the roses before her.

"See what beautiful flowers your husband has just given me," cried Eugenia—"he must have been endowed with second sight, for I was just yearning after such a bouquet."

Had Rosamond beheld the leaves of the Bohon-Upas, instead of the blossoms she loved, she could not have experienced a more sickening sensation. She had begged for those flowers —she had pointed out their emblematic beauties—had promised to bind them to her heart, and yet they were wantonly bestowed on another, as if in defiance of her former wretchedness. She grew dizzy from the rapidity of the thoughts that whirled through her brain, and leaning against the mantel-piece, pressed her hand upon her head.

"You are ill, dear Rosamond," cried Eugenia, springing towards her—"lean on me—you are pale and faint."

Rosamond recoiled from her touch, as if a viper were crawling over her. She had lost the power of self-control, and the passion that was threatening to suffocate her, found vent in language.

"Leave me," cried she, "if you would not drive me mad.

You have destroyed the peace of my whole life. You have stolen like a serpent into my domestic bower, and robbed me of the affections of a once doting husband. Take them openly, if you will, and triumph in the possession of your ill-gotten treasure."

"Rosamond!" uttered a deep, low voice behind her. She started, turned, and beheld her husband standing on the threshold of the door, pale, dark and stern as the judge who pronounces the doom of the transgressor. Eugenia, who had dropped the flowers at the commencement of Rosamond's indignant accusation, with a wild, bewildered countenance, which kindled as she proceeded, now met her scorching glance, with eyes that literally flashed fire. Her temple veins swelled, her lip quivered, every feature was eloquent with scorn.

"Rosamond," said she, "you have banished me for ever. You have cruelly, wantonly, causelessly insulted me." She walked rapidly to the door, where Cecil yet stood, and glided by him before he could intercept her passage. Then suddenly returning, she snatched his hand, and pressed it to her forehead and to her lips.

"My benefactor, brother, friend!" cried she, "may Heaven for ever bless thee, even as thou hast blessed me!"

"Stay, Eugenia, stay!" he exclaimed, endeavouring to detain her—but it was too late. He heard her footsteps on the stairs, and the door of her chamber hastily close, and he knew he could not follow her.

"Rash, infatuated girl!" cried he, turning to Rosamond, "what have you done? At a moment too when my whole heart was overflowing with tenderness and love towards you. Remember, if you banish Eugenia from the shelter of my roof, I am bound by every tie of honour and humanity still to protect and cherish her."

"I know it well," replied Rosamond; "I remember too that it was to give a home to Eugenia you first consented to bind yourself by marriage vows. That home may still be hers. I am calm now, Cecil—you see I can speak calmly. The certainty of a misfortune gives the spirit and the power of endurance. Those flowers are trifles in themselves, but they contain a world of meaning."

"These worthless flowers!" exclaimed Cecil, trampling them under his feet till their bright leaves lay a soiled and indistinguishable mass—"and have these raised the whirlwind of jealous passion? These fading playthings, left for a moment in another's keeping, accidentally left, to be immediately reclaimed!"

"You gave them to her—with her own lips she told me—rapture sparkling in her eyes."

"It was all a misunderstanding—an innocent mistake. Oh, Rosamond! for a trifle like this you could forget all my faith and affection, every feeling which should be sacred in your eyes—forget your woman's gentleness, and utter words which seem branded in my heart and brain in burning and indelible characters. I dare not go on. I shall say what I may bitterly repent. I wish you no punishment greater than your own reflections."

Rosamond listened to his retreating footsteps, she heard the outer door heavily close, and the sound fell on her ear like the first fall of the damp clods on the coffin, the signal of mortal separation. She remained pale as a statue, gazing on the withering flowers, counting the quick beatings of her lonely heart, believing herself doomed to a widowhood more cruel than that the grave creates. Cecil's simple explanation, stamped with the dignity of truth, had roused her from the delirium of passion, and seeing her conduct in its true light, she shuddered at the review. Her head ached to agony—one moment she shivered with cold, the next the blood in her veins seemed changed to molten lead. "I feel very strangely," thought she—"perhaps I am going to die, and when I am dead, he will pity and forgive me." She had barely strength to seek her own chamber, where, throwing herself on the bed, she lay till the shades of night darkened around her, conscious of but one wish, that her bed might prove her grave, and Cecil, melted by her early fate, might shed one tear of forgiveness over the icy lips that never more could open to offend. The bell rang for supper—she heeded not the summons. A servant came to tell her that Mr. Dormer was below. Her heart bounded, but she remained immovable. Again the servant came.

"Shall I make tea for Mr. Dormer?" she asked. "Miss Eugenia is gone out."

Rosamond started up, and leaned on her elbow. "Gone!" repeated she, wildly—"when? where?"

"I don't know, ma'am," replied the girl; "she put on her bonnet and shawl an hour ago and went out through the back gate."

" Does Mr. Dormer know it ?" asked Rosamond faintly.

" I don't know, ma'am—he has just come in," was the reply.
—" I saw him reading a note he found on the table in the
hall, and he seemed mightily flustered."

There was an insolent curiosity in the countenance of the
girl, who had hitherto been respectful and submissive. She
laced the lamp near the bedside and left the room ; and
lmost simultaneously, Cecil entered, with an open note in his
. and, which he threw upon the bed without speaking. She
seized it mechanically, and attempted to read it, but the letters
seemed to move and emit electric sparks, flashing on her
aching eyeballs. It was with difficulty that she deciphered
the following lines, written evidently with a trembling
hand :—

" Farewell, kindest, noblest, and best of friends ! May the
happiness which I have unconsciously blighted, revive in my
absence. I go, sustained by the strength of a virtuous resolution, not the excitement of indignant passion. The influence
of your bounty remains, and will furnish me an adequate
support. Seek not, I pray you, to find the place of my abode.
The Heaven in which I trust will protect me. Farewell—
deluded, but still beloved Rosamond ! Your injustice shall
be forgotten, your benefits remembered for ever."

Rosamond dropped the letter, cast one glance towards her
husband, who stood with folded arms, pale and immovable, at
the foot of the bed, then sinking back upon her pillow, a mist
came over her eyes, and all was darkness.

When she again recovered the consciousness of her existence, she found herself in a darkened chamber, the curtains
of her bed closely drawn, saving a small aperture, through
which she could perceive a neat, matronly figure, moving with
soft, careful steps, and occasionally glancing anxiously towards
the bed. She attempted to raise herself on her elbow, but she
had not strength to lift her head from the pillow ; she could
scarcely carry her feeble hand to her forehead, to put back the
moist hair which fell heavily over her brow.

" How weak I am !" said she faintly. " How long have I
slept ?"

" Be composed," said the stranger, approaching her gently,
"and do not speak. You have been very ill. Everything
depends on your keeping perfectly quiet."

Rosamond began to tremble violently as she gazed up in
the stranger's face. Why was she committed to *her* charge?

Was she forsaken by him whom awakening memory brought before her as an injured and perhaps avenging husband?

"Where is he?" cried she, in a voice so low, the woman bent her ear to her lips, to hear.

"The doctor?" replied she. "Oh, he will soon be here. He said if you waked, no one must come near you, and you must not be allowed to speak one word. It might cost you your life."

Rosamond tried to gasp out her husband's name, but her parched lips were incapable of further articulation. Her eyes closed from exhaustion, and the nurse, supposing she slept, drew the curtains closer, and moved on tiptoe to the window. At length the door slowly opened, and the footstep of a man entered the room. Rosamond knew it was not her husband's step, and such a cold feeling fell on her heart, she thought it the precursor of death. She heard a whispered conversation which set every nerve throbbing with agony. Then the curtains were withdrawn, and she felt a stranger's hand counting the pulsations of her chilled veins. "I am forsaken," thought she, "even in my dying hour. Oh God! it is just." Again the chamber was still, and she must have fallen into a deep slumber, for when she again opened her eyes, she saw a lamp glimmering through the curtains, and the shadow of her nurse reflected in them, seated at a table, reading. She was reading aloud, though in a low voice, as if fearful of disturbing the slumbers she was watching. Rosamond caught the sound, "I the Lord thy God am a jealous God." She repeated it to herself, and it gave her an awful sensation. The commanding claims of her Maker upon her affections, for the first time rose before her in all their height, depth, power, and majesty. "A jealous God!" How tremendous, how appalling the idea. If she, a poor worm of the dust, was so severe and uncompromising in her demands upon a fellow being, what terrible exactions might a neglected Deity make from the creature he had formed for his glory? She remembered the command from which that fearful sentence was extracted. She had broken it, trampled it under her feet. She had bowed down in adoration to an earthly idol, and robbed her God, her *jealous God*, of the homage due to his august name. The light that poured in upon her conscience was like the blazing of a torch through a dark mine. She had felt before the madness of her bosom passion, she now felt its sin and its sacrilege. "I am forsaken," again repeated she to herself,

"but I had first forsaken thee, O my God! Thou art drawing me home unto thee." Tears gathering thick and fast,
fell down her pale cheeks, till the pillow they pressed was wet
as with rain-drops. She wept long, and without one effort
to restrain the gushing forth of her melting heart, when
exhausted nature once more sought relief in sleep. Her first
consciousness, on awakening, was of a soft hand laid gently on
her brow, a warm breath stealing over her cheek, and a trembling lip gently pressed upon her own. Had she awakened in
the abodes of the blest, in the midst of the hierarchy of heaven,
she could hardly have experienced a deeper rapture than that.
which flooded her breast. Slowly, as if fearing to banish by the
act the image drawn on her now glowing heart, she lifted her
eyes, and met the eyes of her husband looking down upon her,
no longer stern and upbraiding, but softened into woman's
tenderness. The next moment he was kneeling by the bedside, his face buried in the covering, which shook from the
strong emotion it concealed.

When Rosamond learned that Cecil, instead of having left
her to her bitter consequences of her rashness, in just and un-
appeasable resentment, had never left her in her unconsciousness, and since her restoration to reason had hovered near the
threshold of her chamber day and night, forbidden to enter,
lest his presence should produce an agitation fatal to a frame
apparently trembling on the brink of the grave, she again reproached herself for believing he could have been capable of
such unrelenting cruelty. When she was assured too that
Eugenia was safe under the protection of an early friend,
whom she had most unexpectedly encountered, and only
waited a passport from the physician, to come to her bedside,
her soul swelled with gratitude that found no language but
prayer.

"I have sinned against Heaven and thee, my husband!"
exclaimed Rosamond, from the depth of a penitent and chastened spirit—"I am no more worthy to be called thy wife."

"We have both erred, my beloved Rosamond; we have lived
too much for the world and ourselves, regardless of higher
and holier relations. Never, till I feared to lose thee for
ever, did I feel the drawings of that mighty chain which links
us inseparably to Him who created us. Let us both commence
life anew—awakened to our responsibilities as Christians, and,
profiting by the sad experience of the past, let us lay the
foundations of our happiness too deep and broad for the storms

of passion to overthrow. Let us build it on the Rock of Ages."

And who was the friend whom Eugenia had so providentially discovered? When she left the dwelling of Cecil Dormer, to seek the lady who wished for an instructress for her daughters, one of the first persons who crossed her path was the terrific Mrs. Grundy. This woman, whose hatred for her seemed implacable as the injuries she had inflicted were deep, seeing her alone and in evident disorder of mind, began to revile and threaten her. A stranger, observing the terror and loathing with which a young and attractive-looking girl shrunk from a coarse and masculine woman, paused and offered his protection. The remarkable resemblance which Eugenia bore to her ill-fated mother led to a discovery as unexpected as it was interesting. The melancholy stranger was no other than her own father, who believed his wife and child had perished in their flight, having heard of the destruction of the boat in which they fled. Thus mysteriously had Providence transmuted into a blessing, what seemed the greatest misfortune of her life.

The history of Mr. St. Clair and his unfortunate wife, which he subsequently related to Cecil and Rosamond, was fraught with the most intense interest. Like Rosamond, he had cherished a *bosom serpent*, remorseless as death, "cruel as the grave;" but he had not, like her, found, before it was too late, an antidote for its deadly venom.

MY GRANDMOTHER'S BRACELET.

WE were all seated in a piazza, one beautiful summer's night. The moonbeams quivered through the interlacing vines that crept fantastically over the latticework that surrounded it. My grandmother sat in an arm-chair in the centre of the group, her arms quietly folded across her lap, her hair white and silvery as the moonbeams that lingered on its parted folds. She was the handsomest old lady I ever saw, my revered grandmother, and in the spring of her years had been a reigning belle. To me she was still beautiful, in the gentle quietude of life's evening shades, the dignity of chastened passions, waiting hopes, and sustaining religious faith. I was her favourite grandchild, and the place near her feet, the arm laid across her lap, the uplifted eye fixed steadfastly on her face, constant as the recurrence of the still night hour, told a story of love and devotion on my part, which defied all competition. As I sat this night, leaning on her lap, I held her hand in mine, and the thought that, a few more years, that hand must be cold in the grave, incapable of answering the glowing pressure of mine, made me draw a deep inspiration, and I almost imagined her complexion assumed an ashen hue, prophetical of death. The weather was warm, and she wore a large loose wrapper, with flowing sleeves, left unconfined at the wrist. As I moved her hand, the folds of the sleeve fell back, and something pure and bright glittered in the moonlight. She made a movement to draw down the sleeve, but the eager curiosity of childhood was not to be eluded. I caught her wrist, and baring it to the gaze of all, exclaimed—

"Only think—grandmother has got on a bracelet—a pearl

(234)

bracelet ! Who would think of her indulging in such finery ? Here are two sweet pearl lilies set together in a golden clasp, with golden leaves below them. Why, grandmother, you must be setting up for a bride !"

" It was a bridal gift," replied she, sliding the bracelet on her shrunken arm; "a bridal gift, made long ago. It was a foolish thought, child. I was looking over a casket, where I have deposited the choicest treasures of my youth, and I clasped it on my wrist, to see how my arm had fallen from its fair proportions. My mind became so lost in thinking of the story of this gem, I forgot to restore it to the place where it has so long lain, slumbering with the hoarded memories of other days."

" A story !" we all eagerly exclaimed,—"please tell it—you promised us one to-night."

" Ah ! children, it is no fairy tale, about bright genii, and enchanted palaces, and ladies so beautiful that they bewitch every one who comes within the magic reach of their charms. It is a true tale, and has some sad passages in it."

" Grandmother," said I, in a dignified manner, "I hope you don't think me so silly as not to like anything because it is true. I have got over the Arabian Nights long ago, and I would rather hear something to make me feel sorry than glad —I always do feel sad when the moon shines on me, but I can't tell the reason why."

" Hush ! Mina, and let grandmother tell her story—you always talk so much," said little Mitty, who sat on the other side of her venerable relative.

The old lady patted with one hand the golden head of the chider, but the arm clasped by the magic bracelet was still imprisoned by my fingers, and as she proceeded in its history, my grasp tightened and tightened from the intenseness of my interest, till she was compelled to beg me to release her.

" Yes," said she, in a musing tone, " there is a story depending on this, which I remember as vividly as if the events were of yesterday. I may forget what happened an hour ago, but the records of my youth are written in lines that grow deeper as time flows over them."

She looked up steadily for a few moments, appearing to my imagination like an inspired sibyl, then began as follows :

" When I was a young girl, I had no brothers or sisters, as you have, but was an only, I might say a lonely child, for my father was dead and my mother an invalid. When I returned

from school, I obtained permission to invite a sweet young
cousin of mine, whose name was Eglantine, to be my companion. We were affluent, she was poor; and when my mother
proposed to make our house her home, she accepted the offer
with gratitude and joy. She was an interesting creature, of
a peculiar temperament and exquisite sensibility. She was
subject to fits of wonderful buoyancy, and equal despondency;
sometimes she would warble all day, gay and untiring as the
bird perched on yonder spray, then a soft melancholy would
sit brooding on her brow, as if she feared some impending
misfortune. This was probably owing to the peculiar circumstances of her infancy, for she was born during her mother's
widowhood, and nursed by a mother's tears. A poetical friend
had given her the name of Eglantine, and well did her beauty,
sweetness, delicacy, and fragility justify the name. In our
girlhood we grew together, like the friends of the Midsum-
mer's Night, almost inseparable in body, and never divided in
heart, by those little jealousies which sometimes interpose their
barriers to young maidens' friendships. But I see little Mitty
has fallen asleep already. My story is too grave for the light
ears of childhood. I shall be obliged, too, to say something
about love, and even you, Mina, are entirely too young to
know anything of its influence."

"Oh! but I do know something, grandmother," exclaimed
I, impulsively; "that is, I have read—I have thought"—I
stammered and stopped, unable to express my own vague
ideas.

"You may not be too young to sympathize, but certainly
too young to feel," said my grandmother, mildly; "but,
ardent and sympathizing as your nature is, it will be hard for
you to carry back your mind to the time when all the warm
passions and hopes of youth were glowing in my bosom. It
is enough to say that there was one who came and rivalled
Eglantine in my affections, one to whom I was betrothed, and
to whom I was to be shortly wedded. It was on such an eve
as this, so clear and bright, that he gave me the pledge of our
betrothal, this bracelet of pearl, and clasped it on an arm which
then filled the golden circlet. Perhaps you wonder that the
first token of love should not have been a ring; but Ronald
did not like to follow the track of other men, and even in
trifles marked out for himself a peculiar and independent
course. That night, when I retired to my chamber, I found
Eglantine seated at the open window, apparently absorbed in

the contemplation of the starry heavens. She sat in a loose undress, her hair of paly gold hung unbound over her shoulders, and her head, being slightly thrown back, allowed the moonlight to flood her whole face with its unearthly radiance.

" ' You look very beautiful and romantic, dear Eglantine,' said I, softly approaching her, and throwing my arms round her neck ; ' but come down from the stars a little while, my sweet cousin, and share in my earthborn emotions.' My heart was too full of happiness, my spirits too excited, not to overflow in unreserved confidence in her bosom. She wept as I poured into her ears all my hopes, my recent vows, and future schemes of felicity. It was her usual manner of expressing deep sympathy, and I loved her the better for her tears. ' All I wonder at and blame in Ronald is,' and I spoke this in true sincerity, ' that he does not love you better than me. Never, till this evening, was I sure of his preference.'

" Eglantine withdrew herself from my arms, and turned her face to the shadow of the wall. There was something inexplicable in her manner that chilled, and even alarmed me. A thought, too painful to be admitted, darted for a moment to my mind. Could she be jealous of Ronald's love for me? Was my happiness to be built on the ruin of hers? No! it could not be. She probably feared my affections might become alienated from her in consequence of my new attachment. Such a fear was natural, and I hastened to remove it by the warmest professions, mingled with covert reproaches for her doubts and misgivings.

" I had a young waiting-maid, who, next to Eglantine, was the especial object of my regard. She was the daughter of a gentlewoman, who, from a series of misfortunes, was reduced to penury, to which was added the helplessness of disease. To relieve her mother from the pressure of immediate want, the young Alice offered herself as a candidate for a state of servitude, and I eagerly availed myself of the opportunity of securing the personal attendance of one so refined in manner and so winning in appearance. Alice now came forward, as was her custom, to assist me in preparing for my nightly rest. She was about to unclasp the bracelet from my wrist, but I drew back my arm. ' No, no, Alice,' said I, ' this is an amulet. Sweet dreams will come to my pillow, beckoned by its fairy power. I cannot sleep without it. See how beautifully the lilies gleam in the moonlight that gilds my couch.' Alice seemed as if she could never weary in admiring the

116

beauty of the ornament. She turned my arm to shift the rays,
and catch the delicate colouring of the pearls, and looped up
the sleeve of my night-dress in a fantastic manner, to display
it fully to her gaze. Once or twice I thought I saw the eyes
of Eglantine fastened upon it with a sad, wistful expression,
and the same exquisitely painful thought again darted to my
mind. I struggled against its admission, as degrading both to
myself and her, and at last fell asleep, with my arm thrown
on the outside of the bed, and the bracelet shining out in the
pure night-beams. Alice slept in a little bed by the side of
mine, for I could not bear that a creature so young and delicate, and so gentle bred, should share the apartments devoted
to the servants, and be exposed to their rude companionship.
She generally awoke me with her light touch or gentle voice,
but when I awoke the next morning, I saw Alice still sleeping, with a flushed cheek and an attitude that betokened excitement and unrest. Eglantine sat at her window, reading,
dressed with her usual care by her own graceful fingers. In
the school of early poverty she had learned the glorious lesson
of independence, a lesson which, in my more luxurious life,
I had never acquired. 'Alice must be ill,' said I, rising, and
approaching her bedside; 'she looks feverish, and her brows
are knit, as if her dreams were fearful.' I bent down over
her, and laid my hand upon her shoulder, to rouse her from
her uneasy slumbers, when I started—for the precious bracelet
was gone. Eglantine laid down her book at my sudden exclamation, and Alice, wakening, looked round her with a bewildered expression. 'My bracelet!' repeated I—'it is gone.'
I flew to my couch; it was not there. I looked upon the carpet,
in the vain hope that the clasp had unloosed, and that it had
fallen during the night. 'Alice,' cried I, 'rise this moment,
and help me to find my bracelet. You must know where it is.
It never could have vanished without aid.' I fixed my eyes
steadfastly on her face, which turned as hueless as marble.
She trembled in every limb, and sunk down again on the side
of the bed.

"'You do not think *I* have taken it, Miss Laura?" said
she, gasping for breath.

"'I do not know what to think,' I answered, in a raised
tone; 'but it is very mysterious, and your whole appearance
and manner is very strange this morning, Alice. You must
have been up in the night, or you would not have slept so unusually late——

" 'Do not be hasty, Laura,' said Eglantine, in a sweet, soothing voice; 'it may yet be found. Perhaps it is clinging to your dress, concealed in its folds. Let me assist you in searching.' She unfolded the sheets, turned up the edges of the carpet, examined every corner where it might have been tossed, but all in vain. In the mean while Alice remained like one stupefied, following our movements with a pale, terrified countenance, without offering to participate in the search.

" 'There is no use in looking longer, Eglantine,' said I, bitterly. 'I suspect Alice might assist us effectually to discover it, if she would. Nay, I will not say suspect—I believe —I dare to say, I know—for conscious guilt is written in glaring characters on her countenance.'

" 'Do not make any rash accusations, Laura,' cried Eglantine; 'I acknowledge appearances are much against her, but I cannot think Alice capable of such ingratitude, duplicity, and meanness.'

" Alice here burst into a passionate fit of weeping, and declared, with wringing hands and choking sobs, that she would sooner die than commit so base and wicked a deed.

" 'Oh! Miss Eglantine,' she exclaimed, 'didn't you take it in sport? It seems as if I saw you in a dream going up to Miss Laura, while she was asleep, and take it from her wrist, softly, and then vanish away. Oh! Miss Eglantine, the more I think of it the more I am sure I saw you,—all in sport, I know,—but please return it, or it will be death to me.'

" The blood seemed to boil up in the cheeks of Eglantine, so sudden and intense was the glow that mantled them.

" 'I thought you innocent, Alice,' said she, 'but I see, with pain, that you are an unprincipled girl. How dare you attempt to impose on me the burthen of your crime? How dare you think of sheltering yourself under the shadow of my name?'

" The vague suspicions which the assertion of Alice had excited, vanished before the outraged looks and language of the usually gentle Eglantine. Alice must have been the transgressor, and in proportion to the affection and confidence I had reposed in her, and the transcendent value of the gift, was my indignation at the offence, and the strength of my resolution to banish her from me.

" 'Restore it,' said I, 'and leave me. Do it quietly and immediately, and I will inflict no other punishment than your own reflections, for having abused so much love and trust.'

" 'Search me, if you please, Miss Laura, and all that be longs to me,' replied Alice, in a firmer tone, 'but I cannot give back what I have never taken. I would not, for fifty thousand worlds, take what was not mine, and least of all from you, who have been so kind and good. I am willing to go, for I would rather beg my bread from door to door, than live upon the bounty of one who thinks me capable of such guilt :' with a composure that strangely contrasted with her late violent agitation, she arranged her dress, and was walking towards the door, when Eglantine arrested her—

" 'Alice, Alice, you must be mad to persist in this course. Confess the whole, return the bracelet, and Laura may yet forgive you. Think of your sick mother. How can you go to her in shame and disgrace ?'

"At the mention of her mother, Alice wept afresh, and putting her hand to her head, exclaimed—

" 'I feel very, very sick. Perhaps we shall die together, and then God will take pity on us. The great God knows I am innocent of this crime.'

"Grandmother," interrupted I, unable to keep silence any longer, "tell me if she was not innocent. I know she must have been. Who could have taken it ?"

"Do you think Eglantine more likely to have stolen it from her cousin, who was to her, as it were, another soul and being ?"

"Oh ! no," I replied, "but I shall feel unhappy till I discover the thief. Please, grandmother, go on. Did Alice really go away ?"

"Yes, my child," answered my grandmother, in a faltering voice, "she went, though my relenting heart pleaded for her to linger. Her extreme youth and helplessness, her previous simplicity and truthfulness, and her solemn asseverations of innocence, all staggered my belief in her guilt. It was a mystery which grew darker as I attempted to penetrate it. If Alice were innocent, who could be guilty—Eglantine ? Such thought was sacrilege to her pure and elevated character, her tried affection for me, her self-respect, dignity, and truth. Alice returned to her mother, in spite of our permission for her to remain till the subject could be more fully investigated.

"When the door closed upon her retreating form, I sat down by the side of Eglantine, and wept. The fear that I had unjustly accused the innocent, the possibility, nay, the probability that she was guilty, the loss of the first pledge of plighted love, indefinite terrors for the future, a dim shade of superstition brooding over the whole, all conspired to make me gloomy and desponding. We were all unhappy. Ronald tried to laugh at my sadness, and promised me 'gems from the mine, and pearls from the ocean,' to indemnify me for my loss, yet I watched every change of his expressive countenance, and knew he thought deeply and painfully on the subject. The strange suspicion which had risen in my mind the preceding night, with regard to Eglantine's feelings towards him, revived when I saw them together, and I wondered I had not observed before the fluctuations of her complexion, and the agitation of her manner whenever he addressed her. He had always treated her with the kindness of a brother—that kindness now made me unhappy. I was becoming suspicious, jealous, and self-distrustful, with a settled conviction that some strange barrier existed to my union with Ronald, a destiny too bright and too beautiful to be realized in this world of dreams and shadows. My mother was firm in her belief of the guilt of Alice, who had never been a favourite of hers. Perhaps I lavished upon her too many indulgences, which displeased my mother's soberer judgment. She forbade all intercourse with her, all mention of her name, but she was ever present to my imagination; sometimes the shameless ingrate and accomplished deceiver, at others the eloquent pleader of her outraged innocence. One day Eglantine came to me, and laid her hand on mine with a look of unspeakable dismay—

"'I have heard,' said she, 'that Alice is dying. Let us go to her, Laura, and save her, if it be not too late.'

"What I felt at hearing these words I never can tell,—they pressed upon me with such a weight of grief—her innocence seemed as clear to me as noonday—my own unkindness as cruel as the grave. Quickly as possible we sought the cottage where her mother dwelt, and a piteous spectacle met our eyes. There lay Alice, on a little bed, pale, emaciated, and almost unconscious; her once bright hair dim and matted; her sweet blue eyes sunk and half closed; her arms laid listlessly by her side, the breath coming faint and flutteringly from her parted lips. On another bed lay her poor, heart-broken mother, unable to relieve the sufferings of her she would gladly have died to save. Frantic with grief, I threw myself by the side of Alice, and disturbed the solemn stillness of the death-hour with my incoherent ravings. I declared her innocence; I called upon her to live, to live for my sake, and throwing my arms wildly round her wasted form, struggled to hold her back from the grave yawning beneath her. It was in vain to cope with Omnipotence. Alice died, even in the midst of my agonies, and it was long before I was able to listen to the story of her illness, as related by her disconsolate mother. She had returned home sick and feverish, and sick and feverish she evidently was on her first awakening, and that wounded spirit, which none can bear, acting on a diseased frame, accelerated the progress of her fever till it settled on her brain, producing delirium, and ultimately death. During all her delirium, she was pleading her cause with an angel's eloquence, declaring her innocence, and blessing me as her benefactress and friend."

Here my grandmother paused, and covered her eyes with her handkerchief. I laid my head on her lap, and the ringlets of little Mitty's hair were wet with my tears. I felt quite broken-hearted, and ready to murmur at Providence for placing me in a world so full of error and woes.

"Did you ever feel happy again, dear grandmother?" asked I, when I ventured to break the silence,—curiosity was completely merged in sympathy.

"Yes, Mina, I have had hours of happiness, such as seldom falls to the lot of woman, but those bright hours were like the shining of the gold that comes forth purified from the furnace of fire. The mother of Alice soon followed her to the grave, and there they sleep, side by side, in the lonely churchyard. Eglantine soothed and comforted me, and endeavoured to stifle the self-upbraidings that ever sounded dolefully to my heart. Alice had been the victim of inexplicable circumstances, and so far from having been cruel, I had been kind and forbearing, considering the weight of evidence against her. Thus reasoned Eglantine, and I tried to believe her, but all my hopes of joy seemed blighted, for how could I mingle the wreath of love with the cypress boughs that now darkened my path? Ronald pressed an immediate union, but I shrunk with superstitious dread from the proposition, and refused the ring, with which he now sought to bind my faith. 'No, no,' I cried, 'the pledges of love are not for me—I will never accept another.'

"My mother grew angry at my fatalism. 'You are nursing phantasies,' said she, 'that are destroying the brightness of your youth. You are actually making yourself old, ere yet in your bloom. See, if there are not actually streaks of gray threading your jetty hair.' I rose and stood before'a mirror, and shaking my hair loose from the confining comb, saw that her words were true. Here and there a gleam of silver wandered through those tresses which had always worn that purple depth of hue peculiar to the raven's plumage. The chill that penetrated my heart on the death-bed of Alice, had thus suddenly and prematurely frosted the dark locks of my youth. My mother became alarmed at my excessive paleness, and proposed a journey for the restoration of my spirits and health. Ronald eagerly supported the suggestion, but Eglantine declined accompanying us. She preferred, she said, being alone. With books at home, and Nature, in the glory of its summer garniture, abroad, she could not want sources of enjoyment. I did not regret her determination, for her presence had become strangely oppressive to me, and even Ronald's manners had assumed an embarrassment and constraint towards her very different from their usual familiarity. The night before our departure I felt more melancholy than ever. It was just such a night as the one that witnessed our ill-starred betrothal. The moon came forth from behind a bed of white clouds, silvering every flake as it floated back from her beauteous face, and diffusing on earth the wondrous secret of heavenly communion. I could not sleep; and as I lay gazing on the solemn tranquillity of the night heavens, I thought of the time when 'those heavens should be rolled together as a scroll, and the elements melt with fervent heat,' and I, still thinking, living, feeling, in other, grander, everlasting scenes, the invisible dweller of my bosom's temple assumed such magnitude and majesty in my eyes, the contemplation became overwelming and awful. The sublime sound of the clock striking the midnight hour— and all who have heard that sound in the dead silence of the night, can attest that it is sublime—broke in on my deep abstraction. Eglantine, who had lain wrapped in peaceful slumbers, here softly drew back the bed-cover, and rising slowly, walked round with stilly steps to the side where I reclined, and stood looking fixedly upon me. 'Eglantine!' I exclaimed, terrified at her attitude and singular appearance. 'Eglantine, what is the matter?' She answered not, moved not, but remained standing, immovable, with her eyes fixed and expressionless as stone. There she stood, in the white moonlight, in her long, loose night-dress, which hung around her, in her stillness, like the folds of the winding-sheet, her hair streaming down her back in long, lifeless tresses, and lighted up on

her brow with a kind of supernatural radiance—and then those
death-resembling eyes! I trembled, and tried to draw the sheet
over my face, to shut out the appalling vision. After a few
moments, which seemed interminable to me, she bent over me,
and taking my right hand, felt of my wrist again and again. Her
fingers were as cold as marble. My very blood seemed to congeal under her touch. 'It is gone,' murmured she, 'but it
is safe—I have it safe. It fits my wrist as well as hers.' Terrified as I was at this unexpected apparition, my mind was
clear, and never were my perceptions more vivid. The mystery of the bracelet was about to be unravelled. Poor Alice's
assertion that she had seen Eglantine standing by my side,
and taking the bracelet from my wrist, came back thundering
in my ears. 'It is gone,' replied Eglantine, in the same low,
deep voice, 'but I know where it is laid; where the bridegroom or the bride can never find it. Perhaps the moon shines
too brightly on it, and reveals the spot.' Thus saying, she
glided across the floor, with spirit-like tread, and opening the
door, disappeared. In the excess of my excitement I forgot
my fears, and hastily rising, followed her footsteps, determined
to unravel the mystery, if I died in the act. I could catch
the glimpses of her white garments through the shadows of
the winding staircase, and I pursued them with rapid steps,
till I found myself close behind her, by the door which opened
into the garden. There she stood, still as a corpse, and again
the cold dew of superstitious terror gathered on my brow. I
soon saw a fumbling motion about the keyhole, and the door
opening, she again glided onward towards the summer-house,
my favourite retreat, the place where I had received this mysterious bracelet—the place where Flora had collected all her
wealth of bloom. She put aside the drooping vines, sending
out such a cloud of fragrance on the dewy air, I almost fainted
from their oppression, and stooping down over a white rose-
bush, carefully removed the lower branches, while the rose-
leaves fell in a snowy shower over her naked feet. 'Where is
it?' said she, feeling about in the long grass. 'It isn't in the
spot where I hid it. If she has found it, she may yet be a
bride, and Ronald still her own.' She stooped down lower
over the rose-bush, then rising hastily, I saw, with inexpressi-
ble agitation, the lost bracelet shining in the light that quivered
with ghostlike lustre on her pallid face. With a most unearthly smile she clasped it on her wrist, and left the arbour,
muttering in a low voice, 'I will not leave it here—lest she

find out where it lies, and win back her bridal gift. I will keep it next my own heart, and she cannot reach it there.' Once more I followed the gliding steps of Eglantine, through the chill silence of night, till we ascended the stairs, and entered our own chamber. Quietly she laid herself down, as if she had just risen from her knees in prayer, and I perceived by her closed lids and gentle breathing, that a natural sleep was succeeding the inexplicable mysteries of somnambulism."

"She was walking in her sleep, then, grandmother!" I exclaimed, drawing a long breath. "I thought so all the time; and poor Alice was really innocent! And what did Eglantine say the next morning, when she awaked, and found the bracelet on her arm?"

"She was astonished and bewildered, and knew not what to think; but when I told her of all the events of the night, the truth of which the bracelet itself attested, she sunk back like one stricken with death. So many thoughts crowded upon her at once in such force, it is no wonder they almost crushed her with their power. The conviction that her love for Ronald could no longer be concealed, the remembrance of the accusation of Alice, which she had so indignantly repelled, the apparent meanness and turpitude of the act, though performed without any conscious volition on her part, the belief that another had been the victim of her involuntary crime, all united to bow her spirit to the dust. My heart bled at the sight of her distress, and, every feeling wrought up to unnatural strength by the exciting scenes I had witnessed, I promised never to wed Ronald, since the thought of our union had evidently made her so unhappy. Eglantine contended against this resolution with all her eloquence, but, alas! she was not destined long to oppose the claims of friendship to the pleadings of love. Her constitution was naturally frail, a fragility indicated by the extreme delicacy and mutability of her complexion, and the profusion of her pale golden hair. Day by day she faded —night by night she continued her mysterious rambles to the spot where she had first deposited the bracelet, till she had no longer strength to leave her bed, when her soul seemed to commune with the cherubim and seraphim, which, I doubt not, in their invisible glory surrounded her nightly couch. As she drew near the land of shadows, she lost sight of the phantom of earthly love in aspirations after a heavenly union. She mourned over her ill-directed sensibilities, her wasted opportunities, her selfish brooding over forbidden hopes and imaginings. She gave herself up in penitence and faith to her Redeemer, in submission to her Father and her God; and her soul at last passed away as silently and gently as the perfume from the evening flower into the bosom of eternity."

"Oh! grandmother, what a melancholy story you have told," cried I, looking at the bracelet more intently than ever, the vivid feelings of curiosity subdued and chastened by such sad revealings; "but did not you marry Ronald at last?"

"Yes," replied she, looking upward with mournful earnestness; "the beloved grandfather, who has so often dandled you in his arms, in this very spot where we are now seated, whose head, white with the snows of threescore years and ten, now reposes on the pillow all the living must press,—who now awaits me, I trust, in the dwellings of immortality, was that once youthful Ronald, whose beauty and worth captivated the affections of the too sensitive Eglantine. Many, many years of happiness has it been my blessed lot to share with him on earth. The memories of Alice and Eglantine, softened by time, were robbed of their bitterness, and only served to endear us more tenderly to each other. The knowledge we had gained of the frailty and uncertainty of life, led us to lift our views to a more enduring state of existence, and love, hallowed by religion, became a sublime and holy bond, imperishable as the soul, and lofty as its destinies. I have lived to see my children's children gather around me, like the olive branches of scripture, fair and flourishing. I have lived to see the companion of my youth and age consigned to the darkness of the grave, and I have nothing more to do on earth but to fold the mantle of the spirit quietly around me, and wait the coming of the Son of Man."

I looked up with reverence in my grandmother's face as she thus concluded the eventful history of the Pearl Bracelet, and I thought what a solemn and beautiful thing was old age when the rays of the Sun of Righteousness thus illumed its hoary hair, and converted it into an emblematic crown of glory.

MYSTERIOUS RETICULE.

"I own," said Fitzroy, "that I have some foolish preju-dices, and this may be one. But I cannot bear to see a lady with a soiled pocket-handkerchief. I never wish to see any-thing less pure and elegant than this in the hand of a beauti-ful maiden." He lifted, as he spoke, a superb linen handker-chief, decorated with lace, that lay carelessly folded in the lap of Mary Lee.

"Ah, yes," exclaimed her cousin Kate, laughing, "it looks very nice now, for she has just taken it from her drawer. See, the perfume of the lavender has not begun to evaporate. But wait till to-morrow, and then it will look no nicer than mine."

"To-morrow!" cried the elegant Fitzroy, with an expression of disgust; "surely no lady would think of using a handker-chief more than once. If I were in love with a Venus de Medici herself, and detected her in such an unpardonable act, I believe the spell would be broken."

"I would not give much for your love, then," cried Kate, "if it had no deeper foundation—would you, Mary?"

Mary blushed, for she was already more than half in lov with the handsome Fitzroy, and was making an internal reso lution to be exceedingly particular in future about her pocket-handkerchiefs.

Fitzroy was a young man of fashion and fortune, of fine person, elegant manners, cultivated mind, and fastidiously re-fined taste. He had, however, two great defects—one was, attaching too much importance to trifles, and making them the criterion of character; the other, a morbid suspicion of the sincerity of his friends, and a distrust of their motives, which might become the wildest jealousy in the passion of love. He had a most intense admiration of female loveliness, and looked upon woman as a kind of super-angelic being, whose food should be the ambrosiæ and nectar of the gods, and whose garments the spotless white of vestal purity. He had never known misfortune, sickness, or sorrow, therefore had never been dependent on those homely, domestic virtues, those tender, household cares, which can alone entitle woman to the poetical appellation of a ministering angel. He was the spoiled child of affluence and indulgence, who looked, as Kate said, "as if he ought to recline on a crimson velvet sofa, and be fanned with peacocks' feathers all the day long." He was now the guest of Mr. Lee, and consequently the daily companion of the beautiful, sensitive Mary and her gay cousin. With his passionate admiration for beauty, it is not strange that he should become more and more attracted towards Mary, who never forgot, in the adornments of her finished toilet, the robe of vestal white and the pure, delicate, perfumed handkerchief, which Fitzroy seemed to consider the *ne plus ultra* of a lady's perfections. The cousins walked, rode, and visited with the elegant stranger, and never did weeks glide more rapidly away. Mary was happy, inexpressibly happy, for life began to be invested with that soft, purple hue, which, like the rich blush of the grape, is so easily brushed away, and can never be restored.

Fitzroy had often noticed and admired, among the decorations of Mary's dress, a beautiful reticule of white embroidered satin. One evening, on returning from a party, Mary's brow became suddenly clouded. "Oh, how could I be so careless?" exclaimed she, in a tone of vexation; "I have left my reticule behind. How unfortunate!"

Fitzroy immediately offered his services, but Mary persisted in refusing them, and dispatched a servant in his stead.

"You must have something very precious in that bag," said Kate. "I have no doubt it is full of billetdoux or love-letters. I intend to go after it myself, and find out all Mary's secrets."

"How foolish!" cried Mary. "You know there is no such thing in it—nothing in the world but——" She stopped, in evident embarrassment, and lowered her eyes, to avoid Fitzroy's searching glance.

The servant came without the bag, and again Fitzroy renewed his offers of search in the morning.

"No, indeed," said Mary; "I am very grateful, but I cannot allow you to take that trouble. It is of no consequence; I insist that you do not think of going. I am very sorry I said anything about it."

Mary's ill-concealed embarrassment and flitting blushes awakened one of Fitzroy's bosom enemies. Why this strange anxiety and confusion about a simple reticule? It must be the receptacle of secrets she would blush to have revealed. Kate's suggestion was probably true. It contained some confessions or tokens of love which she was holding in her heart's treasury, while her eye and her lip beamed and smiled encouragement and hope of him.

The next morning he rose from his bed at an early hour with a feeling of restlessness and anxiety, and resolved to go himself in search of the lost treasure. He found it suspended on the chair in which he remembered to have seen her last seated, leaning against the window, with the moonbeams shining down on her snowy brow. The soft satin yielded to his touch, and the exquisite beauty of the texture seemed to correspond with the grace and loveliness of the owner. He was beginning to be ashamed of his suspicions, when the resistance of a folded paper against his fingers recalled Kate's laughing assertions about love-letters and billetdoux, and jealous thoughts again tingled in his veins. For one moment he was tempted to open it and satisfy his tantalizing curiosity, but pride and honour resisted the promptings of the evil spirit.

Poor Mary! had she known what sweeping conclusions he brought against her during his homeward walk, she would have wished her unfortunate bag in the bottom of the ocean. She was false, coquetish, and vain! He would never bestow another thought upon her, but bid adieu, as soon as possible, to her father's hospitable mansion, and forget his transient fascination. When he entered the room where Mary and Kate were seated, Mary sprang forward with a crimsoned cheek and extended her hand with an eager, involuntary motion. "I thank you," said she, coldly; "but I am very, very sorry you assumed such unnecessary trouble."

She thanked him with her lips, but her ingenuous countenance expressed anything but gratitude and pleasure. Fitzroy gave it to her with a low, silent bow, and threw himself wearily on the sofa.

"I will know what mystery is wrapped up in this little bag!" exclaimed Kate, suddenly snatching it from her hand. "I know it contains some love talisman or fairy token."

"Ah, Kate, I entreat, I pray you to restore it to me," cried Mary.

"No—no—no," answered Kate, laughing, and holding it .igh above her head.

Mary sprang to catch it, but Kate only swung it higher and higher with triumphant glee. Fitzroy looked on with a scornful glance; Mary's unaffected alarm confirmed all his suspicions, and he felt a selfish gratification in her increasing trepidation.

"Kate, I did not think you could be rude or unkind before," said Mary, looking reproachfully at Fitzroy, for not assisting her in the contest.

"Since Miss Lee evidently endures so much uneasiness lest the mysteries of her bag should be explored," cried Fitzroy, with a sarcastic smile, "I am sure her friends must sympathize in her sufferings."

"Oh, if you are in earnest, Mary," cried Kate, tossing the reticule over her head, "I would not make you unhappy for the world."

There was a beautiful child, about two or three years old, a little sister of Kate's, who was playing on the carpet with the paraphernalia of her dolls. The bag fell directly in her lap, and she caught it with childish eagerness. "I got it—I got it!" cried she, exultingly; and before Mary could regain possession of it, she had undrawn the silken strings, and emptied the contents in her lap—a parcel of faded rose-leaves scattered on the floor, from a white folded paper that opened as it fell. Fitzroy beheld it, and his jealous fears vanished into air; but another object attracted his too fastidious gaze— a soiled, crumpled pocket-handkerchief lay maliciously displayed in the little plunderer's lap, and then was brandished in her victorious hand. Mary stood for a moment covered with burning blushes, then ran out of the room, stung to the soul by the mocking smile that curled the lip of Fitzroy.

"Cousin Mary been eating cake," said the child, exposing the poor handkerchief still more fully to the shrinking, ultra-refined man of taste and fashion.

The spell was broken, the goddess thrown from her pedestal —the charm of those exquisite, transparent, rose-scented hand-kerchiefs for ever destroyed. Kate laughed immoderately at the whole scene. There was something truly ridiculous to her in the unfathomable mystery, Mary's preposterous agitation, and Fitzroy's unconcealed disgust. There was a very slight dash of malice mingled with the gayety of her character, and when she recollected how much Fitzroy had admired and Mary displayed her immaculate and superb handkerchiefs, pure from all earthly alloy, she could not but enjoy a *little* her present mortification. She ridiculed Fitzroy so unmercifully that he took refuge in flight, and then the merry girl sought the chamber of Mary, whither she had fled to conceal her mortification and tears.

"Surely you are not weeping for such a ridiculous cause?" said Kate, sobered at the sight of Mary's real suffering. "I had no idea you were so foolish."

Mary turned away in silence; she could not forgive her for having exposed her weakness to the eyes of Fitzroy.

"Mary," continued Kate, "I did not mean to distress you; I did not imagine there was anything in the bag you really wished concealed, and I am sure there was not. What induced you to make such a fuss about a simple pocket-handkerchief? It looks as nice as mine does, I dare say."

"But he is so very particular," sobbed Mary, "he will never forget it. I have always carried a handkerchief in my bag for use, so that I could keep the one which I held in my hand clean and nice. I knew his peculiarities, and thought there was no harm in consulting them. He will never think of me now without disgust."

"And if he never will," cried the spirited Kate, with flashing eyes, "I would spurn him from my thoughts as a being unworthy of respect or admiration. I would not marry such a man were he to lay at my feet the diadem of the East. Forgive me for having made myself merry at your expense, but I could not help laughing at your overwrought sensibility. Answer me seriously, Mary, and tell me if you think that if Fitzroy really loved you, and was worthy of your love, he would become alienated by a trifle like this?"

Mary began to be ashamed of her emotions in the presence of her reasonable cousin;—she was ashamed, and endeavoured to conceal them, but they were not subdued. She was conscious she must appear in a ridiculous light in the eyes of the scrupulously elegant Fitzroy, whose morbid tastes she had so unfortunately studied. When they met again, it was with feelings of mutual estrangement. She was cold and constrained—he polite, but reserved. Mary felt with anguish that the soft, purple hue which had thrown such an enchantment over every scene, was vanished away. The realities of existence began to appear.

Fitzroy soon after took his leave, with very different feelings from what he had once anticipated. He blamed himself, but he could not help the chilled state of his heart. Mary was a mortal, after all; she ate cake, drank lemonade, and used her handkerchiefs like other ladies, only she kept them out of sight. Her loveliness, grace, and feminine gentleness of manner no longer entranced him. He departed, and Mary sighed over the dissolving of her first love's dream; but notwithstanding her weakness on this subject, she had a just estimation of herself, and a spirit which, when once roused, guided her to exertions which astonished herself. Her gay cousin, too, departed, and she was thrown upon her own resources. She read much, and reflected more. She blushed for her past weakness, and learned to think with contempt upon the man who had so false an estimate of the true excellence and glory of a woman's character. "Oh," repeated she to herself a hundred times, as, interested in domestic duties, she devoted herself to the comfort of her widowed father, "how miserable I should have been as the wife of a coxcomb, who would desire me to sit all day with folded hands, holding an embroidered handkerchief, with fingers encased in white kid gloves! How could I ever have been so weak and foolish?" Mary generally concluded these reflections with a sigh, for Fitzroy was handsome, graceful, and intellectual, and he was, moreover, the first person who had ever interested her young heart.

The following summer she accompanied her father to a fashionable watering-place. She was admired and caressed, but she turned coldly from the gaze of admiration, and cared not for the gayety that surrounded her. While others hurried to the ball-room, she lingered over her book, or indulged in meditations unfamiliar to the lovely and the young. One evening, when she had been unusually dilatory, she heard her father call, and taking a lamp, began to thread the passage, which led through a long suite of apartments occupied by the visiters of the spring. As she passed by one of the rooms, the door of which was partially opened, she heard a faint, moaning sound, and paused to listen. It returned again and again, and she was sure some stranger was suffering there, probably for-

gotten in the gay crowd that filled the mansion. Her first
impulse was to enter, but she shrunk from the thought of
intruding herself, a young maiden, into the apartment of a
stranger. "My father will go in and see who the sufferer is,"
cried she, hastening to meet him on the stairs.

Mr. Lee required no entreaties from his daughter, for his
kind and humane feelings were immediately excited by the
idea of a lonely and perhaps dying stranger, in the midst of a
heartless crowd. Mary gave the lamp into her father's hand,
and stood in the passage while he entered. A sudden exclamation, echoed by a faint low voice, made her heart palpitate
with vague apprehensions. Who could this lonely stranger
be whom her father evidently recognised? She stood holding her breath painfully, fearing to lose the sound of that
faint voice which awakened strange emotions within her, when
her father suddenly came to the door and beckoned her to
him. "I do believe he is dying," said he, in an agitated tone.
"It is Fitzroy himself! You must come to him, while I call
a physician."

Mary almost mechanically obeyed the summons, and stood
the next moment, pale and trembling, by the bedside of the
man she had once loved. Could that, indeed, be the elegant
Fitzroy?—with disordered hair, half-closed eyes, parched and
trembling lips, which now vainly endeavoured to articulate a
sound?—the pillows tossed here and there, as if in wrestling
with pain; the white counterpane twisted and tumbled—were
these the accompaniments of this fastidious exquisite? These
thoughts darted through Mary's mind, as the vision of her
soiled handkerchief came ghost-like before her. But she was
no longer the weak girl who wept tears of bitter agony at the discovery that she was made of mortal mould; she was a woman
awakened to the best energies and virtues of her sex She
found herself alone with the sick man, for her father had flown
for the assistance he required, and left her to watch till his
return. She saturated her handkerchief with cologne, and
bathed his burning temples and feverish hands. Her hear'
softened over the invalid in his prostrate and dependent state
"Ah, proud Fitzroy," thought she, "this handkerchief i
now more soiled and defaced than the one which alienated your
fancy from me, and yet you shrink not from its contact. No
pride or scorn now flashes from those dim eyes, or curl those
pallid lips. Alas! he is very, very ill—I fear even unto
death " The tears gathered into her eyes at this appalling

117

idea, and even mingled with the odorous waters with which she embalmed his forehead.

Her father soon came in with the physician, and Mary resigned her watch by his bedside. She withdrew to her own apartment, and waited with intense anxiety the tidings which he promised to bring her. She was surprised at her own emotions. She thought Fitzroy perfectly indifferent to her—nay, more, that she disliked him; but now, when she saw him in suffering and danger, she remembered the charm with which her imagination had once invested him, and accused herself of harsh and vindictive feelings.

"Yes," said Mr. Lee, in answer to her earnest inquiries, "he is very ill—dangerously ill. Imprudent exposure to the burning mid-day sun has brought on a sudden and violent fever, the consequences of which are more to be dreaded, as he has never been sick before. Could he have commanded immediate attention, perhaps the disease might have been arrested. But in this scene of gayety and confusion—though got up for the express accommodation of invalids—Heaven save the sick and the dying."

"Who will take care of him, father? He has no mother or sister near. Oh, surely we must not let him die for want of these!"

"I know what you are thinking of, Mary," said Mr. Lee, shaking his head; "but I cannot consent to it. The fever may be contagious, and you are too young and too delicate for such a task. Besides, there might be remarks made upon it. No; I will remain with him to-night, and to-morrow we will see what can be done for him."

"But to-night may be the crisis of his fate," pleaded Mary; "to-morrow it may be too late. You are very kind, father, but you are not a woman, and you know there are a thousand gentle cares which only a woman's hand can tender. I am a stranger here; I don't care if they do censure me. Let me act a true woman's, a kind sister's part. You know, by your own experience, what a skilful nurse I am."

Mary pleaded earnestly, and wound her arms caressingly around her father's neck, and looked up into his face with such irresistible eyes, that he could not refuse her. The pallid face of Fitzroy seemed to be leaning beside her own, clothed with that authority which sickness and approaching death impart. So Mary twisted up her shining ringlets, and took the rings from her jeweled fingers, and donned a loose, flowing robe.

Behold her, one of the loveliest nurses that ever brought the blessings of Hygea to the chamber of disease. There is a great deal said in romances of the interesting appearance of invalids, of a languor more lovely than the bloom of health, of a debility more graceful than the fullness of strength; but this is all romance. It has been said by one of the greatest moralists of the age, that the slow consuming of beauty is one of the greatest judgments of the Almighty against man for sin. Certainly a sick chamber is not the place for romantic beings to *fall in love*, but it is the place where love, once awakened, can exert its holiest influences, and manifest its death-controlling power; it is the place where religion erects its purest altar, and faith brings its divinest offerings. Yea, verily, it is hallowed ground. Thus Mary thought through the vigils of that long night. She had never been dangerously sick herself, but she felt the entire dependence of one human being upon another, and of all upon God. She felt, too, a kind of generous triumph, if such an expression may be used, in the conviction that this proud and over-sensitive being was so completely abandoned to her cares. Fitzroy lay in the deep lethargy of a burning fever, unconscious whose soft footsteps fell "like snow on snow" around his bed. "He never shall know it," said Mary, to herself. "He would probably feel disgust, instead of gratitude. If he saw this handkerchief, all impregnated with camphor, and stained with medicine, he might well think it unfit for a lady's hand. Shame on me, for cherishing so much malice against him—he so sick and pale!"

For more than a week Fitzroy languished in that almost unconscious condition, and during that interval Mary continued to lavish upon him every attention a kind and gentle sister could bestow. At length he was declared out of danger, and she gradually withdrew from her station in the sick chamber. Her mission was fulfilled, and an angelic one it had been. The physician, her father, and a youthful, unimpaired constitution accomplished the rest.

"What do I not owe you?" said Fitzroy, when, liberated from confinement, he was slowly walking with her through one of the green, shady paths of the enclosure. Now he, indeed, looked interesting. The contrast between his dark brown hair and pale cheek was truly romantic. That dark hair once more exhaled the odours of sweet-scented waters, and his black dress and spotless linen were as distinguished for their elegance as in former days. "What do I not owe you?" repeated he, with more fervour.

Mary smiled. "You were sick, and I ministered unto you. I only obeyed a divine command. A simple act of obedience deserves no reward."

"Then it was only from a sense of duty that you watched over me so kindly?" repeated he, in a mortified tone. "You would have done the same for any stranger?"

"Most certainly I would," replied Mary; "for any stranger as helpless and neglected as you appeared to be."

"Pardon me," said he, evidently disconcerted, "but I thought —I dared to think—that——"

Mary laughed, and *her* rosy lip began to curl with a slight expression of scorn. She was a woman, and her feelings had once been chafed, humiliated through him, if not by him. Her eyes sparkled, not vindictively, but triumphantly. "You dared to think that I was in love with you! Oh, no; that is all passed—long, long ago."

"Passed? Then you acknowledge that you *have* loved?"

"Yes," replid she, in the same laughing tone, though she blushed deeply all the while; "I did love you, Fitzroy, and I could have loved you with a life-long passion. To win your affection I tried to pass myself off as an angel, to whose garments the dust of mortality never adhered. You discovered my folly, and turned from me in contempt. It was a bitter lesson at first, but I thank you for it now. I am not the foolish girl that I was when I first knew you, Fitzroy. You must not think that I am——"

"And *I* am not the fool I was then," interrupted he. "I know now what constitutes the perfection of a woman's character. You only captivated my fancy then, now you have won my whole heart."

"Better lost than won," cried Mary, in the same careless accents. "I could not keep the treasure, and I cannot take it. You think you love me now, but I might fall sick, you know, and people do not look so pretty when they are sick, and you might not like the scent of camphor and medicine, and then one's handkerchiefs get so terribly soiled!"

She stopped, and looked archly at Fitzroy's clouded countenance.

"I understand it all," cried he, bitterly; "you pitied me in sickness, and watched over me. But I must have looked shockingly ugly and slovenly, and you became disgusted. I cannot blame you, for I deserve such a punishment."

"No, no—not ugly, Fitzroy, but helpless, weak, and dependent, proud man that you are. But, oh! you ought to know that this very helplessness and dependence endear the sufferer ten thousand times more to a fond woman's heart than all the pride of beauty and the bloom of health. I have had my revenge; but believe me, Fitzroy, the hours passed in our chamber of sickness will be remembered as the happiest of my life."

The tone of playful mockery which she had assumed, subsided into one of deep feeling, and tears gathered in her downcast eyes. Fitzroy—but it is no matter what Fitzroy said—certainly something that pleased Mary, for when they returned, more than an hour afterwards, her cheeks were glowing with the roses of Eden.

It was about six months after this that Cousin Kate visited Mary—but not *Mary Lee*—once more. Fitzroy, who now often complained of a headache, was leaning back in an easy chair, and Mary was bathing his temples, which she occasionally pressed with her linen handkerchief.

"Oh, shocking!" exclaimed Kate; "how can you bear to see Mary touch anything so rumpled and used, about your elegant person?"

"The hand of affection," replied Fitzroy, pressing Mary's gently on his brow, "can shed a beautifying influence over every object. Mary is a true alchemist, and has separated the gold of my heart from the worthless dross that obscured its lustre. She put me in the crucible, and I have been purified by the fires through which I passed."

THE END

T. B. PETERSON AND BROTHERS' PUBLICATIONS

NEW BOOKS ISSUED EVERY WEEK.

Comprising the most entertaining and absorbing Works published, suitable for the Parlor, Library, Sitting Room, Railroad or Steamboat Reading, by the best writers in the world.

☞ Orders solicited from Booksellers, Librarians, Canvassers, News Agents, and all others in want of good and fast selling books, which will he supplied at very Low Prices. ☜

MRS. ANN S. STEPHENS' WORKS.

Complete in eighteen large duodecimo volumes, bound in cloth, gilt back, price $1.75 each; or $31.50 a set, each set is put up in a neat box.

The Reigning Belle,............	$1 75	The Soldiers' Orphans,...........	$1 75
A Noble Woman,..................	1 75	Silent Struggles,...................	1 75
Palaces and Prisons,.............	1 75	The Rejected Wife,...............	1 75
Married in Haste,...............	1 75	The Wife's Secret,...............	1 75
Wives and Widows,.............	1 75	Mary Derwent,...................	1 75
Ruby Gray's Strategy............	1 75	Fashion and Famine,.............	1 75
The Curse of Gold,..............	1 75	The Old Homestead,.............	1 75
Mabel's Mistake, ...	1 75	The Heiress.......................	1 75
Doubly False,...................	1 75	The Gold Brick,.................	1 75

Above are each in cloth, or each one is in paper cover, at $1.50 each.

MRS. EMMA D. E. N. SOUTHWORTH'S WORKS.

Complete in thirty-five large duodecimo volumes, bound in cloth, gilt back, price $1.75 each; or $61.25 a set, each set is put up in a neat box.

A Noble Lord,..................	$1 75	The Deserted Wife,...............	$1 75
Lost Heir of Linlithgow,........	1 75	The Bridal Eve,...............	1 75
Tried for her Life,..........	1 75	The Lost Heiress,...............	1 75
Cruel as the Grave,......	1 75	The Two Sisters,...................	1 75
The Maiden Widow,.............	1 75	Lady of the Isle,...................	1 75
The Family Doom,.............	1 75	The Three Beauties,.............	1 75
Prince of Darkness,.............	1 75	Vivia; or the Secret of Power,	1 75
The Bride's Fate,.................	1 75	The Missing Bride,.............	1 75
The Changed Brides,...........	1 75	Love's Labor Won,.............	1 75
How He Won Her,.............	1 75	The Gipsy's Prophecy,...........	1 75
Fair Play,..	1 75	Haunted Homestead.............	1 75
Fallen Pride, ...	1 75	Wife's Victory,...................	1 75
The Christmas Guest,...........	1 75	The Mother-in-Law,.............	1 75
The Widow's Son,......	1 75	Retribution.......................	1 75
The Bride of Llewellyn,........	1 75	India; Pearl of Pearl River,..	1 75
The Fortune Seeker,.............	1 75	Curse of Clifton,...................	1 75
Allworth Abbey, ...	1 75	Discarded Daughter,.............	1 75
The Fatal Marriage,.............	1 75		

Above are each in cloth, or each one is in paper cover, at $1.50 each.

RIDDELL'S MODEL ARCHITECT.

Riddell's Model Architect. With 22 large full page colored Illustrations, and 44 plates of ground plans, with plans, specifications, costs of building, etc. One large quarto volume, bound,............$15 00

☞ Above Books will be sent, postage paid, on receipt of Retail Price by T. B. Peterson & Brothers, Philadelphia, Pa. (1)

MRS. CAROLINE LEE HENTZ'S WORKS.

Green and Gold Edition. Complete in twelve volumes, in green morocco cloth, price $1.75 each; or $21.00 a set, each set is put up in a neat box.

Ernest Linwood,....................$1 75	Love after Marriage,...............$1 75
The Planter's Northern Bride,.. 1 75	Eoline; or Magnolia Vale,..... 1 75
Courtship and Marriage,........ 1 75	The Lost Daughter,............... 1 75
Rena; or, the Snow Bird,...... 1 75	The Banished Son,............... 1 75
Marcus Warland.................. 1 75	Helen and Arthur,............... 1 75
Linda; or, the Young Pilot of the Belle Creole,............ .... 1 75
Robert Graham; the Sequel to "Linda; or Pilot of Belle Creole,"... 1 75

Above are each in cloth, or each one is in paper cover, at $1.50 each.

BEST COOK BOOKS PUBLISHED.

Every housekeeper should possess at least one of the following Cook Books, as they would save the price of it in a week's cooking.

The Young Wife's Cook Book.....................................Cloth, $1 75
Miss Leslie's New Cookery Book,.............................Cloth, 1 75
Mrs. Hale's New Cook Book,....................................Cloth, 1 75
Mrs. Goodfellow's Cookery as it Should Be,..............Cloth, 1 75
Petersons' New Cook Book,......................................Cloth, 1 75
Widdifield's New Cook Book.....................................Cloth, 1 75
The National Cook Book. By a Practical Housewife,.........Cloth, 1 75
Miss Leslie's New Receipts for Cooking,......................Cloth, 1 75
Mrs. Hale's Receipts for the Million,.........................Cloth, 1 75
The Family Save-All. By author of "National Cook Book," Cloth, 1 75
Francatelli's Modern Cook. With the most approved methods of
French, English, German, and Italian Cookery. With Sixty-two
Illustrations. One volume of 600 pages, bound in morocco cloth, 5 00

JAMES A. MAITLAND'S WORKS.

Complete in seven large duodecimo volumes, bound in cloth, gilt back, price $1.75 each; or $12.25 a set, each set is put up in a neat box.

The Watchman,...................$1 75	Diary of an Old Doctor,........$1 75
The Wanderer,................... 1 75	Sartaroe,......................... 1 75
The Lawyer's Story............. 1 75	The Three Cousins,............. 1 75
The Old Patroon; or the Great Van Broek Property,................... 1 75

Above are each in cloth, or each one is in paper cover, at $1.50 each.

T. A. TROLLOPE'S WORKS.

Complete in seven large duodecimo volumes, bound in cloth, gilt back, price $1.75 each; or $12.25 a set, each set is put up in a neat box.

The Sealed Packet,...............$1 75	Dream Numbers,...................$1 75
Garstang Grange,................. 1 75	Marietta, ... 1 75
Gemma,............................. 1 75	Beppo, the Conscript,........... 1 75
Leonora Casaloni,............... 1 75	

Above are each in cloth, or each one is in paper cover, at $1.50 each.

FREDRIKA BREMER'S WORKS.

Complete in six large duodecimo volumes, bound in cloth, gilt back, price $1.75 each; or $10.50 a set, each set is put up in a neat box.

Father and Daughter,...........$1 75	The Neighbors,.....................$1 75
The Four Sisters,................. 1 75	The Home,......................... 1 75

Above are each in cloth, or each one is in paper cover, at $1.50 each.

Life in the Old World. In two volumes, cloth, price, ...3 50

☞ Above Books will be sent, postage paid, on receipt of Retail Price,
by T. B. Peterson & Brothers, Philadelphia, Pa.

MISS ELIZA A. DUPUY'S WORKS.

Complete in six large duodecimo volumes, bound in cloth, gilt back, price $1.75 each; or $10.50 a set, each set is put up in a neat box.

The Cancelled Will,..............$1 75	How He Did It, ...$1 75
Who Shall be Victor,............ 1 75	The Planter's Daughter,......... 1 75
Why Did He Marry Her?...... 1 75	Michael Rudolph,.............. 1 75

Above are each in cloth, or each one is in paper cover, at $1.50 each.

EMERSON BENNETT'S WORKS.

Complete in seven large duodecimo volumes, bound in cloth, gilt back, price $1.75 each; or $12.25 a set, each set is put up in a neat box.

The Border Rover,..............$1 75	Bride of the Wilderness,........$1 75
Clara Moreland,.................... 1 75	Ellen Norbury,.................... 1 75
The Forged Will,................. 1 75	Kate Clarendon,.................... 1 75
Viola; or Adventures in the Far South-West,............................ 1 75	

Above are each in cloth, or each one is in paper cover, at $1.50 each.

Heiress of Bellefonte, and Walde-Warren,................... 75	Pioneer's Daughter and the Unknown Countess,........... 75

DOESTICKS' WORKS.

Complete in four large duodecimo volumes, bound in cloth, gilt back, price $1.75 each; or $7.00 a set, each set is put up in a neat box.

Doesticks' Letters,................$1 75	The Elephant Club,...............$1 75
Plu-Ri-Bus-Tah, ... 1 75	Witches of New York,.......... 1 75

Above are each in cloth, or each one is in paper cover, at $1.50 each.

GREEN'S WORKS ON GAMBLING.

Complete in four large duodecimo volumes, bound in cloth, gilt back, price $1.75 each; or $7.00 a set, each set is put up in a neat box.

Gambling Exposed,..............$1 75	Reformed Gambler,..............$1 75
The Gambler's Life,............. 1 75	Secret Band of Brothers,........ 1 75

Above are each in cloth, or each one is in paper cover, at $1.50 each.

DOW'S PATENT SERMONS.

Complete in four large duodecimo volumes, bound in cloth, gilt back, price $1.50 each; or $6.00 a set, each set is put up in a neat box.

Dow's Patent Sermons, 1st Series, cloth,....................$1 50	Dow's Patent Sermons, 3d Series, cloth, ...$1 50
Dow's Patent Sermons, 2d Series, cloth,.................. 1 50	Dow's Patent Sermons, 4th Series, cloth...................... 1 50

Above are each in cloth, or each one is in paper cover, at $1.00 each.

WILKIE COLLINS' BEST WORKS.

The Crossed Path; or Basil,...$1 75	The Dead Secret. 12mo........$1 75

Above are each in 12mo. cloth, or in paper cover, at $1.50 each.

The Dead Secret, 8vo............... 50	Mad Monkton,........................... 50
Basil; or, the Crossed Path,...... 75	Sights a-Foot,........................... 50
Hide and Seek,........................ 75	The Stolen Mask,.................... 25
After Dark,.............................. 75	The Yellow Mask,.................... 25
The Queen's Revenge, ... 75	Sister Rose,............................. 25

The above books are each issued in paper cover, in octavo form.

FRANK FORRESTER'S SPORTING BOOK.

Frank Forrester's Sporting Scenes and Characters. By Henry William Herbert. With Illustrations by Darley. Two vols., cloth,...$4 00

BOOKS FOR SCHOOLS AND PRIVATE STUDY.

The Lawrence Speaker. A Selection of Literary Gems in Poetry and
Prose, designed for the use of Colleges, Schools, Seminaries, Literary
Societies, and especially adapted for all persons desirous to excel in
declamation and public speaking. By Philip Lawrence, Professor
of Elocution. One volume of over 600 pages, half morocco,........$2 00
Comstock's Elocution and Model Speaker. Intended for the use of
Schools, Colleges, and for private Study, for the Promotion of
Health, Cure of Stammering, and Defective Articulation. By An-
drew Comstock and Philip Lawrence. With 236 Illustrations.
In one large volume of 600 pages, half morocco,..................... 2 00
The French, German, Spanish, Latin and Italian Languages Without
a Master. Whereby any one of these Languages can easily be
learned by any person without a Teacher, with the aid of this
book. By A. H. Monteith. One volume, cloth,...................... 2 00
Comstock's Colored Chart. Being a perfect Alphabet of the English Language, Graphic and Typic, with exercises in Pitch, Force
and Gesture, and Sixty-Eight colored figures, representing the various postures and different attitudes to be used in declamation.
On a large Roller. Every School should have a copy of it.......... 5 00
Liebig's Complete Works on Chemistry. By Baron Justus Liebig... 2 00

WORKS BY THE VERY BEST AUTHORS.

*The following books are each issued in one large duodecimo volume,
bound in cloth, at $1.75 each, or each one in paper cover, at $1.50 each.*

A Lonely Life. By the author of "Wise as a Serpent," etc............$1 75
Rome and the Papacy. A History of the Men, Manners and Tempo-
ral Government of Rome in the Nineteenth Century, as admin-
istered by the Priests. With a Life of Pope Pius IX.,.............. 1 75
The Initials. A Love Story. By Baroness Tautphœus,.............. 1 75
The Macdermots of Ballycloran. By Anthony Trollope,............. 1 75
Lost Sir Massingberd. By the author of "Carlyon's Year,"............ 1 75
The Forsaken Daughter. A Companion to "Linda," 1 75
Love and Liberty. A Revolutionary Story. By Alexander Dumas, 1 75
Family Pride. By author of "Pique," "Family Secrets," etc......... 1 75
Self-Sacrifice. By author of "Margaret Maitland," etc.............. 1 75
The Woman in Black. A Companion to the "Woman in White," ... 1 75
A Woman's Thoughts about Women. By Miss Muloch,.............. 1 75
Flirtations in Fashionable Life. By Catharine Sinclair,.............. 1 75
Rose Douglas. A Companion to "Family Pride," and "Self Sacrifice," 1 75
False Pride; or, Two Ways to Matrimony. A Charming Book,...... 1 75
Family Secrets. A Companion to "Family Pride," and "Pique,"... 1 75
The Morrisons. By Mrs. Margaret Hosmer,....................... 1 75
My Son's Wife. By author of "Caste," "Mr. Arle," etc.............. 1 75
The Rich Husband. By author of "George Geith,"................... 1 75
Harem Life in Egypt and Constantinople. By Emmeline Lott,...... 1 75
The Rector's Wife; or, the Valley of a Hundred Fires,................ 1 75
Woodburn Grange. A Novel. By William Howitt,.................. 1 75
Country Quarters. By the Countess of Blessington,.................. 1 75
Out of the Depths. The Story of a "Woman's Life,".................. 1 75
The Coquette; or, the Life and Letters of Eliza Wharton.............. 1 75
The Pride of Life. A Story of the Heart. By Lady Jane Scott,.... 1 75
The Lost Beauty. By a Noted Lady of the Spanish Court,.......... 1 75
Above books are each in cloth, or each one is in paper cover, at $1.50 each.

☞ Above Books will be sent, postage paid, on Receipt of Retail Price,
by T. B. Peterson & Brothers, Philadelphia, Pa.

WORKS BY THE VERY BEST AUTHORS.

The following books are each issued in one large duodecimo volume, bound in cloth, at $1.75 each, or each one is in paper cover at $1.50 each.

My Hero. By Mrs. Forrester. A Charming Love Story,.............$1 75
The Count of Monte-Cristo. By Alexander Dumas. Illustrated,... 1 75
The Countess of Monte-Cristo. Paper cover, price $1.00; or cloth,.. 1 75
Camillo; or, the Fate of a Coquette. By Alexander Dumas,......... 1 75
The Quaker Soldier. A Revolutionary Romance. By Judge Jones,.... 1 75
The Man of the World. An Autobiography. By William North,... 1 75
The Queen's Favorite; or, The Price of a Crown. A Love Story,... 1 75
Self Love; or, The Afternoon of Single and Married Life,............ 1 75
The Dead Secret. By Wilkie Collins, author "The Crossed Path,",... 1 75
Memoirs of Vidocq, the French Detective. His Life and Adventures, 1 75
The Clyffards of Clyffe, by author of "Lost Sir Massingberd,"...... 1 75
Camors. "The Man of the Second Empire." By Octave Feuillet,.. 1 75
Life, Speeches and Martyrdom of Abraham Lincoln. Illustrated,... 1 75
The Crossed Path; or Basil. By Wilkie Collins,................... 1 75
Indiana. A Love Story. By George Sand, author of "Consuelo," 1 75
The Belle of Washington. With her Portrait. By Mrs. N. P. Lasselle, 1 75
Cora Belmont; or, The Sincere Lover. A True Story of the Heart,. 1 75
The Lover's Trials; or Days before 1776. By Mrs. Mary A. Denison, 1 75
High Life in Washington. A Life Picture. By Mrs. N. P. Lasselle, 1 75
The Beautiful Widow; or, Lodore. By Mrs. Percy B. Shelley,...... 1 75
Love and Money. By J. B. Jones, author of the "Rival Belles,"... 1 75
The Matchmaker. A Story of High Life. By Beatrice Reynolds,.. 1 75
The Brother's Secret; or, the Count De Mara. By William Godwin, 1 75
The Lost Love. By Mrs. Oliphant, author of "Margaret Maitland," 1 75
The Roman Traitor. By Henry William Herbert. A Roman Story, 1 75
The Bohemians of London. By Edward M. Whitty,........... 1 75
The Rival Belles; or, Life in Washington. By J. B. Jones,......... 1 75
The Devoted Bride. A Story of the Heart. By St. George Tucker, 1 75
Love and Duty. By Mrs. Hubback, author of "May and December," 1 75
Wild Sports and Adventures in Africa. By Major W. C. Harris, 1 75
Courtship and Matrimony. By Robert Morris. With a Portrait,... 1 75
The Jealous Husband. By Annette Marie Maillard,................. 1 75
The Refugee. By Herman Melville, author of "Omoo," "Typee," 1 75
The Life, Writings, and Lectures of the late "Fanny Fern,"......... 1 75
The Life and Lectures of Lola Montez, with her portrait,............. 1 75
Wild Southern Scenes. By author of "Wild Western Scenes,"...... 1 75
Currer Lyle; or, the Autobiography of an Actress. By Louise Reeder. 1 75
Coal, Coal Oil, and all other Minerals in the Earth. By Eli Bowen, 1 75
The Cabin and Parlor. By J. Thornton Randolph. Illustrated,..... 1 75
Jealousy; or, Teverino. By George Sand, author of "Consuelo," etc. 1 75
The Little Beauty. A Love Story. By Mrs. Grey.................... 1 75
Secession, Coercion, and Civil War. By J. B. Jones,...... .... 1 75
Six Nights with the Washingtonians. By T. S. Arthur,............... 1 75
Lizzie Glenn; or, the Trials of a Seamstress. By T. S. Arthur,...... 1 75
Lady Maud; or, the Wonder of Kingswood Chase. By Pierce Egan, 1 75
Wilfred Montressor; or, High Life in New York. Illustrated........ 1 75
The Old Stone Mansion. By C. J. Peterson, author "Kate Aylesford," 1 75
Kate Aylesford. By Chas. J. Peterson, author "Old Stone Mansion,". 1 75
Lorrimer Littlegood, by author "Harry Coverdale's Courtship,"..... 1 75
The Earl's Secret. A Love Story. By Miss Pardoe,................... 1 75
The Adopted Heir. By Miss Pardoe, author of "The Earl's Secret," 1 75
Above books are each in cloth, or each one is in paper cover, at $1.50 each.

☞ Above Books will be sent, postage paid, on receipt of Retail Price,
by T. B. Peterson & Brothers, Philadelphia, Pa.

WORKS BY THE VERY BEST AUTHORS.

The following books are each issued in one large duodecimo volume, bound in cloth, at $1.75 each, or each one is in paper cover, at $1.50 each.

Cousin Harry. By Mrs. Grey, author of "The Gambler's Wife," etc.$1 75
The Conscript. A Tale of War. By Alexander Dumas, ... 1 75
Saratoga. An Indian Tale of Frontier Life. A true Story of 1787,.. 1 75
Married at Last. A Love Story. By Annie Thomas,.................... 1 75
The Tower of London. By W. Harrison Ainsworth. Illustrated,... 1 75
Shoulder Straps. By Henry Morford, author of "Days of Shoddy," 1 75
Days of Shoddy. By Henry Morford, author of "Shoulder Straps," 1 75
The Coward. By Henry Morford, author of "Shoulder Straps,"..... 1 75
The Cavalier. By G. P. R. James, author of "Lord Montagu's Page," 1 75
Rose Foster. By George W. M. Reynolds, Esq.,......................... 1 75
Lord Montagu's Page. By G. P. R. James, author of "Cavalier,"... 1 75
Mrs. Ann S. Stephens' Celebrated Novels. Eighteen volumes in all, 31 50
Mrs. Emma D. E. N. Southworth's Popular Novels. 35 vols. in all, 61 25
Mrs. Caroline Lee Hentz's Novels. Twelve volumes in all,........... 21 00
Frederika Bremer's Novels. Six volumes in all,...................... 10 50
T. A. Trollope's Works. Seven volumes in all,......................... 12 25
James A. Maitland's Novels. Seven volumes in all,.................... 12 25
Q. K. Philander Doestick's Novels. Four volumes in all,........... 7 00
Cook Books. The best in the world. Ten volumes in all,........... 17 50
Henry Morford's Novels. Three volumes in all,...................... 5 25
Mrs. Henry Wood's Novels. Sixteen volumes in all,.................... 28 00
Emerson Bennett's Novels. Seven volumes in all,..................... 12 25
Green's Works on Gambling. Four volumes in all,..................... 7 00
Miss Eliza A. Dupuy's Works. Six volumes in all,................... 10 50
Above books are each in cloth, or each one is in paper cover, at $1.50 each.

The following books are each issued in one large octavo volume, bound in cloth, at $2.00 each, or each one is done up in paper cover, at $1.50 each.

The Wandering Jew. By Eugene Sue. Full of Illustrations,........$2 00
Mysteries of Paris; and its Sequel, Gerolstein. By Eugene Sue,..... 2 00
Martin, the Foundling. By Eugene Sue. Full of Illustrations,..... 2 00
Ten Thousand a Year. By Samuel Warren. With Illustrations,.... 2 00
Washington and His Generals. By George Lippard... .... 2 00
The Quaker City; or, the Monks of Monk Hall. By George Lippard, 2 00
Blanche of Brandywine. By George Lippard,............................ 2 00
Paul Ardenheim; the Monk of Wissahickon. By George Lippard,. 2 00
Above books are each in cloth, or each one is in paper cover, at $1.50 each.

The following are each issued in one large octavo volume, bound in cloth, price $2.00 each, or a cheap edition is issued in paper cover, at 75 cents each.

Charles O'Malley, the Irish Dragoon. By Charles Lever,......Cloth, $2 00
Harry Lorrequer. With his Confessions. By Charles Lever,...Cloth, 2 00
Jack Hinton, the Guardsman. By Charles Lever,..............Cloth, 2 00
Davenport Dunn. A Man of Our Day. By Charles Lever,...Cloth, 2 00
Tom Burke of Ours. By Charles Lever,..........................Cloth, 2 00
The Knight of Gwynne. By Charles Lever,......................Cloth, 2 00
Arthur O'Leary. By Charles Lever,................................Cloth, 2 00
Con Cregan. By Charles Lever,....................................Cloth, 2 00
Horace Templeton. By Charles Lever,...........................Cloth, 2 00
Kate O'Donoghue. By Charles Lever,............................Cloth, 2 00
Valentine Vox, the Ventriloquist. By Harry Cockton,........Cloth, 2 00
Above are each in cloth, or each one is in paper cover, at 75 cents each.

☞ **Above Books will be sent, postage paid, on Receipt of Retail Price, by T. B. Peterson & Brothers, Philadelphia, Pa.**

NEW AND GOOD BOOKS BY BEST AUTHORS.

Beautiful Snow, and Other Poems. *New Illustrated Edition.* By J. W. Watson, author of "The Outcast and Other Poems." With Original Illustrations by Edward L. Henry. One volume, green morocco cloth, gilt top, side, and back, price $2.00; or in maroon morocco cloth, full gilt edges, full gilt back, full gilt sides, etc.,......$3 00

The Outcast, and Other Poems. By J. W. Watson, author of "Beautiful Snow and Other Poems." One volume, green morocco cloth, gilt top, side and back, price $2.00; or in maroon morocco cloth, full gilt edges, full gilt back, full gilt sides, etc.,............... 3 00

Hans Breitmann's Ballads. By Charles G. Leland. *Volume One.* Containing "Hans Breitmann's Party, with Other Ballads," "Hans Breitmann About Town, and Other Ballads," and "Hans Breitmann In Church, and Other New Ballads," *being the "First," "Second," and "Third Series" of the "Breitmann Ballads,"* bound in morocco cloth, gilt, beveled boards,...................... 3 00

Hans Breitmann's Ballads. By Charles G. Leland. *Volume Two.* Containing "Hans Breitmann as an Uhlan, with other New Ballads," and "Hans Breitmann's Travels in Europe, with Other New Ballads," *being the "Fourth" and "Fifth Series" of the "Breitmann Ballads,"* bound in morocco cloth, gilt, beveled boards,............... 2 00

Hans Breitmann's Ballads. By Charles G. Leland. Being the above two volumes complete in one. Containing all the Ballads written by "Hans Breitmann." Complete in one large volume, bound in morocco cloth, gilt side, gilt top, and full gilt back, with beveled boards. With a full and complete Glossary to the whole work,...... 4 00

Meister Karl's Sketch Book. By Charles G. Leland, (Hans Breitmann.) Complete in one volume, green morocco cloth, gilt side, gilt top, gilt back, with beveled boards, price $2.50, or in maroon morocco cloth, full gilt edges, full gilt back, full gilt sides, etc.,....... 3 50

John Jasper's Secret. A Sequel to Charles Dickens' "Mystery of Edwin Drood." With 18 Illustrations. Bound in cloth,........... 2 00

The Last Athenian. From the Swedish of Victor Rydberg. Highly recommended by Fredrika Bremer. Paper $1.50, or in cloth,...... 2 00

Across the Atlantic. Letters from France, Switzerland, Germany, Italy, and England. By C. H. Haeseler, M.D. Bound in cloth,... 2 00

The Ladies' Guide to True Politeness and Perfect Manners. By Miss Leslie. Every lady should have it. Cloth, full gilt back,.... 1 75

The Ladies' Complete Guide to Needlework and Embroidery. With 113 illustrations. By Miss Lambert. Cloth, full gilt back,......... 1 75

The Ladies' Work Table Book. With 27 illustrations. Cloth, gilt,. 1 50

The Story of Elizabeth. By Miss Thackeray, paper $1.00, or cloth,... 1 50

Dow's Short Patent Sermons. By Dow, Jr. In 4 vols., cloth, each.... 1 50

Wild Oats Sown Abroad. A Spicy Book. By T. B. Witmer, cloth,... 1 50

Aunt Patty's Scrap Bag. By Mrs. Caroline Lee Hentz, author of "Linda," etc. Full of Illustrations, and bound in cloth,......... 1 50

Hollick's Anatomy and Physiology of the Human Figure. Illustrated by a perfect dissected plate of the Human Organization, and by other separate plates of the Human Skeleton, such as Arteries, Veins, the Heart, Lungs, Trachea, etc. Illustrated. Bound,........ 2 00

Life and Adventures of Don Quixote and his Squire Sancho Panza, complete in one large volume, paper cover, for $1.00, or in cloth,.. 1 75

The Laws and Practice of the Game of Euchre. By a Professor. This is the book of the "Laws of Euchre," adopted and got up by the Euchre Club of Washington, D. C. Bound in cloth,............. 1 00

☞ **Above Books will be sent, postage paid, on receipt of Retail Price, by T. B. Peterson & Brothers, Philadelphia, Pa.**

NEW AND GOOD BOOKS BY BEST AUTHORS.

Treason at Home. A Novel. By Mrs. Greenough, cloth,..............$1 75
Letters from Europe. By Colonel John W. Forney. Bound in cloth, 1 75
Moore's Life of Hon. Schuyler Colfax, with a Portrait on steel, cloth, 1 50
Whitefriars; or, The Days of Charles the Second. Illustrated,....... 1 00
Tan-go-ru-a. An Historical Drama, in Prose. By Mr. Moorhead,.... 1 00
The Impeachment Trial of President Andrew Johnson. Cloth,....... 1 50
Trial of the Assassins for the Murder of Abraham Lincoln. Cloth,... 1 50
Lives of Jack Sheppard and Guy Fawkes. Illustrated. One vol., cloth, 1 75
Consuelo, and Countess of Rudolstadt. One volume, cloth,.............. 2 00
Monsieur Antoine. By George Sand. Illustrated. One vol., cloth, 1 00
Frank Fairleigh. By author of " Lewis Arundel," cloth,.............. 1 75
Lewis Arundel. By author of " Frank Fairleigh," cloth,.............. 1 75
Aurora Floyd. By Miss Braddon. One vol., paper 75 cents, cloth,... 1 50
Christy and White's Complete Ethiopian Melodies, bound in cloth,... 1 00
The Life of Charles Dickens. By R. Shelton Mackenzie, cloth, ... 2 00
Poetical Works of Sir Walter Scott. One 8vo. volume, fine binding, 5 00
Life of Sir Walter Scott. By John G. Lockhart. With Portrait,..... 2 50
The Shakspeare Novels. Complete in one large octavo volume, cloth, 4 00
Miss Pardoe's Choice Novels. In one large octavo volume, cloth,... 4 00
The Waverley Novels. *National Edition.* Five large 8vo. vols., cloth, 15 00
Charles Dickens' Works. *People's* 12mo. *Edition.* 21 vols., cloth, 32 00
Charles Dickens' Works. *Green Cloth* 12mo. *Edition.* 21 vols., cloth, 40 00
Charles Dickens' Works. *Illustrated* 12mo. *Edition.* 34 vols., cloth, 50 00
Charles Dickens' Works. *Illustrated 8vo. Edition.* 18 vols., cloth, 31 50
Charles Dickens' Works. *New National Edition.* 7 volumes, cloth, 20 00

HUMOROUS ILLUSTRATED WORKS.

Each one is full of Illustrations, by Felix O. C. Darley, and bound in Cloth.

Major Jones' Courtship and Travels. With 21 Illustrations,.........$1 75
Major Jones' Scenes in Georgia. With 16 Illustrations,................. 1 75
Simon Suggs' Adventures and Travels. With 17 Illustrations,...... 1 75
Swamp Doctor's Adventures in the South-West. 14 Illustrations,... 1 75
Col. Thorpe's Scenes in Arkansaw. With 16 Illustrations,............. 1 75
The Big Bear's Adventures and Travels. With 18 Illustrations,...... 1 75
High Life in New York, by Jonathan Slick. With Illustrations,.... 1 75
Judge Haliburton's Yankee Stories. Illustrated,....................... 1 75
Harry Coverdale's Courtship and Marriage. Illustrated,.............. 1 75
Piney Wood's Tavern; or, Sam Slick in Texas. Illustrated,.......... 1 75
Sam Slick, the Clockmaker. By Judge Haliburton. Illustrated,... 1 75
Humors of Falconbridge. By J. F. Kelley. With Illustrations, ... 1 75
Modern Chivalry. By Judge Breckenridge. Two vols., each........ 1 75
Neal's Charcoal Sketches. By Joseph C. Neal. 21 Illustrations,... 2 50

CHARLES LEVER'S BEST WORKS.

Charles O'Malley,....................	75	Arthur O'Leary,.....................	75
Harry Lorrequer,.....................	75	Con Cregan,......................	75
Jack Hinton,..........................	75	Davenport Dunn,....................	75
Tom Burke of Ours,...............	75	Horace Templeton,..................	75
Knight of Gwynne,.............. ..	75	Kate O'Donoghue,..................	75

Above are in paper cover, or a fine edition in cloth at $2.00 each.

A Rent in a Cloud,................ 50 | St. Patrick's Eve,.......... 50

Ten Thousand a Year, in one volume, paper cover, $1.50; or in cloth, 2 00
The Diary of a Medical Student, by author " Ten Thousand a Year," 75

DUMAS', REYNOLDS', AND OTHER BOOKS IN CLOTH.

The following are cloth editions of the following good books, and they are each issued in one large volume, bound in cloth, price $1.75 each.

The Three Guardsmen; or. The Three Mousquetaires. By A. Dumas,$1 75
Twenty Years After; or the *" Second Series of Three Guardsmen,"*... 1 75
Bragelonne; Son of Athos; or *" Third Series of Three Guardsmen,"* 1 75
The Iron Mask; or the *" Fourth Series of The Three Guardsmen."*.... 1 75
Louise La Valliere; or the *"Fifth Series and End of the Three Guardsmen Series,"* 1 75
The Memoirs of a Physician. By Alexander Dumas. Illustrated,... 1 75
Queen's Necklace; or *" Second Series of Memoirs of a Physician,"* 1 75
Six Years Later; or the *" Third Series of Memoirs of a Physician,"* 1 75
Countess of Charny; or *" Fourth Series of Memoirs of a Physician,"* 1 75
Andree De Taverney; or *" Fifth Series of Memoirs of a Physician,"* 1 75
The Chevalier; or the *"Sixth Series and End of the Memoirs of a Physician Series,"* 1 75
The Adventures of a Marquis. By Alexander Dumas.. .... 1 75
Edmond Dantes. A Sequel to the " Count of Monte-Cristo,".......... 1 75
The Forty-Five Guardsmen. By Alexander Dumas. Illustrated,... 1 75
Diana of Meridor, or Lady of Monsoreau. By Alexander Dumas,... 1 75
The Iron Hand. By Alex. Dumas, author "Count of Monte-Cristo," 1 75
The Mysteries of the Court of London. By George W. M. Reynolds, 1 75
Rose Foster; or the *" Second Series of Mysteries of Court of London,"* 1 75
Caroline of Brunswick; or the *" Third Series of the Court of London,"* 1 75
Venetia Trelawney; or *"End of the Mysteries of the Court of London,"* 1 75
Lord Saxondale; or the Court of Queen Victoria. By Reynolds,...... 1 75
Count Christoval. Sequel to "Lord Saxondale." By Reynolds,....... 1 75
Rosa Lambert; or Memoirs of an Unfortunate Woman. By Reynolds, 1 75
Mary Price; or the Adventures of a Servant Maid. By Reynolds,... 1 75
Eustace Quentin. Sequel to "Mary Price." By G. W. M. Reynolds, 1 75
Joseph Wilmot; or the Memoirs of a Man Servant. By Reynolds,... 1 75
Banker's Daughter. Sequel to "Joseph Wilmot." By Reynolds,...... 1 75
Kenneth. A Romance of the Highlands. By G. M. Reynolds, 1 75
Rye-House Plot; or the Conspirator's Daughter. By Reynolds,...... 1 75
Necromancer; or the Times of Henry the Eighth. By Reynolds,...... 1 75
Within the Maze. By Mrs. Henry Wood, author of " East Lynne,". 1 75
Dene Hollow. By Mrs. Henry Wood, author of " Within the Maze," 1 75
Bessy Rane. By Mrs. Henry Wood, author of " The Channings,".... 1 75
George Canterbury's Will. By Mrs. Henry Wood, author " Oswald Cray," 1 75
The Channings. By Mrs. Henry Wood, author of " Dene Hollow,"... 1 75
Roland Yorke. A Sequel to "The Channings." By Mrs. Wood,...... 1 75
Shadow of Ashlydyatt. By Mrs. Wood, author of " Bessy Rane,"..... 1 75
Lord Oakburn's Daughters; or The Earl's Heirs. By Mrs. Wood,... 1 75
Verner's Pride. By Mrs. Henry Wood, author of " The Channings," 1 75
The Castle's Heir; or Lady Adelaide's Oath. By Mrs. Henry Wood, 1 75
Oswald Cray. By Mrs. Henry Wood, author of " Roland Yorke,".... 1 75
Squire Trevlyn's Heir; or Trevlyn Hold. By Mrs. Henry Wood,...... 1 75
The Red Court Farm. By Mrs. Wood, author of " Verner's Pride,"... 1 75
Elster's Folly. By Mrs. Henry Wood, author of " Castle's Heir,".... 1 75
St. Martin's Eve. By Mrs. Henry Wood, author of " Dene Hollow," 1 75
Mildred Arkell. By Mrs. Henry Wood, author of " East Lynne,".... 1 75
Cyrilla; or the Mysterious Engagement. By author of " Initials," 1 75
The Miser's Daughter. By William Harrison Ainsworth, ... 1 75
The Mysteries of Florence. By Geo. Lippard, author " Quaker City," 1 75

CHARLES DICKENS' WORKS.

☞ GREAT REDUCTION IN THEIR PRICES. ☜

PEOPLE'S DUODECIMO EDITION. ILLUSTRATED.

Reduced in price from $2.50 to $1.50 a volume. ·

This edition is printed on fine paper, from large, clear type, leaded, that all can read, containing Two Hundred Illustrations on tinted paper.

Our Mutual Friend,......Cloth, $1.50	Little Dorrit, ...Cloth, $1.50
Pickwick Papers,.........Cloth, 1.50	Dombey and Son,........Cloth, 1.50
Nicholas Nickleby,.......Cloth, 1.50	Christmas Stories,........Cloth, 1.50
Great Expectations,......Cloth, 1.50	Sketches by "Boz,".....Cloth, 1.50
David Copperfield,.......Cloth, 1.50	Barnaby Rudge,..........Cloth, 1.50
Oliver Twist,.............Cloth, 1.50	Martin Chuzzlewit,......Cloth, 1.50
Bleak House,.............Cloth, 1.50	Old Curiosity Shop,.....Cloth, 1.50
A Tale of Two Cities,...Cloth, 1.50	Dickens' New Stories,..Cloth, 1.50

Mystery of Edwin Drood; and Master Humphrey's Clock,......Cloth, 1.50
American Notes; and the Uncommercial Traveller,..............Cloth, 1.50
Hunted Down; and other Reprinted Pieces,........................Cloth, 1.50
The Holly-Tree Inn; and other Stories,............................Cloth, 1.50
The Life and Writings of Charles Dickens,........................Cloth, 2.00
Price of a set, in Black cloth, in twenty-one volumes,..................$32.00
   "   "   Full sheep, Library style,............................... 42.50
   "   "   Half calf, sprinkled edges,.............................. 53.00
   "   "   Half calf, marbled edges,......................... 58.00
   "   "   Half calf, antique, or half calf, full gilt backs, etc. 63.00

GREEN MOROCCO CLOTH, DUODECIMO EDITION.

This is the "People's Duodecimo Edition" in a new style of Binding, in Green Morocco Cloth, Bevelled Boards, Full Gilt descriptive back, and Medallion Portrait on sides in gilt, in Twenty-one handy volumes, 12mo., fine paper, large clear type, and Two Hundred Illustrations on tinted paper. Price $40 a set, and each set put up in a neat and strong box. This is the handsomest and best edition ever published for the price.

ILLUSTRATED DUODECIMO EDITION.

Reduced in price from $2.00 to $1.50 a volume.

This edition is printed on the finest paper, from large, clear type, leaded, that all can read, containing Six Hundred full page Illustrations, on tinted paper, from designs by Cruikshank, Phiz, Browne, Maclise, McLenan, and other artists. This is the only edition published that contains all the original illustrations, as selected by Mr. Charles Dickens.

The following are each contained in two volumes.

Our Mutual Friend,......Cloth, $3.00	Bleak House,..............Cloth, $3.00
Pickwick Papers,.........Cloth, 3.00	Sketches by "Boz,"......Cloth, 3.00
Tale of Two Cities,.......Cloth, 3.00	Barnaby Rudge,.........Cloth, 3.00
Nicholas Nickleby,.......Cloth, 3.00	Martin Chuzzlewit,......Cloth, 3.00
David Copperfield,.......Cloth, 3.00	Old Curiosity Shop, ...Cloth, 3.00
Oliver Twist,.............Cloth, 3.00	Little Dorrit,.............Cloth, 3.00
Christmas Stories,........Cloth, 3.00	Dombey and Son,........Cloth, 3.00

The following are each complete in one volume.

Great Expectations,...............$1.50 | Dickens' New Stories,...Cloth, $1.50
Mystery of Edwin Drood; and Master Humphrey's Clock,....Cloth, 1.50
American Notes; and the Uncommercial Traveller,.............Cloth, 1.50
Hunted Down: and other Reprinted Pieces,........................Cloth, 1.50
The Holly-Tree Inn; and other Stories,............................Cloth, 1.50
The Life and Writings of Charles Dickens,........................Cloth, 2.00
Price of a set, in thirty-five volumes, bound in cloth,................. $50.00
   "   "   Full sheep, Library style,............................ 68.00
   "   "   Half calf, antique, or half calf, full gilt backs, etc. 100.00